Anarchy and Elegance

Anarchy and Elegance

Confessions of a Journalist
at Yale Law School

Chris Goodrich

AN AUTHORS GUILD BACKINPRINT.COM EDITION

Anarchy and Elegance
Confessions of a Journalist at Yale Law School

AN AUTHORS GUILD BACKINPRINT.COM EDITION
Published by iUniverse, Inc.

For information address:
iUniverse
2021 Pine Lake Road, Suite 100
Lincoln, NE 68512
www.iuniverse.com

Originally published by Little Brown

ISBN: 0-595-26405-0

Printed in the United States of America

FIRST EDITION

Acknowledgments of permission to reprint previously copyrighted material
appear on page 285.

LIBRARY OF CONGRESS CATALOGING-IN-PUBLICATION DATA
Goodrich, Chris, 1956—
    Anarchy and elegance: confessions of a journalist at Yale Law
School / Chris Goodrich. — 1st ed.
        p.   cm.
    1. Law — Study and teaching — United States. 2. Practice of law —
United States. 3. Yale Law School. I. Title.

To Lisa, with love,
and without whom this book
would not have been written

Law reflects but in no sense determines the moral worth of a society. The values of a reasonably just society will reflect themselves in a reasonably just law. The better the society, the less law there will be. In Heaven there will be no law, and the lion will lie down with the lamb. The values of an unjust society will reflect themselves in an unjust law. The worse the society, the more law there will be. In Hell there will be nothing but law, and due process will be meticulously observed.

GRANT GILMORE
The Ages of American Law
1974

Contents

Acknowledgments

I would not have attempted to write this book without the knowledge that I could rely on much goodwill and cooperation from many people. Some lent moral support; some literary advice; some legal skills; some all three. First thanks must go to the members of my "small group," who, alas, remain nameless: I have changed the identities of all the students encountered in this book, but most of you know who you are. Thanks also to those who read my manuscript or listened to my ideas: Lisa Miles, Paul Kahn, Cathy Iino, Geoffrey Hazard, Guido Calabresi, Paul Gewirtz, Jefferson Powell, Dan Ortiz, Burr Henly, Sue Henly, Rob Cohen, Tim Appelo, Jay Schaefer, Bobbi Welling, Meg Perry, Bill Lindsay, Christie Archibald, Mike Mattil, Gary Torre, my parents, my siblings and siblings-in-law, and others unnamed because of faulty memory or my sense that they would prefer to remain anonymous.

Special thanks and admiration to my editor, Pat Mulcahy, and Rafe Sagalyn, my agent, for being willing to take a chance. Thanks, too, to the others in law and publishing who responded, if not always favorably, to my ideas about professional value systems.

I have attempted to make this book as accurate, from a legal point of view, as possible, but mistakes no doubt remain. They are solely my responsibility.

Anarchy and Elegance

Prologue

I had no intention of going to law school when I graduated from Yale College in 1978. I had taken the Law School Admissions Test, of course, because all my friends did, but a career in law wasn't the least appealing; it struck me as a sterile, uncreative occupation. Writing seemed a more congenial profession to my way of thinking, and I subsequently spent two years in Berkeley, my hometown, getting a master's degree in journalism.

Eight years later, however, I was a first-year student at Yale Law School. I wasn't, to be sure, a typical first-year; I was a freelance legal reporter on a one-year fellowship, which I received after persuading the law school that my practical knowledge of the field would be greatly complemented by a large dose of theory. My experience at Yale Law proved to be among the most rewarding in my life, but I remain thankful, nonetheless, that I decided against law years earlier.

There's some irony in that conclusion, for I've come to understand that while my undergraduate decision was correct, it was right for the wrong reasons. Law, I discovered in the course of my belated legal education, can be exceedingly creative, even constructive, and as fascinating as it is challenging. For all that, however, today I would again avoid the

3

legal profession — but this time for fear of seduction, not boredom. My year in law school convinced me that legal education has a way of replacing everyday human values with what I can only call "legal" values — values that sustain the system of law rather than the people that system was created to serve. Law schools commonly boast that they teach students to "think like lawyers," but I learned that some important things are lost, to both the culture and the individual, in the course of this intellectual transformation. Legal training doesn't create selfish, aggressive people — but it does provide the intellectual equipment with which recipients can justify and give force to beliefs and actions most people would wholeheartedly condemn.

I no longer doubt that such a transformation occurs among students at most law schools, particularly the "elite" schools that emphasize intellectual achievement. At Yale Law I took the same classes and did the same assignments as every other first-year student, and the pressure to be somebody else was heavy and constant. The experience often felt a staged event — hence this book's division into acts — with the all-important difference that students were supposed to leave the legal theater with a distinctly superior understanding of the world. I wasn't alone in that feeling; it seemed impossible for anyone to go through a single day of law school without sensing that he or she didn't measure up — that the ability to think like a lawyer was demonstrably different, and better, than the ability to think as one once did, like an ordinary person.

From the humiliation that often concluded the professors' Socratic cross-examinations to their scoffing dismissal of our early written work, it was clear that only one worldview — hyperrational, adversarial, and positivistic — was acceptable in law school. Most of us eventually realized that the professors' aggressive assurance about the law masked a deep and abiding ambivalence, but that didn't redeem the anguish we had previously endured; in me, certainly, the realization provoked resentment, for it demonstrated that law valued *appearing* to be right more than actually *being* right. One came very close to deep truths in law school, it seemed, only to discover that those truths, for the lawyer, were beside the point.

These pronouncements may sound improbable and presumptuous, coming as they do from someone who spent only a year in law school, without intending to make law a career. In fact, however, I think the limited nature of my exposure forced me to approach law school at least as seriously as my fellow students; having but nine months to pick up three years' worth of law, I wanted to make the most of the opportunity. As a journalist, too, my concerns transcended legal rules, language, and thought; I found myself needing to comprehend the inner workings of law school in a way the typical student — for professional, financial, emotional, and psychological reasons — did not. The fact that I could walk away from law school, self-respect intact, regardless of what happened there actually seemed to liberate me to experience it fully. Indeed, I determined to write this book when I realized that my special status enabled me to trace the development of the legal frame of mind in a way no lawyer could; the vast majority of law school graduates have learned to "think like lawyers" so successfully that they can hardly recall what it was like to think another way.

The deeply transformative nature of legal education struck me even in the early weeks of law school. For a time I believed I was onto a truly original idea, but in fact it was ancient, practically a cliché. Even then, however, the idea seemed worth pursuing, for I wasn't just observing the transformation through which tens of thousands of lawyers have passed; at some level I was actually experiencing it. In a very personal way I had come to understand — as I would learn in my second semester of law school, upon reading *Democracy in America* — what Alexis de Tocqueville meant when he wrote, more than one hundred fifty years ago, that American lawyers

> secretly oppose their aristocratic propensities to the nation's democratic instincts, their superstitious attachment to what is old to its love of novelty, their narrow views to its immense designs, and their habitual procrastination to its ardent impatience.

And again:

> This notion of their superiority perpetually recurs to [lawyers] in the practice of their profession: [and] the habit of directing to their purpose the blind passions of parties in litigation, inspires them with a certain contempt for the judgment of the multitude.

And most damningly,

> The lawyers of the United States form a party which is but little feared and scarcely perceived. . . . [It] acts upon the country imperceptibly, but finally fashions it to suit its own purposes.

The world's most famous democracy wasn't so democratic, Tocqueville discovered, as it initially appeared.

These and other passages reinforced my instinctive belief that lawyers had a substantially different outlook on life than nonlawyers — and probably even more different now than in Tocqueville's time, for today's three-year law schools ensure that only students who have internalized legal values will be admitted to practice. More importantly, Tocqueville's observation about the legal profession's ability to absorb power, to fashion the country to suit its own purposes, has proved all too accurate. Consider the following statistics:

- The United States has three times as many lawyers per capita as Germany, ten times as many as Sweden, twenty times as many as Japan.
- The number of civil lawsuits filed in federal court tripled between 1970 and 1986, from 87,300 to 254,800, and now hovers around 220,000 annually.
- The number of federal agencies rose from twenty in 1962 to seventy in 1982; the number of pages of federal regulation tripled in the 1970s alone.

There are more than 750,000 lawyers in the United States, less than one-third of one percent of the total population, yet

- in the 1990–1992 Congress, almost two-thirds of our senators and more than two-fifths of our congressmen were lawyers;
- 59 percent of U.S. presidents (24 of 41) have been lawyers;
- about 40 percent of all Rhodes scholars go on to law school, a fact that Harvard president Derek Bok, himself a lawyer, has cited as representative of the "massive diversion of exceptional talent into pursuits that often add little to the growth of the economy, the pursuit of culture, or the enhancement of the human spirit."

The cost of all this law?

- $34 to $43 billion, according to a 1987 study;
- $12.4 billion — the 1989 earnings of the hundred highest-grossing U.S. law firms.

- $2 to $3 billion — the legal fees generated, at a minimum, by the savings and loan bailout;
- $85,000, the starting salary for many newly minted lawyers at top law firms in 1990. By one estimate, law firms spend $250 million annually recruiting new lawyers.

And the trend, today, is toward the creation of even more lawyers.

- More than 40,000 students graduate from law school every year.
- Applications to law schools have increased dramatically during four of the last five years. The increase is attributed to the Iran/contra hearings, the hearings over Robert Bork's nomination to the Supreme Court, the declining attraction of Wall Street, and, most of all, to the television show *L.A. Law*.

I didn't go to law school, obviously, to justify Tocqueville's view of the legal profession. But his analysis has proved frighteningly accurate, and boils down to a single, paramount question: Do we really want the United States to be run, in effect, by a group of people trained to think quite differently from the rest of us, especially when that training entails the inculcation of (in Tocqueville's words) a "secret contempt of the government of the people"? I doubt it; but in this book I am less concerned with determining the appropriateness of the legal profession's influence than demonstrating its distinctiveness and relation to legal education. The courtroom attorney's cardinal rule is "Never ask a question to which you don't already know the answer," but my task as a journalist is almost the reverse — to ask questions that have been too long overlooked.

Act I: Disorientation

Logic across your path, and history, and the social bearings
of the rules, Hohfeld's analysis, and clashing schools of
jurisprudence. Details, unnumbered, shifting, sharp, disordered,
unchartable, jagged. And all of this that goes on in class but
an excuse to start you on a wilderness of other matters you need.
The thicket presses in, the great hooked spikes rip clothes and
hide and eyes. High sun, no path, no light, thirst and the
thorns. — I fear there is no cure. No cure for law but more
law. No vision save at the cost of plunging deeper. But men do
say that if you stand these thousand vicious gaffs, if you fight
through to the next bush, the gashing there brings sight.

KARL LLEWELLYN

Yale Law 1918

The Bramble Bush

1930

One

Off the Treadmill

I was much troubled in spirit, in my first years on the bench,
to find how trackless was the ocean on which I had embarked.
I sought for certainty. I was oppressed and disheartened when I
found that the quest for it was futile. I was trying to reach
land, the solid land of fixed and settled rules, the paradise of
justice that would declare itself by tokens plainer and
more commanding than its pale and glimmering reflections
in my own vacillating mind and conscience.

JUSTICE BENJAMIN CARDOZO
Yale Law School lectures published as
The Nature of the Judicial Process
1921

I realized, soon after I opened the acceptance letter from Yale
Law, that I knew very little about it. A few of my college
friends had gone there — in fact, a number of relatives —
but I still had no clear idea what made Yale Law such a
prestigious institution. I had heard from many people that
law school was pretty much the same no matter where you
went, but I had also listened to many lawyers and law professors talk about the distinctions that do exist. Harvard Law
has connections to both big business and radical legal
thought; it is the standard against which other law schools
are judged. The law school at the University of Chicago is

deeply influenced by economic thinking, perhaps best known for producing such controversial legal figures as Richard Epstein and Judge Richard Posner. Stanford Law is almost the inverse of Chicago, being progressive but far removed from the corridors of power; its reputation outstrips its influence. Many other schools were talked about, but for the most part only as variations on the Harvard theme — though without its occasional radicalism.

The adjective I invariably heard applied to Yale Law was *philosophical*. That characterization meant little to me until I interviewed a Yale Law professor while writing an article on the peculiar fact that while two hundred–odd law reviews are published in the United States, almost all of them are edited by law students. The professor defended the practice of letting novices act as the profession's intellectual gatekeepers by painting this anomaly as a positive attribute. Student editing, he said, allows the publication of a much greater number of law reviews, which in turn ensures the presence of many points of view in the "ongoing conversation" about law. I was reminded of this comment when I read my acceptance letter, for the encouragement of differing viewpoints did seem a hallmark of a "philosophical" law school. At the same time, however, I couldn't help wondering whether Yale Law expected me to participate in law's conversation or had invited me strictly to listen.

A week before leaving for New Haven I went to Boalt Hall, the law school of the University of California at Berkeley, to investigate Yale Law further. I found, predictably, that 90 percent of Yale Law's sixty-odd faculty members had Ivy League degrees, but beyond that their backgrounds were surprisingly diverse.

A number had been born abroad — in Italy, Yugoslavia, Poland, Germany — and many of the visiting professors for the upcoming year were from foreign countries — Britain, Argentina, Israel (the last also being a justice on his country's supreme court). One professor had been Lyndon Johnson's point man for the 1964 Civil Rights Act; another, a federal judge who taught part-time, was often mentioned during the Reagan administration as a leading Supreme Court nominee. Two professors were psychoanalysts, one had an M.B.A., another a divinity degree, and countless numbers had Ph.D.s in economics, anthropology, and other social sciences. One assistant professor was just twenty-eight years old; one emeritus professor had argued more than a hundred cases before the Supreme Court, more than all but a handful of lawyers in the history of the United States. One professor wasn't even a lawyer — he had a doctorate in philosophy, but his only law degree was a Master of Studies in the Law, the same one I would earn. The faculty was distinguished, clearly, and the school's very low student-to-faculty ratio — less than 11-to-1, compared to Harvard's 24-to-1 — meant I could get to know some of them well.

As a student in the M.S.L. program I would be taking the courses assigned every entering Yale Law student — Constitutional Law, Torts, Procedure, and Contracts. Though M.S.L. students — four journalists and a professor of philosophy during my year — were allowed to replace one of those classes with an upper-level course, they were discouraged from doing so; I had planned to skip Contracts, but didn't after the journalists' dean said the principles of contract law would come up again and again in other courses. The M.S.L.s were also allowed to pick their own "small groups" — the dozen or so subsets of the first-year class which take all of their courses together, three as lectures and one, the "small group" itself, as a seminar. The ability to choose one's own small group, I later learned, was something for which most first-years would give their eyeteeth, since it determined the field of law studied in depth in the seminar format as well as which professors one drew for the lecture courses.

Each of the journalists had to be in a different small group, so I had to decide quickly which course I wanted to get most involved in. That seemed easy enough. Contracts and Procedure sounded boring; Torts or Constitutional Law seemed more appropriate for seminar discussions. I wasn't sure of my choices, however, so I called up a friend and recent Yale Law graduate who had recommended me for the M.S.L. program. Dan, a law professor himself after clerking at the Supreme Court, explained that my instincts were all wrong. Law school, he said, was like high school; the classes were big, you often learned more from the other students than from the teachers, and it didn't really matter what you studied so long as you had a good professor.

I was skeptical. How could anyone inject life into Contracts and Procedure, let alone courses like Corporations and Taxation? More significantly, how could the professor matter more than the course — the messenger be more valuable than the message? That seemed a bad sign. I pressed Dan further, and he finally suggested that Constitutional Law, provided it was taught by a good professor, was probably the best course to take as a small-group seminar. Con Law was often more complex and thus more interesting than the other courses, Dan said — sufficiently advanced, in fact, that it isn't even offered to first-years at many law schools. Dan gave me thumbnail sketches of the professors teaching Constitutional Law seminars that fall. Joe Goldstein, one of the lawyer/psychoanalysts, could be harsh but was supposed to like journalists. Burke Marshall, the Civil Rights Act orchestrator, was a safe bet — a gentleman, very traditional, but soft-spoken almost to a fault. Akhil Amar was young, a whiz kid who acted like one. Paul Kahn had started teaching at Yale only a year earlier, and Dan didn't know much about him.

I eventually decided to pencil myself into Kahn's small group, listing Goldstein's as my second choice. Only with Kahn could I have a Con Law seminar plus classes taught by two of Yale Law's best-known professors — Guido Calabresi, the school's new dean, for Torts, and Geoffrey Hazard, the legal profession's Mr. Ethics, for Procedure. Dan had said it was worth tinkering with my schedule to get Guido; he was the one teacher, by all accounts, who was not to be missed. As for Kahn — well, I'd take my chances, for the devil I didn't know couldn't be that much worse than the devil I did. Within two weeks of sending in my seminar request, the M.S.L. dean wrote back to say I could get into Kahn's small group. "Believe me," she added, referring to the Byzantine small-group selection process, "law school gets easier."

By this time I also knew where I was going to live in New Haven. I had applied for housing in the law school, hoping to get the complete law school experience, but Dan told me that would be a big mistake. Left to themselves, he said, law students talked of little besides law; I would go crazy between their constant arguing and obsession with detail. I took this counsel to heart, and not long after I had asked David, my brother in New Haven, whether he could find me a place to live close to campus, he reported I was the proud renter of a first-floor garden apartment on Lynwood Place, just two blocks from the law school.

I spent my last week in California visiting old friends. A day before leaving I stopped by Berkeley's central hospital to see Alice and Mark, a couple I had known for ten years, and their brand-new baby girl. Alice, a lawyer, was obviously exhausted from twenty-odd hours of labor, but I had never seen her so happy — certainly not when we had met up after work. As I held Katy for the first time, Mark reminded me of a pact we had made when I had taken a job at *California Lawyer*, the magazine of the state bar association, four years earlier. If he ever became a landlord, I was supposed to shoot him; if I ever became a lawyer, he was supposed to shoot me. I told Mark the deal was still on.

The orientation for new students took place in the Yale Law auditorium on a warm September afternoon. I went to school by way of the Old Campus — the undergraduate quadrangle — curious to see how it had changed since 1978, when I had graduated. The scene was virtually the same: students playing lacrosse and soccer, others carrying stereos, parents looking awed or preoccupied. I was a little taken aback by a banner that read "Welcome Class of 1990"; it was hard to believe I had been away that long.

The law school sits on an inconspicuous block surrounded by edifices of marble and granite. To the south is the enormous freshman dining hall, the Beinecke rare book library, and Book and Snake, a secret-society building that looks like a mausoleum. To the east, out the law school's back door, is the Grove Street Cemetery, its crypto-Egyptian gateway announcing "The Dead Shall Be Raised"; to the north and west sit the graduate studies building and the main library, Sterling. The library and the law school look somewhat alike, since both were built in the 1920s in warm, yellow stone; but the law school's neo-Gothic spires and gargoyles give it an unexpected sense of humor.

I walked along High Street admiring the stone tracery on the large upper-floor windows. Ducking in a little-used entrance I recalled from my undergraduate days, I noticed a carving above the door. It showed a student collapsed from too much drink, spiders wrapping him in webs while an owl looks on without expression. I turned right and into the law school auditorium.

I had forgotten how regal it was. Leaded glass, heavy curtains, dark varnished wood — and the same old leather seats in a memorably dingy shade of green. I had last sat here nine years earlier, to watch *Behind the Green Door*; it was the end-of-term Porn Night, an event sponsored by the Law School Film Society and, no doubt, long since discontinued. One moment from the evening instantly came back to me — a friend bringing down the house by yelling "Moving violation!" when the screen showed a naked woman being wheeled around on a gurney while other women fondled her. The legal angle escaped me at the time.

The atmosphere was different this day. The students gathered in the auditorium had been admitted to the most selective law school in the country; of some 3,700 applicants (since exploded to over 5,600) these were the lucky 175. In three years employers from coast to coast, four hundred strong, would be falling all over themselves to hire the new graduates at outrageously high salaries. The exhilaration in the air was palpable . . . but there was nervousness too, an essence of fear. This wasn't Harvard, of course, where it was rumored that students regularly dropped out, stole library books, razored cases from closed-reserve material, and occasionally committed suicide. But it wasn't a cakewalk, either. Unspoken questions floated about the room like the dialogue balloons of comic strips. What if the computer sent the wrong letter? What if I don't make it? What if I don't *like* it? What if I simply can't handle the pressure?

Law school would be so much easier for me; lawyers never

seem to expect much of journalists (sometimes for good reason). Only pride, not a prestigious career or the chance to make a lot of money, was riding on my performance. I was relaxed, happy that this year had very little downside.

Dean after dean welcomed us to Yale Law, many of them telling jokes. One said the incoming class outweighed the second-year class; another that the school seemed to teach everything except law; a third that it was fueled by anarchy. The deans were emphatic and charming, concerned and friendly; they spoke as if they lived to help students, which I found hard to believe.

I perked up, however, when Dean Calabresi spoke. He looked like Santa's head elf — indeed, he would play an elf at the law school's Christmas party (the hefty tax professor would play Santa Claus). Guido, as he is universally known, spoke by waving his hands, and the effect would have been comic if his words weren't so serious.

"You are off the treadmill here," he said. "Take advantage of this opportunity to stretch yourself. You don't have to get a notch ahead of anyone else." Students should love and take care of one another, he continued, and allow that sense of caring to become a habit. Excellence was a necessary part of becoming a good lawyer, but without humanity and decency, skill in the law was worthless — not merely wrong, but dangerous.

I liked what I heard. But I wondered whether Guido was also playing a role, a game. After years of interviewing attorneys I had found it virtually impossible to take what they said at face value; I had spent an inordinate amount of my professional life trying to figure out how — and occasionally, whether — a lawyer was manipulating the law, and me, to the advantage of his clients and himself.

I gave Guido the benefit of the doubt. At least I understood the words and ideas he used: love, honesty, cooperation. This was law with a human face, and it was the first time I had heard a lawyer discuss law in such common human terms.

The small groups met for the first time immediately after orientation. Mine gathered in a room that doubled, like many law school classrooms, as a student court, complete with bench and jury box. Seventeen students showed up and most of them looked incredibly young to me, the proverbial bright-eyed and bushy-tailed. Their nervous energy — talking, twitching, flirting — made me feel, at twenty-nine, like a holdover from the ancien régime.

Paul Kahn had a short grizzled beard and was going bald and gray at the same time. The hair he had was fairly long and wild, and made me think of 1930s movie scientists who narrowly avoid blowing themselves up with nitroglycerine. That impression was only heightened by Kahn's intense gaze. He looked students right in the eye when they spoke, but even then I got the sense he'd much prefer to be back in his office solving legal riddles. He didn't seem very comfortable playing professor.

Kahn asked the students to introduce themselves. About half were directly out of college, the other half having worked at a surprisingly diverse range of jobs. Bill, the one student older than I, had put himself through college working full-time in a postal distribution center not far from my house in Berkeley. Denise, the daughter of a Yale Law alumnus, had negotiated contracts for a theater company in Manhattan. Sam had been a reporter for a small southern newspaper; Vicky had worked for a health plan; Kate, a graduate of a midwestern college best known for its football teams, had been a legal assistant in a high-powered New York law firm.

Kahn quickly returned to the business at hand. Our first assignment was to read the U.S. Constitution, printed in the back of our Con Law casebook, and *Bowers v. Hardwick*, a decision handed down by the Supreme Court just a few months earlier.

The case meant nothing to me by name, but I remembered the situation when Kahn described it. In upholding a Georgia law prohibiting sodomy, the court had determined that homosexuals had no constitutional right to practice that act. *Bowers* had caused a furor in San Francisco, of course, for it seemed intent on turning gay people into second-class citizens. I was surprised, and pleased, that Kahn started Con Law with a case of ongoing significance, especially one about which I had strong feelings. I hoped he was going to tear it apart.

After a few organizational questions, the class dispersed. Sam, tall and apple-cheeked, came over to talk about reporting and the news media. He was friendly, but I sensed from the way he zeroed in on me that he wasn't keen on law school. Sam later told me that for a time he really believed his admission to Yale was the result of a clerical error or a prank played by his friends; his undergraduate grades and LSAT scores were sufficiently below those of the average Yale Law admittee, apparently, that Sam assumed he wouldn't get in. When his acceptance letter arrived, he said, he called up the registrar to make sure it was authentic.

I hung around the law school for another hour trying to exorcise my nostalgia. It was hauntingly familiar, yet at the same time I didn't seem to know the place at all. I had walked these halls a hundred times as an undergraduate, seen the message centers and bulletin boards that held the school together, but now they had different meanings for me. Hallways and stairways now represented destinations, not ways of leaving; phrases that had been obscure to me a decade earlier — the Barristers' Union, Moot Court, TRO, LSO, Green Haven Prison Project — now made sense. I seemed to belong in this building for the first time; I could go up to professors' offices, down to the student locker room, and not feel an intruder.

I wandered the law school absorbing this new culture. Outside one office was a clipping from a legal newspaper announcing the names of the clerks hired by the U.S. Supreme Court for the upcoming term. Nine had graduated from Yale Law, three from Harvard, and the rest from other top law schools around the country. (The "top ten" are sometimes said to be Harvard, Yale, Stanford, Columbia, the universities of Virginia, Michigan, Pennsylvania, and Chicago, and UC Berkeley and UCLA, but a number of schools are of equal caliber.) It was an astounding accomplishment — Yale's sending three times as many graduates to the Supreme Court as Harvard with less than a third of the enrollment. I knew law clerks did virtually all of the research and even much of the writing of Supreme Court decisions, and I found myself wondering whether the outcome of a case could depend on where the clerk went to school.

I climbed the stairwell in the center of the school. I stopped at the second-floor landing, where the building bows out into an apse overlooking the main courtyard. Below me, the lawn was full of students playing free-for-all volleyball and catching up with friends and the last of the afternoon sun.

Turning to ascend the next flight of stairs, I felt a visceral jolt. There, at the landing, was the law library — or rather a deluge of light, pouring like an annunciation through the library's cathedral windows. These were the tracery windows I had seen from High Street, and they made the library seem a glass ship riding on a stone sea. I saw why Guido had referred to Yale Law at the orientation as the "Temple of Truth." If truth could be found, here, surely, was the place.

A quick tour told me the library would be a pleasant place to work. With those towering windows on three sides it was the airiest I had ever encountered. The study carrels seemed plentiful and uncrowded, and at both ends of the room were deep leather chairs that looked good for reading (and perhaps catnapping). And there were books, of course, too — lots of them, in bookshelves that lined the perimeter and extended like fingers into the library's center. Thousands of volumes showed the familiar spines of case "reporters," as they are called, and one particular set told me where I'd be spending much of my time over the next nine months — in the south-western corner of the room, home to the Supreme Court Reporter.

Having finished my initial tour of duty, I set off for the Yale Co-op to buy the necessary course material. That was one advantage of the first-year law student's prescribed curriculum: you didn't have to delay book-buying while figuring out what classes to take.

The law school section was easy to spot, marked by a pallet of doorstop-weight books bound in navy blue. I browsed among the readings required for some upper-level classes, and some of them made law school sound fascinating. Plato, Aeschylus, Aquinas, More, Rousseau, Bentham, Kant, Freud — if by some fluke a student went directly to

Yale Law from high school, he or she could still get a pretty good liberal arts education.

Eventually I picked up the casebooks for my own courses, plus their updating supplements, and staggered into the checkout line. Seeing a law student approach, the clerk reached for the store's sturdiest plastic bag and doubled it. The books cost me $140.

That evening I sat down with the school's catalogue and discovered that it contained a short history of Yale Law. The first professor of law at Yale College, I read, was appointed in 1801, and he lectured undergraduates "on general aspects of municipal and international law." His name, I learned to my surprise, was Elizur Goodrich, my great-great-great-great-grandfather.

Classes began the following morning. I was scheduled to be in class four hours that day and thanked God the semester had started in the middle of the week — on Mondays I had five and a half hours of classes. I didn't know whether I could sit still that long anymore.

Before my first class, over morning coffee in the dining hall, I heard some of the scuttlebutt on Kahn. A second-year widened his eyes when I mentioned that I had Kahn for my small group, and shook his head when I said I had requested the assignment. Kahn had been so hard on the previous year's small group, the second-year said, that he had been dubbed "Genghis."

I grinned in reply, a mixture of horror and stupefaction (I assume) on my face. Had I made a big mistake? But there wasn't much I could do about it, for the class was about to begin.

Con Law — or Kahn Law, as it inevitably became — met in probably the least comfortable classroom in the school.

Hidden in a basement corridor behind a locked hallway-to-nowhere door, it was almost impossible to find and, upon discovery, hardly seemed worth the trouble. The room was cramped by a large rectangular table and a low ceiling; it had windows, but all you could see through them, and only if you sat in the right chair, was the hosiery of passing pedestrians.

Students straggled in, looking relieved to have found the classroom at all. Kahn waited silently in his shirtsleeves at the far end of the table, occasionally sipping from a Styrofoam cup of coffee. There was some jockeying for chairs, for the one thing every incoming student knows about law school is that you are likely to remain all semester in the seat you take the first day of class. I had expected to stay above this unspoken game of musical chairs, but in fact, being newly single, I probably took it more seriously than anyone. Coming into the classroom I paused only a few seconds while deciding which young woman to sit by, but the delay was costly; Michelle, who had a lovely big smile, and Audrey, serious but with an engaging laugh, were already surrounded. I sat next to Sam.

I waited all through the first class for the Genghis treatment, but it never came. Kahn didn't hector or mock anyone and didn't appear annoyed by simple questions and ignorant answers — in fact, he almost seemed to welcome them. Kahn was nervous, just as he was at the introductory meeting, but I took that to be a good sign. If he wasn't a confident teacher, I thought, he couldn't give us a legal snow job.

Kahn soon began to lecture on *Bowers*. He was nothing if not prepared — his class notes were typed and filed in a binder, and seemed to include a lot of information that didn't show up in the published decision. I felt a little guilty. Kahn had obviously spent many hours getting ready for class, and I had taken only ninety minutes the night before to read *Bowers* once and the Constitution twice. I didn't yet know I was supposed to *think* about what I read.

If Kahn called on me, I was prepared only to say that the decision was bad for minority rights. It quickly became clear that Kahn believed the implications of *Bowers* ran much deeper than that. "This case," he said, "is about abortion."

I was startled. If there was one thing I knew about judicial opinions, it was that they tended to be narrow in scope. A court generally tailors a decision closely to the facts of a situation so attorneys can't later argue that it would also apply to a superficially similar set of facts. I was intrigued by the connection Kahn made, even though it made no sense to me. What did abortion have to do with gay rights?

The explanation emerged slowly. Kahn laid out the facts of the case in detail and demonstrated convincingly that they weren't nearly so simple as Justice Byron White — for whom Kahn had clerked a few years earlier — had suggested in his harsh majority opinion.

Michael Hardwick, a homosexual man, was charged with sodomy after a policeman tracking down a disorderly conduct infraction had found him *in flagrante* with another man. The two men weren't having sex on the sidewalk; they were in Hardwick's bedroom, but the policeman saw them after a roommate, thinking Hardwick had gone out, invited the officer inside to see for himself that the man he sought wasn't home. The district attorney declined to prosecute the case but kept the charge open, meaning that Hardwick could have been prosecuted at a later date. Hardwick decided to challenge the constitutionality of the Georgia statute prohibiting sodomy, charging that it placed him in imminent danger of arrest and violated his constitutional right of privacy.

At trial, a federal judge found that Hardwick had failed to "state a claim" — that the statute did not breach a fundamental right, as Hardwick argued. That decision was reversed on appeal, however, and Michael Bowers, Georgia's attorney general, appealed in turn to the U.S. Supreme Court.

Most of these facts were in the written decision. The one I thought most important was Bowers's admission, at one point, that the Georgia sodomy statute would be unconstitutional if enforced against a married couple. That fact, which I found in a footnote in the dissent of Justice John Paul Stevens, was enough for me. The law was applied in a discriminatory fashion; it ran afoul of the equal protection clause of the Fourteenth Amendment. Shouldn't that be the end of it? I said as much, and Kahn found the comment worth talking about.

The failure of Hardwick's attorneys to base their argument on equal protection grounds, Kahn said, was one plausible explanation for their losing the case. In fact, as some of the other justices in *Bowers* noted, they had not pressed a number of good claims. Hardwick could have stressed that he was subject, if convicted, to "cruel and unusual punishment," prohibited by the Eighth Amendment; he could have argued that his actions were protected by the "privileges and immunities" clause of the Fourteenth Amendment. But from reading Justice White's opinion, it appeared he didn't.

Why not? What was going on here?

It was a complicated explanation. Hardwick's attorneys, first, had accepted the legal truism that the privileges and immunities clause, as Kahn put it, had "dropped into a black hole." As much as the transparent words of that clause might seem to support the idea that no one should be subject to prosecution for private, voluntary acts, it didn't; a century of legal interpretation had invested such protections in much less obvious places in the Constitution, such as the "due process" clauses of the Fifth and Fourteenth amendments. Instead of scouring the Constitution, in other words, to find language that seemed to provide the best protection for Hardwick's conduct, his attorneys followed the standard legal technique of trying to pour their case into constitutional terms that have proved effective in the recent past. And one of the most fashionable in recent years has been the "right to privacy" — a term that can't be found in the Constitution, was said in previous Supreme Court decisions to have emerged somehow from the Bill of Rights (the first ten constitutional amendments) as a whole, and that had achieved its greatest reach to date in the abortion case *Roe v. Wade*.

Kahn's argument began falling into place. Hardwick's attorneys thought it made sense to argue that if the right to privacy, as articulated in *Roe*, guaranteed a woman's right to control her body, then gays should enjoy a similar right over their own bodies. But the attorneys hadn't anticipated how the Supreme Court would react to that argument — that Justice White, who had dissented in *Roe* and had long believed the right of privacy to rest on a poor constitutional foundation, would take the opportunity provided by *Bowers* to turn around what Hardwick's attorneys apparently thought was a right-to-privacy juggernaut. *Bowers* wasn't about the right of privacy, the justice said, but about whether there was "a fundamental right to engage in homosexual sodomy." After setting up the argument in those terms, he apparently didn't have much trouble getting a majority of the court to agree with him.

As Kahn pointed out, however, Hardwick's attorneys weren't entirely to blame for being hoisted on their own petard. Justice White's characterization of the case was disingenuous, for *Bowers* involved a procedural rather than a substantive right. Hardwick was appealing not a decision that had gone against him after trial, but the fact that the original judge in Georgia had refused to grant him a trial at all; Hardwick was only asking for the opportunity to present his argument in court. The case shouldn't have been decided on its merits, consequently, at least at this point; Justice White simply took the occasion to deny a right preemptively even before hearing a complete argument on its behalf. Kahn noted wryly that Hardwick would probably have had a better chance if he had actually been convicted of sodomy, for then the reasonableness of a claim under the equal protection and cruel and unusual punishment clauses of the Constitution would have been obvious to both his lawyers and his judges.

I felt angry, almost ill, when I understood that Hardwick's prosecution had been reduced to a game of strategy. His attorneys said their client's action fit into this pigeonhole; Justice White said it didn't, then gratuitously added that the action stood entirely outside the Constitution. Ultimately, *Bowers* didn't seem to have anything to do with sodomy or gay rights — it was about abstract constitutional theory, about legal ingenuity and tactical mistakes, about personal agendas dressed up in legal form. And the most important message of *Bowers*, which only those in the legal community would be likely to get, was its threat to *Roe* — its implication that the right to privacy was no longer expanding and might even be ready to contract.

Our first Con Law class was an eye-opener. To understand fully the subtext of Supreme Court decisions, to be able to see the movement beneath the surface — I was in awe not only of the power of the law but of the chance I had to comprehend how law changed the world. I saw for the first time the deep seduction of the law. How could you witness that power, analyze it, walk around it, and not want to harness it yourself?

Two

The Art of Massage

I am well aware that one can't get along without domineering or
being served. Every man needs slaves as he needs fresh air.
Commanding is breathtaking. . . . Somebody has to have the last
word. Otherwise, every reason can be answered with another and
there would never be an end to it. Power, on the other hand, settles
everything. . . . We no longer say as in simple times, "This is the
way I think. What are your objections?" We have become lucid. For
the dialogue we have substituted the communiqué: "This is the
truth," we say. "You can discuss it as much as you want;
we aren't interested. But in a few years there'll be the police
who will show you we are right."

CLAMENCE
the lawyer-narrator in Albert Camus's
The Fall
1956

The students from the small group were talking about the
premiere episode of *L.A. Law* when I walked into Room 127
the following Monday. It was the one room on campus that
followed the stereotypical law school lecture-class design: a
raised stage encircled by tiers of long, arcing tables that
marched upward to the rear wall. Every seat was clearly
visible from the podium and every sound seemed to funnel
in that direction. I could hear Sam call *L.A. Law* "trash, but

fun trash," from twenty feet away. The room felt chill and exposed.

This was the first meeting of Procedure, and the air was heavy with anticipation. Geoffrey Hazard was known to be an intimidating practitioner of the Socratic method, Yale's answer to Professor Kingsfield of *Paper Chase* fame. When he called on someone, it was said, the student was likely to be in the hot seat for twenty minutes and would not escape without embarrassment, no matter how good the answers provided. I sat in a low tier on the northwest side of the room, guessing the seat was outside the central area toward which Hazard would direct most of his questions. I had forgotten, of course, that professors called on students by name, not face, a system guaranteeing that no seat is safer than any other.

Conversation faded away when Hazard pushed through the swinging doors on the far side of the room and placed his books and papers on the podium. He strode into the room, I thought, as if he were about to argue a case — he looked more like a lawyer than a law professor. He wore a well-tailored business suit and his short hair was exactly combed; he seemed tall, though that impression was largely due to his posture, which was ramrod straight. Hazard sat silently for a time before glancing at his watch and asking the class to come to order.

Hazard told us his course required a book called *Cases on Pleading and Procedure, State and Federal,* and the Federal Rules of Civil Procedure. The class laughed obediently when he told us to buy new copies of the casebook because, as one of its authors, he received royalties on every sale. The housekeeping taken care of, Hazard stepped down from the podium and began pacing before it.

Litigation, he began in a penetrating tone, is "a means to

correct human fallibility." The procedures entailed by litigation were not to be taken lightly simply because they involved the internal, technical rules of the justice system; it was essential to know and apply them well, for they often determined who won and who lost. "Each *procedural* issue can become a *skirmish* of its *own*," Hazard said, inflecting every word that could conceivably be stressed. "What you do *procedurally* is *informed* by your understanding of *substantive* law."

Hazard halted in front of the first row of students on the far side of the room. He looked down at them and paused. Two students continued to lean over their notebooks, writing furiously — already too intimidated, I was sure, to sit up and find Hazard staring into their skulls. There was something about the deliberateness with which Hazard spoke, the confidence with which he stalked the floor and periodically turned his back to the class, that made it seem no movement escaped his attention.

One student in the row returned Hazard's gaze unwaveringly. When he resumed talking he spoke directly to her. "There are plays within plays within plays," he continued. "If you're lucky, the substance of the case *might* come through."

Hazard went on in this vein for several minutes. He larded his speech with words like *predicates, correlatives,* and *dialectics,* and half of the time I didn't know what he was trying to say. I hadn't heard those words in such abundance since making the mistake of signing up for a linguistics class as a college freshman, and they continued to strike me as pseudoscientific, full of misplaced mystical authority. Given Hazard's commanding presence, though, I didn't risk showing an expression other than credulous attention.

Hazard turned to the class list on the podium, and at that

point no minds drifted. You could almost hear the adrenaline rush through the student body as Hazard chose his first victim. After some noisy fidgeting the class became deadly silent.

"*Swann v. Burkett,*" Hazard said, and looked up.

I hadn't read the case. I could have picked it up from the mimeograph room the previous Friday, but I had been in a rush to get to New York to attend the opening of the first-ever exhibit of my brother John, a painter. I had made a choice, I told myself on the drive down, and I would live with it; if Hazard called my name on Monday I would simply say, "Sorry, I'm not prepared," and suffer the consequences.

Sitting in class, I realized in one blind flash how pathetic that would sound. And what an opportunity for the professor! It was easy to imagine Hazard's comeback. Unprepared? After the very first weekend of law school? With days to do the assignment and little else? What did I think Yale Law was, some sort of country club? Why had I bothered to show up for class . . . or law school, for that matter? Hazard had canceled the first scheduled meeting of Procedure to preside over some legal meeting out of town, but I doubted if I would get much mileage by saying that I, too, had obligations that occasionally overrode my commitment to legal education.

"Mr. James — is there a Mr. James here?"

A man replied, in a strained voice, "Yes." In his early twenties with medium-length brown hair and wearing a madras sport shirt, James was sitting halfway up the far section of the amphitheater.

I started breathing again.

The ensuing dialogue went along the following lines:

"Nice to have you with us, Mr. James." Hazard looked

serious. "Now assuming that you have read *Swann v. Burkett* — and that's assuming a lot, I know — can you give us a brief description of the case?"

A lengthy pause followed during which the class flipped through the mimeo. Peering over the shoulder of the student sitting in front of me, I saw the case concerned an apartment house in Berkeley near People's Park, just a couple of blocks from where I once lived. I felt a twinge of pride thinking I was probably the only person in the room besides Hazard who knew the exact building around which the lawsuit revolved.

James said the case concerned housing discrimination against blacks in alleged violation of state law.

"Yes, Mr. James, that's very good," said Hazard, raising his eyebrows. He seemed patronizing and encouraging at the same time. "Could you be more specific? It would help if we had something to talk about."

James tried again. He spoke while leafing through a seven-page section of the mimeo headed "Summary of Facts of *Swann v. Burkett*." The word CONFIDENTIAL was typed in capitals in the right-hand corner.

The summary revealed that in 1960 a black couple named Swann had seen a newspaper advertisement for an apartment at 2709 Benvenue. Mrs. Swann called the landlord, a Mr. Burkett, who said, "You come on by, I'm sure we can work something out." After Mr. and Mrs. Burkett showed them the apartment, the Swanns said they wanted to rent it.

Burkett replied that the apartment had already been spoken for. He then showed them another apartment in a cottage at the back of the building. The Swanns asked to rent this one instead, but Burkett said he had already promised it to another couple. Burkett agreed to call the next day if the second couple decided not to take it.

The Swanns, sensing racial discrimination, immediately asked white friends who lived nearby to look at the cottage apartment while posing as a couple in the same circumstances as the Swanns — childless, petless, wife working and husband in graduate school. They took a look at the cottage apartment, and within a few minutes Burkett offered it to them. He never called the Swanns and was said to be out whenever they called him.

The Swanns sued "in propria persona" — without the aid of an attorney. They based their legal complaint on the Unruh Civil Rights Act, California Civil Code Section 51, which states in part:

> All citizens within the jurisdiction of this State are free and equal, and no matter what their race, color, religion, ancestry or natural origin are entitled to the full and equal accommodations, advantages, facilities, privileges or services in all business establishments of every kind whatsoever.

The Swanns contended that Burkett's apartment building should be considered "a business establishment" under the act because it had to be licensed through the Berkeley Business License Ordinance. If renting apartments wasn't a business, they argued, it wouldn't require a business license.

James had gotten this far in his (less-detailed) summary of the case when Hazard asked how Burkett's attorney, Mr. Wayne, had responded to the Swanns' complaint.

"He filed a demurrer," James said.

Hazard asked James if he knew what a demurrer was. When James said no, Hazard replied, "Ah." A demurrer, he explained, is a document filed by a defendant saying that even if the facts given in a complaint are true, they don't constitute an illegal act under the law cited. Hazard added that demurrers had been abolished for federal civil procedure and in most states as well. Great, I thought — we're going to learn about a legal form that's virtually extinct.

"Mr. James, what are the grounds for Burkett's demurrer?"

James looked very tired as he stared at the mimeo. For a moment he said nothing.

"He . . . Burkett's attorney . . . Wayne says the complaint is ambiguous, that it doesn't state facts sufficient to constitute a cause of action. . . ."

James stopped, his fingers moving down the demurrer.

Hazard walked thoughtfully in front of James's section, nodding, finger on his chin, in no hurry.

". . . and . . . that he, Burkett that is, hasn't violated Section Fifty-one. . . ."

"Ah! And why is that?"

"Because he . . . um . . . I'm not. . . ."

Silence.

"Perhaps, Mr. James, because the Swanns hadn't shown that an apartment building was 'a business establishment'? Does that sound like a term you've heard before?"

More silence.

"In the code section you just read for us?" Hazard continued.

"Uh, yes . . . I, I think so."

"You 'think so'?" Hazard looked pleased. "It's a start, it's a start."

Nervous laughter.

Hazard looked at his watch and explained the dueling legal strategies.

The Swanns had cited Berkeley's business-licensing ordinance in an attempt to show that Burkett's apartment fell under Section 51 of the Unruh Act — that much I understood. But the ordinance was a poor peg on which to hang an argument, Hazard said, because it would be almost impossible to demonstrate that when Berkeley used the word *business* in the ordinance, it intended to regulate the same sort of operation the California legislature intended to regulate when it used the phrase *business establishment* in the Unruh Act. The fact that both the ordinance and the act used the word *business* meant little, and to assume they defined the same thing was to invite ridicule from opposing attorneys.

I didn't quite get this. Doesn't everyone know what a "business" is — an activity performed to make money?

Hazard anticipated the question I didn't dare ask.

Section 51 didn't define the term *business establishment;* it didn't enumerate the various operations that could fit under that label. Moreover, Berkeley's shorthand title for its licensing ordinance could be a misnomer, as Wayne contended in his demurrer. What evidence was there for assuming that the two laws were intended to apply to the same set of businesses? That the city ordinance was intended, like the Unruh Act, to prevent discrimination? An attorney who wanted to base a case on Section 51, Hazard said, had to find a better way to demonstrate that an apartment building could properly be called a "business establishment."

It was about this time that Hazard revealed his reasons for beginning Procedure with this particular case. Hazard had been a law professor at Boalt, and Swann a law student, when the incident with Burkett occurred, and Hazard had become the Swanns' attorney soon after the landlord demurred to the original complaint, which Swann had written himself. Hazard essentially scrapped the student's complaint and submitted his own. As Hazard explained it to us, a plaintiff has the right to file an amended complaint so long as the newer version makes the legal issues "less fuzzy."

Hazard's complaint was much shorter than the original. He dropped all references to the Berkeley ordinance and Section 51; he called the Swanns U.S. citizens as well as California residents, and their allegations a "cause of action." Rather than saying Burkett operated his apartment building in "a business manner," as the Swanns had, he called it one of a number of "establishments" operated by Burkett "for profit." And he asked for fifteen hundred dollars in damages, plus costs, instead of five hundred.

Hazard answered the question on everyone's mind: Why had he eliminated any discussion of the applicable laws?

"When you're composing a complaint, ladies and gentlemen" — Hazard looked around the room — "you map out a scenario, and all its variations, by working backwards from your knowledge of what arguments might prevail. You imply substantive law through description of the historical event at issue. The complaint reveals the cause of action; it describes an event within a class of events which, by the application of substantive law, constitutes a legal grievance. The minor factual premise embeds the major legal premise; it is intended to lead to a narrative the judge can write."

I translated in my head. The less information the attorney volunteers, the better, for two reasons: so he doesn't get caught up in irrelevant, distracting, and arguably contradictory facts, and because the less he says about the law, the more room he has to maneuver. The attorney wants to force an opponent to rely on assumptions subject to later attack; he wants, if possible, to create a situation in which an opponent tips his hand first and inadvertently provides arguments and information that can be used against him. The complaint was a collection of facts into which the judge dropped law, and if the attorney arranged the facts well, only the law most favorable to the client would seem to fit.

It sounded awfully manipulative to me. If you think law supports your side, you try to show how neatly the law's pegs, round or not, correspond to your case's round holes; if you think it doesn't, you whittle the law's pegs, or chisel the facts' holes, to look square. Often, and if properly done, you can distort the facts or the law — usually both — just enough so that the case turns not on the dispute in question but on your skill as an advocate.

I didn't have any argument with the Swanns, with whose cause I agreed. But this was being a good lawyer? "Massaging" the facts and the law — that's the word Hazard used — to suit your client's goals? I had a feeling Hazard was massaging student minds in the very same way.

Procedure haunted me that first week of class much more than Con Law. Kahn had seemed appropriately appalled by the injustice of *Bowers* — had assigned it, I assumed, to ensure that students remembered from day one that bad court decisions could be challenged. The legal issues in *Swann* weren't so different — minority rights at the cutting edge of the law — but Hazard's approach to law seemed to empty it of moral content, made it an intellectual exercise. He glossed over the social context of *Swann;* he seemed more interested in the case's legal maneuvering than the justice of his clients' position. That wasn't only Hazard's doing, of course; Procedure, after all, is a class in methodology. But I was still surprised to the extent to which Hazard glorified technical mastery of the law, for it seemed he could have taken Burkett's side with equal enthusiasm. The ability to read the minds of judges and other lawyers seemed more important to him than the rights and values at stake.

I couldn't figure out what Hazard was up to. Condescending one minute, funny the next; arrogant, then affable; encouraging, then bullying; informal, then didactic. He played so many roles, gave so many contradictory messages, that I felt on edge just wondering what he was going to do next. Hazard seemed to like nothing more than keeping his students off balance. But that was, I eventually came to see, the whole idea behind his teaching method — to keep us treading quicksand. Practicing lawyers constantly encounter difficult, stressful situations; they have no choice but to deal with everything judges and opposing attorneys throw at them. Hazard was training us to think on our feet, to take any idea in stride no matter how outrageous, to be prepared for every eventuality. The lessons would hurt, but for the lawyer they were necessary.

I had already begun to sense, however, that Hazard's teaching methods were not entirely benign. His inducement of mental vertigo was so complete, so far beyond the necessary, that I had no difficulty believing that a deeper agenda lurked beneath the surface disorientation. Many critics of legal education use the word *brainwashing* to describe the process, and I began to understand what they meant. By eliminating all nonlegal points of reference, Hazard forced us to accept his word about law; by implying that every assumption students had made prior to law school was presumptively wrong, he made us doubt our self-worth. And when he hinted at the existence of a legal framework that could encompass *all* thoughts and ideas, accessible only to those who adopted the legal point of view — courageously and altruistically, by implication — he had us eating out of his hand. In those early weeks, we were so relieved to be told that certainty existed somewhere in the legal world that we didn't care whether it was valid.

I had heard from a second-year student that the professor for the other section of Procedure, Owen Fiss, had once begun a semester by throwing the Federal Rules of Civil Procedure out the classroom window while crying, "It's mush, it's pudding!" I began to wish I were in that section. The more I thought about Hazard's approach to Procedure, his love of rules and his professional, professorial authority, the more law seemed a rationalization of the status quo.

I was not in a good mood when Hazard resumed the discussion of *Swann v. Burkett* at the next session.

Hazard walked toward the aisle nearest James's seat. I assumed, like everyone else, that he was going to continue the interrogation where he had left off.

"Mr. Lopat?"

I almost jumped — Hazard wasn't looking anywhere near Lopat when he called his name. Lopat, seated a few feet to Hazard's left, low down in the center section, seemed particularly startled. He may have been prepared, but he certainly wasn't ready.

"Mr. Lopat, what if there were no Section Fifty-one? What if the cause of action was predicated on the Fourteenth Amendment?"

He paused.

"What would the complaint look like?"

Hazard had told us at the close of the previous class to think about arguments that could be made if Section 51 didn't exist. I had bought the *Swann v. Burkett* package and read its 235 pages with some care, but had gotten nowhere. How could Hazard expect us, still profoundly ignorant of the law, to be able to argue a hypothetical situation? We had enough trouble just trying to figure out what happened in *Swann* in real life.

Lopat was apparently as confounded as I. The class became very quiet as he glanced down at the case, then up at Hazard, then down again.

"I believe you'll find the Fourteenth Amendment in the Federal Rules, which, you'll remember, I told you always to bring to class. Section One."

Much flipping of pages.

We read.

AMENDMENT XIV
[1868]

Section 1. All persons born or naturalized in the United States, and subject to the jurisdiction thereof, are citizens of the United States and of the State wherein they reside. No State shall make or enforce any law which shall abridge the privileges or immunities of citizens of the United States; nor shall any State deprive any person of life, liberty, or property, without due process of law; nor deny to any person within its jurisdiction the equal protection of the laws.

Hazard turned away from Lopat, put his hands in his trouser pockets, and looked up at the ceiling.

The class was five minutes old and already I was completely lost. I knew that the Fourteenth Amendment had been passed after the Civil War to prevent the Confederate states from enacting racist laws. But the amendment appeared to concern only state laws, making it appropriate for a case like *Bowers v. Hardwick* — and not, it seemed to me, for the variation on *Swann* that Hazard proposed. If California's Civil Rights Act didn't exist, what state law could bring the case under the Fourteenth Amendment?

"Ahlright, Mr. Lopat," said Hazard, adopting a German accent, "shall ve write a complaint predicated on the Fourteenth Amendment?"

Hazard asked Lopat a series of questions concerning the filing of a case, something we knew nothing about.

"Who should be named as defendants?"

Pause.

"Are you going to sue the city of Berkeley?"

Pause.

Lopat ultimately decided no. The city had deep pockets, but it would be a difficult case to make (for reasons I never understood).

"Co-defendants? Mrs. Burkett? She was there too."

Lopat said yes. The complaint involved a single act by both the Burketts.

Federal or state court?

The student had no idea.

Hazard explained why he filed the real case in state court. In 1960, he said, a California judge on a state claim was more likely to give an activist interpretation of the law than a federal judge on a federal claim. "It's a maxim that the lower the court, the fewer the constitutional rights," Hazard added, "but that isn't always true."

Jury trial?

Lopat looked ahead blankly.

Hazard noted that there is no automatic right to a jury trial in civil suits, as there is in criminal cases, so the lawyer has to look closely at the available jury pool. Berkeley at the time was only 10 to 15 percent black — and moreover, Hazard said, jury panels were then drawn from the voters list, driving the number of potential black jurors even lower and eliminating most University of California students as well.

No, Hazard said, a jury trial wasn't advisable: "You'd get a bunch of people like the Burketts."

Hazard came to the heart of the matter.

"Cause of action?"

Lopat confessed that he didn't see the link to state law
Hazard explained. The city of Berkeley's business-license
ordinance hadn't emerged in a vacuum; it had to be authorized by a state law permitting local communities to establish regulations of their own. It was possible to argue,
consequently, that Berkeley's action was a form of state action, once removed; the city was simply acting as a stand-in
for the state. Hazard could have used that argument himself
in 1960 but did not want to imply that every city licensing
was, in effect, state action. Such a position could have been
disastrous, for it would have allowed Burkett's attorney to
say that the acceptance of this interpretation of the law
opened the floodgates to litigation — usually an effective
argument, since most judges are overworked.

"So, Mr. Lopat. How does your complaint read now?"

Lopat, reading from Hazard's amended complaint:
"Plaintiff is informed and believes that defendant —"

"Jurisdiction, Mr. Lopat, jurisdiction!"

Lopat looked bemused.

"What facts establish jurisdiction?"

Lopat continued to look bemused.

"The first thing you've got to do is establish jurisdiction.
The Swanns live in Berkeley, that's an undisputed fact. Is
that enough?"

Pause.

"Would you like me to spell it out?"

Pause.

"Okay. Are you going to call the Swanns 'residents' of
California or 'citizens' of the U.S.?"

Lopat said nothing. Either his brain was gridlocked, unable to process any more information, or he couldn't believe
it really mattered which characterization he used.

"Both, perhaps, Mr. Lopat?"

Or else Lopat had had enough of Hazard and was about to explode.

Hazard wandered during the lull that ensued.

"Citizens," Lopat finally said.

Hazard turned back to him. "You're saying citizenship is a *legally* relevant fact?"

Lopat, after a moment and with an edge to his voice, said, "I guess not."

"Ah, so you've changed your mind?"

Pause. Lopat turned slightly crimson.

Nobody knew what Hazard was doing besides Hazard, but everyone knew their turn would come too soon.

Hazard walked toward my side of the room, where Lopat could see only his back. He clasped his hands behind him, rocked back and forth on the balls of his feet, and mugged for the students sitting before him.

"Is that your final answer?"

Pause.

I tried to think of this one-sided dialogue as theater.

Grinning, back still turned: "Do you *think* that's your final answer?"

Some laughter.

I noticed that my knees were locked up. Creeping paralysis; there was something hypnotic about power that contained no hint of physical force. I stopped looking at Hazard, hoping to keep myself out of the line of fire.

Hazard, now stone-faced, walked back toward Lopat.

Lopat looked down at the mimeo with intense concentration. He found no salvation there, perhaps because he was preoccupied with the idea that the entire class was wondering how red his face would be when he finally looked up.

"I'm not sure," he said. Fairly red, especially the ears.

" 'I'm not sure'?" Hazard turned to the class and displayed a benevolent smile. "That's a permitted answer. Anyone care to supply a different one?"

No hands went up. I noticed that the doors through which Hazard had come into the classroom now appeared to be chained. My mind was drifting — not for lack of interest, but because I hated the fear Hazard had instilled in the class. I wanted Hazard to call on me just so I could refuse to cooperate, to give him a taste of his own medicine.

It took me two or three minutes to figure out that what I took for a chain was actually the shadow cast by a carved doorstop.

"I see I've reduced you to the status of military recruits who won't reveal a single thought."

The comment was so accurate it evoked no laughter at all. My shirt was growing increasingly clammy.

Someone stretched, feigning ease or boredom, in the back.

"Yes? . . . No? Just a muscle spasm, eh?"

Fidgeting, which had previously been limited to doodling and the sliding about of books and pencils, advanced to leg-crossing and paper-shuffling.

"Mr. Lopat? Any ideas?"

A woman in her thirties spoke up in a clear, strong voice without raising her hand. She gave a confident-sounding answer.

The air became taut. She had taken the pressure off Lopat, certainly, which was a relief . . . but who did she think she was? It was as if she had walked out of the audience to try to clear up a misunderstanding between Estragon and Didi in *Waiting for Godot*.

Hazard nodded and asked the woman's name. He recognized it — he knew her father, a federal judge, and asked that she pass on his regards.

Hazard, to Lopat: "Would you care to respond to your incipient friend and potential competitor in this dog-eat-dog profession?"

Laughter, this time.

To the outspoken woman: "It's always possible that someone may not agree with you."

More laughter, and the tension broke. Hazard, it seemed, was going to spread his sarcasm evenly; an equal opportunity offender.

Hazard smiled crookedly. I was sure he had come up with a further retort and couldn't decide whether it was beyond the bounds of decency.

He thought better of it and backpedaled toward the podium. Had he sensed how close we had come to mutiny? Absolutely — that was his job, to press the edge, to bend the class without breaking it.

"Any more thoughts, Mr. Lopat?" It was one of the few open-ended questions Hazard would ever ask.

Lopat, to my amazement, did have more to say. He explained that while the first section of the Fourteenth Amendment twice referred to "citizens" of the United States, it was with reference to the privileges and immunities clause; the due process and equal protection clauses, by contrast, applied to "any person" within a state's jurisdiction. A statement of the Swanns' residency in California was thus enough to establish the applicability of the amendment to Hazard's hypothetical.

I thought of the *Bowers* discussion in Kahn Law. I read the Fourteenth Amendment again, and again. Was that what happened — the privileges and immunities clause fell out of use because it swept in fewer people, only "citizens," than the amendment's other clauses? Could the explanation really be that simple — and so easy to miss? Law's operative words often seemed to be the very ones I slid over.

Hazard had called the Swanns "citizens" of the U.S. in his amended complaint, apparently, to bring Section 51 squarely into play, but also "residents" of California to make it easier for a judge to issue a decision that applied to non-citizens as well.

"Questions?"

There were only five minutes left. Some brave soul asked what had become of the Swanns' friends — the white couple who had effectively demonstrated Burkett's racism.

"That's a very good question. When we went to trial, they were sitting in an office across the street from the court-house. I didn't want to call them unless I had to; their transaction with Burkett was fictitious, and I didn't want the judge to think the same of the Swanns'.

"Note that Burkett's attorney knew about that couple but didn't do anything about it. His failure to investigate hurt his case but also meant that if he filed a motion for a new trial in light of newly discovered evidence, I could say he should have known about it. But don't forget — the only reason Wayne knew about that couple was because the Swanns mentioned them in their original complaint.

"I hope that makes clear why I hammer away at the idea that there's no such thing as a completely relevant fact. Remember: you *can't plead evidence!*"

Hazard looked benignly at Lopat. He lifted an arm in Lopat's direction, as an actor does when acknowledging a co-star.

Three

Down the Rabbit Hole

The life of the law has not been logic; it has been experience. The felt necessities of the time, the prevalent moral and political theories, intuitions of public policy, avowed or unconscious, even the prejudices which judges share with their fellow men, have had a good deal more to do than the syllogism in determining the rules by which men should be governed. The law embodies the story of a nation's development through many centuries, and it cannot be dealt with as if it contained only the axioms and corollaries of a book of mathematics. . . . The substance of the law at any given time pretty nearly corresponds, so far as it goes, with what is then understood to be convenient; but its forms and machinery, and the degree to which it is able to work out desired results, depend very much upon its past.

OLIVER WENDELL HOLMES, JR.

The Common Law

1881

The dining hall is the social center of Yale Law. The school schedules classes to foster meal-time socializing among first-years, or so it seems; many of the small-group seminars let out around 12:30, which naturally leads to lunch.

My routine was to drop my new book pack — my old one fell apart after a week, unable to cope with five-pound books — just inside the dining hall door, then survey the room to see who else was around. If I didn't decide to hang

out with the other students from Kahn Law, or I failed to
spot another friend or M.S.L. journalist, I would sit by
anyone who looked interesting.

The student grapevine and the "face book" — the student
directory — told me there was no shortage of people worth
getting to know. In the first-year class was a nun always
dressed in her habit, a marine who had recently served in the
Persian Gulf, a man of the Baha'i faith from New Jersey, and
three or four Ph.D.s. Students in the second- and third-year
classes included a former New Haven councilwoman, a couple of students with divinity degrees, three M.D.s, and more
than a dozen Ph.D.s (my class had fallen down, apparently,
in the advanced-degree department). A number of the upper-
class students had well-known fathers like Arthur Liman and
Alan Dershowitz (both Yale Law graduates), but the closest
the school came to student celebrities were the former wife
of Eldridge Cleaver and a one-time member of the singing
group Sha Na Na (which sued him, ironically, for quitting
to go to law school).

I usually ended up eating with Sam, Denise, or Michelle,
who soon became my closest friends at the law school. I
gravitated toward them, I think, because they were among
the least prickly students in the small group. They took law
seriously, but not, like some other students, as an excuse for
unbridled competition.

Sam had acquired a good-ol'-boy veneer during his college years in the South. But he was essentially shy, and had
gone into journalism, I guessed, for the same reason I had —
to overcome diffidence. Sam had eventually tired of reporting because he wanted to participate in life rather than
observe it, and I think he was disappointed to find that while
law school was in many ways as exhilarating as journalism,
it seemed less fun, less involving. Sam was used to asking the

questions, just as I was, and it was difficult suddenly to be on the other side of interrogation.

Michelle was perhaps even more shy than Sam. At first I thought her genuinely outgoing — within a month she seemed to know every other student by name — but I soon saw she was motivated largely by duty, a sense that she should know everyone else. Michelle's expression often said she wished she had more in common with the people around her; raised in the Midwest, she had attended a Catholic college, and was obviously not comfortable in the Ivy League. Like a lot of students, she had enrolled in Yale Law not because she was particularly interested in law but because she had been accepted, and because a law degree seemed to keep all options open. Early on Michelle had said she hoped to use her law degree to "help people," and I often wondered, as did she, how "promissory estoppel" and "contractual consideration" and "trespass *vi et armis*" would allow her to do so.

Students like Sam and Michelle, wary and unconfident, were not unusual at Yale Law. Denise was more typical — brash, talkative, energetic, Ivy League–assured. A New Yorker, she wasn't tentative about law; Denise liked nothing better than a good argument . . . or a bad argument, so long as her position was winning or (in the alternative) outrageously far-out. The way she handled herself in discussions always made me think she must have already graduated from law school and had returned just to brush up on her strategic negotiation skills.

Denise was one of three or four students in the small group who seemed primed for distinction beyond law school. No presidents among them, perhaps, although Yale Law had done well in that department in recent years; Gerald Ford is a graduate, as are one-time presidential aspirants Gary Hart, former California governor Jerry Brown, and, bizarrely, evangelist Pat Robertson. But I was sure the small group would produce a presidential adviser or two, a couple of judges or professors, and certainly some elected officials and lawyers of influence. There was a good chance that someone from this group would eventually affect the way the world worked.

The teaching assistant for Con Law was a third-year student from Seattle. Although Kurt was about the same height as Kahn, and also had a beard, the two were otherwise completely different. While Kahn was uptight but intellectually brilliant — so I had concluded from the *Bowers* discussion — Kurt was homespun and relaxed. He usually wore blue jeans and flannel shirts, and with his dark red hair could have passed for a Norwegian woodsman.

As Kahn's aide-de-camp, Kurt's job was to shepherd us through our initial attempts at legal writing and research. Our first project was the library assignment, intended to familiarize students with the inner workings of law libraries. I looked forward to the exercise because in the past I had found library research rather fun. It was the odd details, the colorful facts, the telling moments one stumbled across in the course of reporting a story that brought to life a subject that would otherwise be deadly dull.

One aspect of the assignment, however, was clearly going to be a royal pain — writing the legal citations we located in the proper legal form. Kahn had told us to buy the "blue book" citation guide, published by the Harvard Law Review, and it proved to be 255 pages of detailed instructions (the index alone spanned 34 pages). Among other fascinating things, the blue book informed the lawyer when to space out the acronym of a law review and when to italicize the letter "l" in a subdivision.

The library assignment consisted of about forty questions, each of which could be answered by looking up a few cases, sometimes just one. None involved analysis, at least directly; all we had to do was supply the information requested. That seemed easy enough, but Kurt told us the assignment was going to take a lot more time than we imagined. If we tried to do it all at once, he said, we would go crazy, either because so many searches resulted in dead ends or because none of the answers we came up with would seem quite right. If we got lost in a question after fifteen minutes of "good faith effort," Kurt said, we should ask for help.

I set to work on the assignment the following day. Whoever put the assignment together — it was a teaching assistant's hand-me-down, apparently — had tried to take the sting out of it. We were supposed to find, among other things, a law review article dedicated to Chuck Berry; a federal case in which someone sued Satan; and two rabbit-related legal references — a Georgia case determining that "hunting rabbits from an automobile cannot be equated with making war on the United States," and a Connecticut statute prohibiting the sale of purple rabbits.

I breezed through the first questions, which asked for "full citations and subsequent history" of a few cases. I had a head start on many students; I already knew that U.S.L.W., P.2d, and L.Ed. meant, respectively, *U.S. Law Week*, *Pacific Reporter Second Series*, and *Lawyer's Edition, U.S. Supreme Court Reporter*, so it took me little time to find them.

Some of the citations, however, were long and off-putting. The cite I found in an official reporter for "473 F.2d 943" was

Wilbur v. Mullaney, 473 F.2d 943 (CA1 1973), va-
cated, 414 U.S. 1139, 94 S. Ct. 889, 39 L. Ed. 2d 96
(1974), on remand, 496 F.2d 1303 (CA1 1974),
aff'd, 421 U.S. 684, 95 S. Ct. 1881, 44 L. Ed. 2d 508
(1975).

It wasn't as complex as it looked. Much of the cite was
redundant; the clause "414 U.S. 1139, 94 S. Ct. 889, 39 L.
Ed. 2d 96," for example, referred to a single decision as
printed by three different publishers. The cross-referencing
was no doubt handy for lawyers and judges and law clerks,
but it made law seem inaccessible to everyone else.

When I finished the simple citation questions, my knowledge of legal research was virtually sapped. From then on I
walked on new ground, and it was rarely firm. Some questions involved only realizing that a specific reference work
existed; it was easy to locate the Supreme Court's "sick
chicken" case once you knew of a book called *Shephard's Acts
and Cases by Popular Names — Federal and State.* Other questions, though, involved spiraling around an issue like a vul-
ture. I would go from one promising reference book to
another, hoping for a scent, and often picking up a trail that
led me to *this* case containing *that* proposition indexing *this*
gloss citing *another* case in *that* state for the given time period
. . . only to discover that I had gone around in a circle. It
wasn't a matter of whether I'd get off track, but when,
where, and how many times. Sometimes it felt as if I were
attempting to complete a connect-the-dots drawing —
except the dots weren't numbered, didn't fall into any obvious pattern, and seemed to hover in a third or fourth
dimension.

Three nights of staying up until 2 A.M., attempting to
answer questions such as whether a Canadian citizen had to

establish United States citizenship before grazing cattle on federally owned land in Alaska, and I was done with the assignment. I learned what one-time Yale Law professor Fred Rodell thought were the two main problems of legal scholarship: "One is its style. The other is its content." I also learned that at least one federal judge has written an opinion in verse, though "not of the calibre," he admitted "of Saint-John Perse." Above all I had the first inklings of what it is like to navigate by the law. The library assignment told me there was nothing upon which the law didn't touch, that every particle of information in the universe could be caught, somehow, in law's web. Give an attorney a library, pen, and paper, and he could tame chaos. It was power of amazing proportions — and only just beyond my grasp.

Michelle and I crossed paths frequently while doing the library assignment. Most students, including me, were reluctant at times to share hard-won information with others, fearful of losing an edge or ignominiously leading someone else down a dead-end trail. But Michelle was different; she welcomed people who stopped by her carrel to talk, and volunteered whatever shortcuts she had uncovered. She wasn't trying to be the best law student or the fastest, and that made her stand out; the law school remained a competitive place, no matter how many times the dean and other professors stressed the need for cooperation and community.

Michelle's immunity to the "law first" ethic came home vividly a few days before the library assignment was due. Seeing her with a paperback at a table in the law school courtyard one afternoon, I walked over to kid her about sloughing off. The book was *Cyrano de Bergerac,* among the works I would have least expected to find in a law student's hands. I said as much, and Michelle grinned in embarrassment.

We talked about the play, about the library assignment, and then I asked Michelle how she was doing, really.

"Fine," she replied, with a melancholy look and not much conviction. I said she seemed a little homesick.

"My father's paying all this money," Michelle said, "and it just doesn't seem worth it. I don't think I'm getting enough out of this place." She didn't feel she was being worked hard enough and was considering a transfer to another law school that had offered a full scholarship.

It was upsetting news. With her deft human touch and open mind, her sense of personal responsibility, Michelle struck me as exactly the sort of person law schools need in abundance. Yet it seemed she was being driven out of Yale Law — and not so much by the high expense, I guessed, as by its atmosphere. She had come to dislike free time because it forced her to see she wasn't the kind of person who succeeded here; her inability to be glib and breezy and quickwitted, her lack of surpassing ambition and confidence, marked her as middling in Yale Law's hyperintellectual terms. So what if she never wanted to play "hide the ball" with Hazard, preferred to collaborate with other people rather than compete with them? Michelle was quite religious, I knew, and I could see that law was trying to drive such beliefs out of her — subtly, of course, by saying that lawyers should value only those beliefs that can be rationally explained.

It was this encounter with Michelle, I think, that first made me consider seriously whether legal education is largely an indoctrination in a new system of belief. On reflection, her reading *Cyrano* wasn't so irrelevant to the law as I had first assumed, for wasn't Rostand describing the difficulties inherent in becoming the agent of another's cause? In focusing on another's problems rather than on one's own?

Unable to separate his desires from Christian's, Cyrano becomes an advocate, blots out honest communication, and ultimately causes tragedy. That is an issue lawyers encounter all the time, but law schools pretend, for the most part, that it doesn't exist.

Before going to Yale Law I had joked with friends that I would consider my year a success if I convinced a few law students to drop out. Now, drawn to law's power as much as repulsed by its effects, I redefined the joke. The year would be worthwhile, I told myself, if I convinced a few law students to stay enrolled — and then, as lawyers, to change the legal culture from within.

Kahn assigned *Marbury v. Madison,* probably the single most important legal decision in the history of American law, for the second week of class.

The case is only eight pages long but it took me three readings and as many hours to make any sense of it. I knew nothing about *Marbury* other than that it established the doctrine of judicial review — the idea that the courts, rather than the legislative or executive branches of government, have final say over the interpretation of the Constitution. Once I understood how the ruling came about, *Marbury* proved quite interesting.

In 1801, on the last day of his presidency, John Adams named forty-two justices of the peace for the District of Columbia. The official commissions, however, were not delivered before Adams left office, and Thomas Jefferson, the incoming president, refused to forward them. One of Adams's appointees, William Marbury, filed a suit of original jurisdiction in the Supreme Court asking for a "writ of mandamus" that would force Jefferson's secretary of state, James Madison, to hand over the commissions.

In his decision for a unanimous court, delivered more than a year after Marbury brought suit, Chief Justice John Marshall — a Federalist like Adams — at first seemed to favor the plaintiff. It was "decidedly the opinion of the court," he wrote, "that when a commission has been signed by the president, the appointment is made; and that the commission is complete when the seal of the United States has been affixed to it" by the secretary of state. All those steps had apparently been taken, which would seem to bring the case to an early close. But it didn't, not by any means; Marshall was only warming up.

After declaiming gloriously that the United States "has been emphatically termed a government of laws, and not of men," the chief justice demonstrated precisely the reverse. Through a combination of tortured logic and a dazzling rhetorical strategy, Marshall single-handedly ensured that American law was a creature of the court system rather than popular or legislative will. He began by discussing the powers of the president, which he determined to be of two forms: the powers granted by the Constitution and the powers authorized by Congress. Marbury was appointed through the latter power, and actions taken under that authority, Marshall said, were subject to review by the courts (because they were directed by law rather than presidential discretion). Again it seemed Marbury was going to win, for this finding effectively meant that a new president could not unilaterally block the pending appointments of his predecessor. Law, not politics, would determine the outcome of the dispute.

But the chief justice was far from finished. The Constitution, Marshall said in a tone that had the hallmarks of an afterthought, gave the Supreme Court original jurisdiction only in certain cases; normally it could take only appellate cases, those for which a judicial record had been established.

But the law under which Marbury brought suit — the Judiciary Act of 1789 — had failed to account for this distinction, Marshall said, and thus had mistakenly extended the court's original jurisdiction beyond constitutional limits. The Supreme Court, in other words, couldn't hear Marbury's case, or at least not until it had worked its way through the proper channels. Yes, Marbury was entitled to his commission . . . but the law with which he hoped to force its delivery brought to the court's attention another law the court was bound to find unconstitutional — and thus sealed Marbury's loss.

My ideas about *Marbury* weren't so clear before we discussed it in class. But I did gather that the case was both brilliant and brilliantly deceptive. Marshall could have said right off that the Supreme Court had no jurisdiction in *Marbury*, but he didn't, because he had other fish to fry. He had the chance, he realized, to make the Supreme Court the ultimate referee of law, and that the best way to ensure that result was to decide that *both* the plaintiff and defendant were wrong. By finding against an appointee of his own party, Marshall appeared to be saying that the Supreme Court was above politics; by striking down the Judiciary Act, Marshall appeared to be saying that the court would accept only such power as was its due. In reality, however, Marshall was eating his cake and having it, too, for he had arrogated to the Supreme Court the right to decide what the Constitution actually means — and thus, to a large extent, to set the terms of the nation's greatest debates. Marshall, in *Marbury*, had acted like a Greek god during wartime. He helped one side, then the other, all the while enjoying the combatants' false conviction that they are following their own free will.

At first I resisted this view of *Marbury*, sensing that I was fishing for conspiracy. The background material given by

Kahn and the casebook, however, only reinforced my skepticism.

Marshall was a member of John Adams's cabinet when the president nominated him to the chief justiceship in January 1801, just a few weeks before Jefferson ascended to the presidency. Marshall was thus aware of Marbury's case long before it went to court — indeed, was deeply involved in it, for he had been Adams's acting secretary of state and thus was personally responsible for Marbury's commission not being delivered! (A few weeks after assuming the chief justiceship Marshall actually admitted, "I should [have] sent out the commissions which had been signed & sealed but for the extreme hurry of the time.") And there was more. The new secretary of state, James Madison, hadn't bothered to defend himself against Marbury's suit. Was there collusion between Adams and Jefferson, Kahn wondered aloud, to test the limits of judicial power? I was finally convinced of the deep fishiness of the case when I read, in the casebook, that constitutional scholar Robert McCloskey had described *Marbury* as "a masterwork of indirection, a brilliant example of Marshall's capacity to sidestep danger while seeming to court it, to advance in one direction while his opponents are looking in another."

By the end of class I was aghast. This wasn't the *Marbury* I had read about in high school. It remained a "great case," to be sure — not because it eliminated politics from the law, however, but because it buried politics so deeply within it. Kahn had criticized this aspect of *Marbury*, yet he seemed to share every lawyer's admiration for the skill with which Marshall enshrined subterfuge as a legitimate judicial tool. Justice White had used the same technique, though much less well, in *Bowers v. Hardwick:* frame the issue in a way that makes the desired end seem an ineluctable result and, *voilà,* there it is. Marshall was simply better at covering his tracks than White, and came out on the side that history has vindicated.

My new understanding of *Marbury* became dramatically relevant a few weeks later, when Attorney General Edwin Meese indirectly assaulted the case during a speech in New Orleans. Although he claimed not to be arguing against the doctrine of judicial review, Meese did just that when he said Supreme Court rulings do not "establish a 'supreme law of the land' that is binding on all persons and parts of government." Since that position seemed directly at odds with Marshall's famous assertion in *Marbury* that it is "emphatically the province and duty of the judicial department to say what the law is," Meese was roundly attacked in legal circles . . . even though the argument had also been advanced by presidents as diverse as Jefferson, Jackson, Lincoln, and FDR.

Days before, happily ignorant, I had understood *Marbury* to be the bedrock of American legal culture. But that illusion was now shattered; the case had come to represent, instead, the idea that the ends justify the means even in law — the credibility of which is *based* on the idea that just ends depend on just means. How could I accept the manipulations of Marshall and not the manipulations of White and Meese — and Robert Bork, for that matter, the judge and former Yale Law professor who argued that the Constitution's framers intended Americans to be bound to the end of time by their "original intent," regardless of the changes the centuries might bring? I began to see why one of Kahn's favorite questions was "Can we go back?" Those who challenged *Marbury* essentially challenged almost two centuries of law;

it was much easier to go along with the status quo, to fight today's battles without worrying whether the battle itself is legitimate.

I was developing a constitutional crisis of my own. As much as Con Law disturbed me, it became my favorite class; it allowed me to examine, and in some cases comprehend, the deepest assumptions of the law. It was a challenge I could not resist — to probe law with its own tools and see how well it measured up to the standards it set for everybody else.

My excitement over Constitutional Law was nearly unique. The problem wasn't the material, however, so much as Kahn, who rubbed many students the wrong way. A number of them vented their anger with Kahn at a pizza party Kurt held for the small group to celebrate the completion of the library assignment.

I got to the party early because I didn't go to one of the "professional responsibility" seminars first-years are required to attend a few evenings during the semester. When the small group trickled in, I learned they had attended a lecture entitled "Judges from Outside the Mainstream," and I was sorry I had passed it up; the guest speakers talked, I gathered, about what it was like to be a member of a minority charged to implement the laws of the majority. The students didn't have much to say about the event, however, and seemed to regard the professional-responsibility lectures as just another class — only worse, because they took place in the evening and thus encroached on study time. The lectures petered out within a few weeks, and represented the only compulsory discussions of ethics at the law school.

During the party I talked for the first time with Liz, who had yet to say a word in Con Law. She had a host of complaints about Kahn. He lectured too much; he didn't acknowledge student comments, just pointed to the next upraised hand; he seemed less interested in what was said than who was saying it. I asked Liz to tell me a little about herself, attempting to gain some insight into her dislike of Kahn and Yale Law in general, and an answer slowly emerged. Unlike many of the other students, Liz had gone to a state school, accepted financial aid, and lacked the country-club social skills and legal connections many other students took for granted; she felt out of place and treated like a second-class citizen. Liz was proud of her achievements, and properly so, but Yale Law made them seem negligible and ordinary, as if life up to law school enrollment were meaningless. She was angry because the early talk about love and fairness and cooperation at Yale Law seemed to be just that: talk.

Liz had applied to law school with the goal of representing patients injured by malpracticing doctors. In a rare show of tact, I didn't ask about the source of her interest, but the specific nature of her ambition told me why she thought Con Law, and indeed almost all of our classes that first semester, was irrelevant — because the courses said so little about the practice of law in real life. That is a common complaint about law school, but Liz was the only student I knew who seemed to regard it as a genuine problem. She acted almost as if she had been duped, and seemed even more likely than Michelle to drop out of law school.

Talking with Liz was depressing, so much so that when Michelle passed by in search of a soda I hastened to intercept her. She had cheered up considerably since mentioning the desire to leave Yale, and we were soon discussing family and friends and personal dreams — anything but law. The chatter seemed daring, almost thrilling, for law school, and on impulse I asked Michelle whether she'd be interested in seeing a play at the Yale Rep, to which I had season tickets. She said she would.

The party broke up soon after, and I felt peculiar about what had gone on. It had something to do with the strong reactions I had toward both Liz and Michelle. Liz was an outsider who acted like one, furious about her status but simultaneously reinforcing her alienation by refusing to try to communicate with insiders; she wouldn't compromise, and thus circumscribed her world. Michelle, on the other hand, was an outsider who could pass for an insider, and did — and subsequently felt compromised, knowing that her dissembling was neither honest nor healthy. I saw that I had long played both those roles in my life — sometimes the rebel, sometimes the accommodator — and that law school seemed bent on making me choose between them. I was a journalist in search of "truth," yes, but also a law student in search of justification.

This conflict had already made itself apparent earlier in the evening. I overheard Grant, the most aggressive and — with Denise — garrulous student in the small group, saying a "well-placed source" had told him that when Antonin Scalia was nominated to the Supreme Court from his appellate judgeship in Washington, he had delayed handing down some potentially controversial decisions so as not to endanger his confirmation.

The revelation, if true, was shocking. But what was I supposed to do about it? Did I have some implicit agreement of confidentiality with Yale Law that prevented me from following up on such information? More important, perhaps, did Grant (whom I had never talked to before) know I was a journalist — that his loose talk had serious implications? The allegations sounded like gossip, an insider's attempt to impress Grant, but shouldn't I at least check out the rumor? My presence at law school obliged me to face a new set of ethics, a new set of loyalties.

Curiously, I had encountered a strikingly similar conflict of values years earlier, when I was a first-year student in journalism school. Conservative politicians in California disliked the state's liberal chief justice, Rose Bird, and tried to discredit her in a nasty campaign when she came up for confirmation in 1978. On election day the *Los Angeles Times* ran a front-page story in which a well-placed source claimed that one of Bird's staunchest allies on the court had delayed a decision that could cost her the election because it made her look soft on crime. The story was picked up all over the state, and few doubt that it almost caused Bird's defeat; she was confirmed by a very narrow margin.

We discussed the *Times*'s action in my newswriting class. I was virtually alone in saying I would not have run the story; the source's claim was an obvious attempt to affect the outcome of the election and thus, in my opinion, likely to prove highly distorted, at the very least. The professor vehemently disagreed, repeating the journalistic creed that "you go with what you've got," regardless of the consequences.

As it turned out, my view of the situation was not far off. A panel appointed to investigate the leak concluded that the decision had simply not completed its journey through the court's opinion-writing process: William Clark — an associate justice of the court best remembered for having failed to graduate from either college or law school — eventually testified that he had confirmed the leak for the *Times* (which convinced many people that he was the leak's true source). Clark would go on to become President Ronald Reagan's national security adviser, while Bird would go down to defeat in a second, even dirtier confirmation campaign while I was attending Yale Law.

I didn't pursue the Scalia story, no longer knowing which side I was on — and doubting, too, whether the notion of "sides" was a good one.

Four

Imagining the Past

> The perfect lawyer . . . should search the human heart,
> and explore to their sources the passions, and appetites, and feelings
> of mankind. . . . He should unlock all the treasures of history for
> illustration, and instruction, and admonition. . . . He will thus see
> man, as he has been, and thereby best know what he is. He will thus
> be taught to mistrust theory, and cling to practical good; to rely
> more upon experience than reasoning; more upon institutions than
> laws. . . . If the melancholy infirmities of his race shall make him
> trust men less, he may yet learn to love man more.
>
> JUSTICE JOSEPH STORY
> inaugural address as professor of law
> *Harvard University*
> 1829

A few weeks into the school year I tried to find a copy of *The Paper Chase,* John J. Osborn, Jr.'s novel about a first-year student's experience at Harvard Law School. Like most people, my impressions of legal education were based on some version of that book, but Osborn's law school — at least as portrayed in the movies and on television — was quite unlike mine. I wanted to read the original to see if I could find some resemblance. Law school was not what I had expected it to be, and I had begun to wonder how I arrived at my expectations. Had my views about legal education really been formed by a book — a novel no less — that I had never read?

I wasn't surprised to discover that the law library didn't have a copy of *The Paper Chase*. I eventually located a well-thumbed one in Cross-Campus, the below-ground, tomblike undergraduate library across High Street from the main library. That evening I found I had little in common with James Hart, Osborn's narrator, and our differences could largely be accounted for by the different eras, and schools, in which we received legal training. No law student I knew showed such interest in either sex or alcohol.

The Paper Chase is dominated, of course, by Professor Kingsfield. His closest counterpart at Yale Law is Hazard, but he doesn't set the tone for Yale Law the way Kingsfield does for Osborn's Harvard. That task is performed by Guido, who opened Torts by telling us that "ignorance is sacred; lack of understanding is where most learning comes from." Small wonder that Osborn, who studied at Yale Law a few years after *The Paper Chase* was published, called the school an "Alice-in-Wonderland anachronism."

Guido scurried into Room 120 on the first day of class looking less like an elf than Nikolai Lenin, with his receding hairline and van Dyke beard (before the week was out someone taped Lenin's portrait on the wall behind the podium). The dean wrote eight telephone numbers on the blackboard and told us to call him at home anytime, even at 3 A.M., as a student once did after losing his course notes on the train from New York. (Guido told the student not to worry; the notebooks would still be right where he left them, for at that time the cars on the New Haven line were never cleaned.) Guido said he preferred to rely on students to volunteer answers and wouldn't resort to the Socratic method unless his questions were consistently received in silence.

"I don't care," he said, "whether you're prepared for class

or not. That's up to you, though it's foolish not to read the material because it'll make it hard for you to figure out what's going on. But your way of studying is your business." He warned, however, that some students might find themselves hurt from time to time by sarcastic remarks and challenging questions. "But *don't* be hurt when I disagree with you, or stop asking questions," Guido said, "because you learn about the law by being skeptical — skeptical, not cynical." Cynicism, he said, was perhaps the lawyer's worst trait.

The dean spent another ten minutes telling stories calculated to put us at ease. He then began talking about the first decision in the casebook, *Ives v. South Buffalo Railroad Co.* . . . and the result was instant and utter confusion.

I had read the case a couple of times the night before and knew from the headnote — the unofficial summary — that it involved a railway switchman injured on the job. But of the case itself I could make neither head nor tail; what had struck me most about *Ives* was the fact that it was an unrelieved wall of print. Paragraphs went on for one, two, three, even four pages; I lost the thread of Judge Werner's argument every other minute amid the catalogue of citations and hypothetical situations, the "ifs" and "buts" and evernarrowing focus of each dependent clause. There were no concessions to the reader: the opinion was written exclusively for attorneys — certainly not for the losing plaintiff, Ives. Werner didn't even bother to give the nature of Ives's injury, let alone his first name.

At home, I had underlined a few points in *Ives* I thought worth talking about. And I had done so reluctantly, almost angrily. Why in God's name had Guido started the course with this particular case? I hadn't a clue what my analysis was supposed to uncover, to be used for; I could re-read *Ives* all night and still fail to understand it.

With *Bowers* and *Marbury* at least I had some sense of the case, but *Ives* was a black box to me. It was much more complicated than most decisions I had read, seemed untypical of tort law, and — having been handed down in 1911 — appeared outdated and historically insignificant, too; what could these long passages on seamen and shipowners, masters and servants, husbands and wives possibly have to do with an injured railwayman? How could we learn anything about torts by studying cases in which the word *tort* was mentioned only in an offhand reference to the "laws of deodands"? That phrase didn't even appear in my 832-page *Black's Law Dictionary*.

I didn't learn much from that first day of Torts. Guido's discussion of *Ives* was on a plane far beyond my comprehension. Within forty minutes he had talked about fault, insurance, test cases, inconsistent pleadings, risk sharing, demurrers, legislative intent, the Constitution's supremacy clause, common law . . . everything, it seemed, but what I considered to be the heart of the matter, the worker's injury. What I thought valuable in the case Guido skipped; what I thought irrelevant he emphasized.

I eventually gathered that the legal significance of *Ives* lay in Werner's holding that New York's workers compensation law violated the due process clauses of the federal and state constitutions. Werner struck down the statute because it acted, he said, as an illegal "taking" of an employer's property; it prevented the railroad from arguing (and perhaps proving) that it wasn't at fault for its employee's accident. There was no way, at the time, I could have pulled that idea out of the case itself, but for Guido it was just the starting point. The students were already supposed to understand, apparently, what I thought we were here to learn.

It was impossible to keep up. I had sat next to Alina, one

of the other M.S.L.s, and every few minutes we would exchange bug-eyed glances. I assumed we were thinking the same thing: that this material was completely over our heads. I kept waiting to hear something that made sense, something I already knew or wanted to know, but I never did — a galling experience, considering I had a better background in law than most of the other students. I didn't know what to do in class. If I wrote down everything Guido said, I might be able to figure out what he meant later — but if I did that, I would miss the preamble to his next point. And the one thing I was absolutely sure of was that I would never be able to follow Guido to his central thought should I miss a single strand of his intellectual web. The net effect of Guido's hundred interesting points, seemingly harnessed together in service of some deep, unknown purpose, was stupefaction.

Yet Guido's forays into sociolegal policy were powerful nonetheless, for they addressed issues I had never considered before. Who should pay for the costs of accidents? Should a loss lie where it falls, with the injured party, regardless of needs or abilities? How much leeway should the legal system give judges in deciding such questions; how much "play in the joints" do we want in legislative statutes? At the same time, however, I wondered why Guido was explaining how societies dealt with torts before we even knew what a tort was. Guido had already said, to much laughter, that we'd be less able to define a tort by the end of the semester than at the beginning, but it was some weeks before I realized he was quite serious.

I was dazed by the time class ended — ten minutes late, which proved typical for Guido. I was learning in Con Law about the importance to law of facts, in Procedure about the importance to law of words, but in Torts something quite different — the importance of legal theory to a culture's value system.

"I don't know about this," Alina said, her voice rich with skepticism, as we signed up for the first row on the seating chart. We might not understand what Guido was talking about, but at least we'd hear every inscrutable word.

The deans had warned from day one that perhaps the biggest difficulty first-years faced was coming to terms with the ambiguity of law. That was especially true in Torts. How do you make rules that control what is essentially uncontrollable — the accident, the tort, the unintentional wrong?

Guido dealt with that oxymoron by speaking in epigrams. Few made sense when they first came out of his mouth, but their mystery was purposeful — each was a koan, a paradox lost. (Webster's New Collegiate Dictionary defines a koan as "a paradox to be meditated upon that is used to train Zen Buddhist monks to abandon ultimate dependence on reason and to force them into gaining sudden intuitive enlightenment.") Guido's epigrams illustrated a belief that though it may be impossible, ultimately, to understand anything, it is the lawyer's duty to understand as much as he possibly can. Over the course of the semester, many of Guido's koans began to resonate.

"The rules you make," the dean said one day, "shape the people you are." I memorized the phrase even though its meaning at first eluded me. Guido continually frustrated the class by defining a rule only after talking about its effects, and for a while I didn't understand why he did so; only gradually did I see he adopted this approach in order to impress upon us the enormity of the temptation to apply a known rule to a new situation, regardless of its fit. And therein lay rules' ability to shape society: by defining limits prematurely, by authorizing the status quo, by confirming present knowledge that time will soon make obsolete. Law only reflected society, in theory, but in practice law can weigh it down as well.

"Imagine the past, remember the future." This was a favored epigram of the late Alexander Bickel, a politically conservative Yale Law professor (who borrowed the phrase from the historian L. B. Namier). It seemed tuneful non-sense when Guido loosed it on the second day of class, but this koan, too, eventually made sense. Lawyers need to imagine the past because appellate court decisions, the version of history upon which they perforce rely, are damagingly in-complete. They are narrow, law-shaped collections of fact, and lawyers who limit their thinking to them — to other lawyers' interpretations and understandings of reality — only perpetuate existing mistakes; they ignore a multitude of issues that invariably remain outside the legal record. Law-yers need to remember the future for the same reason. If they fail to ensure that every pertinent point makes it into the legal record of a case, their omissions will be passed down through the ages and likely never corrected.

My favorite Guidian aphorism, however, was a plain one: "For every maxim there is a countermaxim." Doubling back on itself like a Möbius strip, denying its own truth in the process of illustrating it, the maxim — or was it countermaxim? — captured perfectly the internal contradic-tions of the law. Guido pronounced it on his fifty-fourth birthday, the day he gave a memorable lecture on the doc-trine of the "reasonable man."

It was the middle of October and by then most of the Torts class had grown fond of the dean. A couple of students had made construction-paper party hats in his honor, so when Guido came into the classroom that day he was confronted with what appeared to be a forest of dunce caps. "Ah," he said, "I see you're all wearing academic uniforms!"

Guido put on his birthday hat — on him, it looked like a bishop's miter — and launched into an English case from 1837, *Vaughan v. Menlove.* When Vaughan's hayrick caught fire and burned a neighbor's buildings, the neighbor sued, charging that Vaughan had been negligent in failing to heed warnings that the hay he used, and his method of construction, made the rick susceptible to spontaneous combustion. (Though "Vaughan" appears first in the case's name, that doesn't necessarily mean he is the plaintiff; here, he is the appellant to a higher court, having lost the case at the trial level.) Menlove, the neighbor, sought a ruling that held individuals liable for their damaging actions if they "should have known better." Guido argued against that standard, and his disquisition went essentially as follows:

"Who is this 'reasonably prudent man' the court talks about? I'll talk about the change to 'reasonable person' later, whether it's verbal sexism or something deeper, but right now let's talk about the reasonable man.

"In *Vaughan* the question is whether you're going to use an absolute or a relative standard. The defendant's lawyer says to use a 'good faith' test; that Vaughan's fault should be measured by his own faculties, not those of other men. But the court decides to use the objective, 'reasonably prudent man' standard.

"What we've got here is a moral judgment about what the defendant *should* have done. There's a strong presumption that people know what reasonable men know; in criminal law, if you shoot someone with a gun you can't say it was a banana — unless you've had a history of operations for eating guns."

The class snickered, for *banana* was one of Guido's code words. Sometimes, he was telling us, a fact may be found irrelevant in one case but dispositive in another, or in the very same case before a different judge.

"In fact, people *don't* know what the reasonable man knows, because there's no such being. Yet we hold them to that standard anyhow because we don't like what they did; we want to condemn them.

"But things get tricky if you equate legal fault with moral fault, which is something people do all the time. There's a certain amount of Private Eddie Slovick in this."

Guido reminded us of an earlier lecture in which he criticized the U.S. Army's selecting Slovick for execution from among a group of World War II deserters because the private had once been convicted of petty theft. Outside of both desertion and thievery being morally objectionable acts, what connection was there between shoplifting and treason? Did Slovick deserve to die, in effect, for petty larceny?

"In a fault system, you're asking the person to pay who hasn't lived up to the general test. But we don't have a pure fault system, we sometimes *do* want to make the injurer pay even *without* fault. Workers compensation! *Ives v. South Buffalo!* Old Judge Werner!"

Ah — that was one reason for Guido's assigning *Ives.* Werner had ruled exactly the other way, of course, by declaring the workmen's compensation statute unconstitutional, but that view had long since gone by the boards. *Ives* was indeed ancient history; Guido was demonstrating that a society's values *do* change, and that law was sometimes an instrument of — and sometimes an obstacle to — that change.

Guido had begun calmly but by this time was windmilling his arms in excitement. He had already joked that he'd get workers comp if his arms ever "fell off," because then he couldn't teach. (Body parts are always falling off in Torts — even heads, at least in Guido's version of *Gould v. Slater Woolen Co.*, 147 Mass. 315, 17 N.E. 531 [1888].)

"You've got the flavor of moral fault in *Vaughan*. The defendant didn't do what he ought to have, says the plaintiff. But what happens if you go that way? Doesn't that mean you have to punish wrongdoing that causes *no* damage? What about *Scott v. Shepherd* and the squib that fizzles out?"

Guido cited an eighteenth-century case in which a lighted powder-bomb was hurled from person to person around a marketplace until it blew up in a merchant's face. Who should be liable — the initial, presumably malicious squib-tosser, or those in the middle who caused no harm only by luck, or the final thrower, who saved himself at the expense of another? Or should the court consider everyone liable and spread the costs?

"Legal fault and moral fault are different things, and when you confuse them, you change how a case comes out. Asking 'What did you know at the time?' is very different from asking 'What *ought* you to have known?' And who defines the 'ought'? The judge? The jury? The legislature?"

Guido went into hyperdrive, his eyes popping, his fore-head lined with questions. He stared intensely into a few student eyes — left side of the room, center, right side, in the back — trying to determine whether we were following him.

"That's a more important question than it seems. A sys-tem that confuses these issues may be claiming to do one thing while doing another."

Guido paused.

"What should trouble you about fault as a moral issue is that you're saying people could have done better who couldn't have. What good does it do," Guido almost shouted, "to ask people to do more than they *can* do?"

This was much more interesting than anything I had expected to hear at law school. And Guido wasn't even close to finishing his reflections on the "reasonable man": *Vaughan v. Menlove* — like most cases we studied in law school — had progeny.

Guido took us back down the garden path the following day. This time, however, he started with hypothetical situations. Suppose the defendant in *Vaughan*, the hayrick fire-starter, was a child. What then — do we let Menlove suffer, as would Oliver Wendell Holmes, Jr.?

"Holmes said, 'The general principle of our law is that loss from accident must lie where it falls.' Men must act, and since people generally profit from individual activity, the actor shouldn't necessarily bear the burden of his mistakes."

But what, Guido asked, if Holmes is wrong? Should the child really be held liable for damages he causes? Should his parents? What if he's an orphan? Should we invent the standard of 'reasonable child'? 'Reasonable orphan'? How many categories, how many standards, must we have, and how do we decide when we have enough?

Guido segued into two American cases. In *Charbonneau v. MacRury*, the Supreme Court of New Hampshire decided in 1931 that the conduct of a minor who killed someone while driving should be measured against the conduct of the average driver of the same age and experience. In *Hill Transportation Co. v. Everett*, also from New Hampshire but decided thirteen years later, a federal appellate court decided that a minor who injured someone while employed as a bus driver should be held to the same standards as an adult.

"What's different?" Guido asked. "Is it a case of on the

one hand, fish, on the other hand, fish'? What's going on here? Anybody."

No hands.

"Come on! Is this *Holmes v. Mather?*"

Guido quoted his all-time favorite case, in which England's Baron Bramwell, rather like his contemporary Holmes, found against a pedestrian struck by a carriage. " 'For the convenience of mankind in carrying on the affairs of life, people as they go along roads must expect, or put up with, such mischief as reasonable care on the part of others cannot avoid.' Why not protection for teenage drivers in *Hill?* Anyone!"

More silence.

"Wake up, you shouldn't be asleep yet! It's too early to be confused!"

A tentative arm waved and someone argued that the *Charbonneau* judge was right: teenagers shouldn't be penalized for their inability to drive up to the standards of an adult because they can attain that standard only by more driving. The argument seemed to correspond to Guido's side of the issue — *Charbonneau* was a subjective test, one that acknowledged the naturalness and unpredictability of human differences. I assumed the dean would like the student's analysis, but he didn't seem to.

"So it's correct? Does that mean you make a separate driving standard for teenagers because they can't live up to the general standard? Even when all the statistics show that as a group, drivers between the ages of sixteen and twenty-six are much more likely to kill than anyone else? Do we really want that? Somebody else!"

The scenario repeated itself a few times. Guido played the class as if it were speed chess, responding instantly to each student's comment and calling just as quickly on someone else. No answer was good enough; each failed to address some aspect of the reasonable man issue. This suggestion discriminated against that group; that one would break down over time; the other carried heavy transaction costs. Having found nothing new in our brains, Guido paused dramatically and began telling us what was wrong with the system.

Hill, Guido said, may well have made roads safer by encouraging a higher standard for minor drivers — indeed, it is the general rule of the road in the United States. But the safety fostered by *Hill* comes at a price.

"The only reason for applying a lower standard of care when minors are concerned," wrote the judge in *Hill,* "is to protect them from the normal consequences of their immaturity . . . and we see no reason why an employer of minors should be put in a more advantageous position with respect to the torts of his servants than one who employs adults." Employment, it turned out, was the key difference between the cases; if the standard of *Charbonneau* was applied in *Hill,* employers would have an incentive to hire minors, despite their categorically poor driving records, because the *Charbonneau* standard could allow the minor's employer to escape liability. But as Guido pointed out, *Hill* carried its own problems. It deterred employers from hiring minors as drivers, and probably caused minors to lie about their age.

Guido's outline of the issues, as always, was both compelling and troubling. It crossed my mind why some students had begun to write him off as a self-obsessed, impractical dreamer. His view of law was threatening because it fought complacency; to understand Guido was to feel obliged to try to solve the problems he broached. The dean's underlying message was that lawyers were duty-bound to ensure that the laws they implemented worked no harm, however hidden that harm might be.

Guido began to shop for answers again.

"Are we concerned with letting the punishment fit the tort? If we make exceptions, who's going to decide the exceptions? At what level of generality are we going to apply the rule?"

Audrey, from my small group, ventured an answer, as did another student. Guido shook each of them off. This idea didn't ensure that all automobile-caused losses would be made whole; that one failed to address the special needs of the poor and handicapped.

Liz, who sat to my right, raised her hand. Guido immediately dismissed her comment as well — it didn't provide incentives for bad drivers to get better. Liz grimaced and whispered, "So much for that." She never volunteered to speak in class again.

Guido tried another angle.

"Here's an ugly hypothetical. Suppose it's true that handicapped people have more accidents, more even than minors. Do we keep the same objective standard? If we do, we're discouraging them from driving, and asking them to pay more for insurance. And that seems like discrimination, especially to the person whose handicap doesn't affect his driving."

I found myself making up my own hypotheticals even as I listened — law school had given me the ability to think on two wavelengths at the same time. If a legislature relies heavily on accident statistics when deciding what standard to apply to minor drivers — an obvious choice — what would stop it from making similar choices with regard to other groups? Racial minorities, the aged, the disabled, the newly immigrated — suppose you could show that, as groups, they had more accidents than the "reasonable man." Then what? Do you balkanize the driving standard, set different standards for different groups — and thus, through higher premiums, make poor drivers poorer financially? And if you take that road, how do you determine the nature of the group? Would an older, newly immigrated, handicapped black man be uninsurable because of his group's record, despite his own half-century of accident-free driving?

"We make up such categories all the time," Guido said, "and you've got to look behind them." Perhaps a group has more accidents, for example, because its members have little money and drive older, unreliable, less safe, more accident-prone cars. Should they be further penalized for poverty? And what about the fact that past accidents, Guido said, are not good predictors of future accidents? With that obvious measure proving unhelpful, an insurance company is almost certain to classify drivers by sex, age, wealth, and race, and thus discriminate. Insurers are often prohibited from using such categories in setting rates, but they can achieve the same discriminatory effect indirectly with geographical classifications that capture the old categories under different names. Rates set by residential zip codes may seem neutral at first, but they're not if they demand higher premiums for those who happen to live on the wrong side of the tracks.

Guido had convinced me once again that apparently objective standards are not so objective, and thus unjustified. And that meant, of course, it was time for him to pull the rug out from under the conviction.

"But if we create a lower standard for a high-risk group like teenage drivers, we've made a decision for accidents. Some people will die to allow equality — equality of opportunity, equality of choice. And we do make decisions, from high principle and low convenience, that go against life, even as we say life is a pearl beyond price."

Guido paused to let that sink in.

"When I clerked for Justice Hugo Black the court decided *Cooper v. Aaron,* in which the federal government tried to enforce an order to desegregate the public schools in Little Rock. The solicitor general, in a case he obviously cared very much about, told the Supreme Court that 'People will die if you continue this order, but sometimes we value equality more than life.' And the court agreed with him, in the only opinion I know of that every justice signed.

"If you look at *Roe v. Wade* you see something similar. There are strong feelings on both sides about what is right, yet we can't have things both ways, as we would like. What's unfortunate about the abortion decision is that the Supreme Court said the right-to-life view was wrong. *Roe* said that in our Constitution the fetus is not protected until the third trimester, telling the pro-life advocates, 'Your views are outside the Constitution; life, for our legal system, doesn't begin when you say it does.' And there is of course a backlash from those put outside the law, because their values have been rejected.

"If we can avoid the tendency to attenuate the issues on the other side from our own, if we can try and understand them, it may not make the decision about hard issues like abortion any easier, but it does let us retain the polity. It's odd that this should come out of tort-type situations, but there it is."

Guido wraps up. In the 1970s, ladies' rooms became women's rooms; why didn't men's rooms become gentlemen's rooms? Because our common standards "sound in male attributes" — the standard is masculine, female attributes being acknowledged only as a variation on an existing theme.

Likewise, the notion of the reasonable man standard is driven by male beliefs, and the recent change in the legal standard from reasonable man to "reasonable person" is probably no more than cosmetic. The standard remains the same, except that its internal bias becomes better hidden than ever. We may value women — or racial minorities, or immigrant cultures, or homosexuals — enough to remove verbal discrimination, but not enough to change the way we do things. And the failure to incorporate minority values into the accepted standard, ironically, will likely hurt society in the long run, for it amounts to a rejection of values that, in another context or in a different person, we would have considered positive. The drive to preserve through law, in short, may ultimately destroy.

"These are real problems," Guido concluded, "for you to work out."

When I was working on the library assignment I would have given anything for solid, reliable, you-could-look-it-up answers. Now, however, I was in full flight toward Guido's camp; his practical idealism, however paradoxical, seemed much more compelling, and honest, than black-letter law. It was frustrating to learn rules by being told how unfair and misguided they were, to read about standards only to watch them scrutinized into oblivion, but Guido had shown to my satisfaction that positive things could emerge from this maddening, laborious dialectic. Wrestling with a case at 2 A.M., law often seemed a technical, reductive contrivance, but eight hours later, in Torts, it could appear the last best hope for solving conflicts.

Guido promised we were learning more than we knew. Despite all the evidence to the contrary, I began to believe him. Ambiguity, in Guido's hands, became aspiration.

Five

Anarchy and Elegance

We boast our light; but if we look not widely on the sun itself it
smites us into darkness. . . . The light which we have gained was
given us, not to be ever staring on, but by it to discover onward
things more remote from our knowledge. . . . There be who
perpetually complain of schisms and sects, and make it such a
calamity that any man dissents from their maxims. 'Tis their own
pride and ignorance which causes the disturbing, who neither will
hear with meekness, nor can convince; yet all must be suppressed
which is not found in their [code]. They are the troublers, they are
the dividers of unity, who neglect and permit not others to unite
those dissevered pieces which are yet wanting to the body of Truth.
To be still searching what we know not by what we know, still
closing up truth to truth as we find it . . . this is the golden
rule . . . ; not the forced and outward union of cold,
and neutral, and inwardly divided minds.

JOHN MILTON

Areopagitica

1644

Kahn handed out the memo-writing assignment in late September. I wanted to say, "About time"; the semester was just
three weeks old, but I remained frustrated that the equilibrium I had lost in the first few days of law school had not
returned. I welcomed the opportunity that case research gave
me to figure out the nature of the legal woods.

The memo assignment originated with the decision of a local school board in the hypothetical Dove County, Tennessee, to require the use of a certain series of books in elementary school reading classes. The books were selected from a state-approved list created after a number of public hearings, but when teachers started using the books, some fundamentalist Christian parents notified school principals that they found two volumes offensive to their religious beliefs. Most principals, in response, arranged alternative reading assignments; one refused, however, whereupon the board of education passed a resolution saying that only officially adopted textbooks could be taught in the school system. A number of students were subsequently suspended from school for refusing to attend reading class or to read the required textbooks, which led their parents to threaten to sue the school district on the grounds that the board had violated their First Amendment right to the free exercise of religion.

Each member of the small group was to write a fifteen-page legal memorandum analyzing the parents' challenge. We could consult anything in the library we chose, but Kahn suggested we spend most of our time with U.S. Supreme Court decisions. Half the small group was to represent the school board, the other half the fundamentalist parents, and the memo was intended to advise our clients whether they would be better off litigating the controversy or attempting to reach some kind of accommodation. I was relieved to be assigned to counsel the school board; I didn't think I'd be comfortable, or effective, representing the fundamentalists.

The hypothetical Kahn had chosen, a variation on a real-life lawsuit tried a few months earlier, was a legal classic. The First Amendment says in part that "Congress shall make no law respecting an establishment of religion, or prohibiting the free exercise thereof," but those dual goals can conflict;

one man's free religious exercise may well be another's establishment clause violation. In the 1878 case *Reynolds v. United States*, for example, the Supreme Court upheld a federal statute outlawing bigamy; while Congress could not regulate religious "belief" under the First Amendment, the court found, it could regulate religious "action" deemed "in violation of social duties or subversive of good order." The case has few defenders today . . . but if the Supreme Court had decided otherwise and struck down the antibigamy law, it could have been accused of giving preference to the Mormon religion, effectively "establishing" it. *Reynolds* is still good law, and still studied in law school as the case that set many of the terms of the free exercise/establishment clause debate.

The legal issues in the Dove County case were more complicated than those in *Reynolds,* having yet to be simplified — oversimplified, in truth — by the judicial process. For me, it was also complicated on a personal level, for while I strongly believed in the need to protect the rights of minority groups, I had yet to face the fact that the rights of some politically conservative minorities can also be abrogated. On principle, I should have been just as concerned with the rights of the fundamentalist parents as with those of any other minority, but I found that analogy hard to make. There was something in the fundamentalists' case that made me think that their aims were political rather than religious; their free exercise claim seemed a bit like a front.

Kahn, however, had anticipated that problem. He told us to assume that the parents' beliefs were sincere, which meant that the school board couldn't argue that the fundamentalists' concerns were essentially political and thus incapable of being decided by a court. That meant we couldn't use the "political questions" doctrine, a device I had recently read about that allows a court to avoid deciding issues it considers too complex, or "political," or threatening to judicial legitimacy. We couldn't avoid dealing with the central legal issue — that legitimate rights were in legitimate conflict, and someone's rights were going to be compromised.

Kahn cited four cases to get us started. We had about three weeks to write a first draft, which Kurt would go over before sending us back for another week of rethinking and rewriting.

I didn't believe, upon first reading the memo assignment, that it was going to be particularly difficult. It seemed clear to me that each side had to give ground; a trial, undoubtedly heavily publicized because of the First Amendment issues involved, would polarize Dove County, and that wouldn't do anyone any good. Whoever lost the court decision — at trial or at a later appellate level — would be furious, feeling like the loser in *Roe v. Wade* — put "outside the Constitution." By attempting to impose peace, the legal system might actually ensure slow burns and violent eruptions — hardly something a lawyer could condone, let alone participate in.

On rereading the assignment, however, I was struck by the care with which the fundamentalists' position had been put together. The prospective plaintiffs seemed to have acted quite reasonably, considering their anger; instead of insisting that the school board remove the books to which they objected, for example, they asked only that their children be provided with alternative reading material. I realized then what their lawyers had done, and my spirit sank. They had defined their grievance narrowly, thus preventing the school board from invoking its best defense — the First Amendment, invoked with the assertion that the parents were trying to practice censorship. Strike one against the school board: the parents' legal strategy was sophisticated.

I came across strike two soon after, when I studied more closely the sequence of events leading up to the children's suspension. The parents sought accommodation first, not confrontation; after notifying the school district of their concerns, they negotiated individually with a number of school principals to allow their children to go to different rooms with different books. That approach seemed eminently reasonable, and I would undoubtedly have agreed to it myself had I been one of the principals involved. The education of the excused children would probably suffer, since they got less direct reading instruction from a teacher, but if the parents were willing to pay that price, why not let them?

Only gradually did I grasp that the principals' compromise had seriously damaged the school board's legal defense. First, they had left the board wide open to accusations that it tolerated violations of the establishment clause, by giving special treatment to children for religious reasons. Second, the principals had undermined a basic rationale behind required textbooks — that a mandatory curriculum is the best way to ensure educational standards at reasonable cost. To permit a schoolchild to refuse to read a book because his or her parents disagree with a few passages is to invite all parents to seek similar arrangements for their own children.

The school board was already headed down the "slippery slope," the lawyer's metaphor for the idea that once you make one exception to a rule, it's very difficult to deny other exceptions — making the rule look like Swiss cheese. Unless the board found a convincing rationale for upholding the principals' accommodation, it could find itself presiding over the demise of the required curriculum, and possibly worse. I already knew, from *Bowers,* how difficult it was to get off the slippery slope; unable to give a good explanation for his decision, Justice White had argued, in effect, If we sanction homosexual sodomy here, the next thing you know we'll be asked to legalize adultery and incest! (Chief Justice Burger did no better in his concurrence, pointing to various laws over the centuries that made sodomy a crime. He failed to mention the ancient Greeks . . . a notable oversight, considering their enormous influence over modern concepts of law and justice.)

It is the lawyer's duty to bring relevant slippery slope arguments, pro and con, to a client's attention, even if they seem absurd; a lawyer can never predict which of his arguments may win. And the more I thought about it, the more attractive a this-could-be-the-end-of-the-school-system-as-we-know-it argument became, for by now I was convinced that the Dove County case was, at bottom, a cynical setup. The parents' actions had been orchestrated by some good lawyers; they had been careful to define the case so that it seemed to turn on religious rights rather than free speech, on the school board's willingness to break rules rather than the parents'. It was going to be difficult to attack the fundamentalists without making the school board look like a bully.

I wondered, too, whether this situation was the first volley in a skirmish or the prelude to all-out war. Was Dove County a test case, or were the fundamentalists preparing suits like this all over the country? Were they about to launch a barrage of make-us-an-exception lawsuits, in employment and taxation as well as education? Once I believed — or assumed or projected or established, it didn't matter which — that the other side was advised by a lawyer, I had no choice but to think like a lawyer myself. If my opponent had already thrown his net, I had to throw mine before his fell; if he hadn't thrown it, or didn't have one, well, a first strike would only further my client's cause. Now it was my job to spin out worst-case scenarios, to see every dam as a potential flood, every agreement or accommodation as a lawsuit-in-waiting. Having seen the slippery slope, I was prepared to make it serve my own ends. From casual accommodation to religious war; where I once saw a single grain of sand I now saw a vast beach.

I still wanted to negotiate a settlement, but the legal system allowed me to do so only after I had paraded my heavy artillery before the enemy. My battle plan was simple — to reshape history. I would ratchet time back to before any accommodation was made: I would say that the compromising principals had acted without authority, that they would be disciplined. I would create Hazard's legal "template" — arrange favorable facts in ways that implied only laws that helped my client, unfavorable facts in ways that made laws helpful to my opponent seem inapplicable. I would tell my client, first, whether it could win, and second, how it could win. That this was a non sequitur didn't occur to me at the time; preemptive attack, in the legal frame of mind I had begun to adopt, seemed the only appropriate response.

I started the library research in a mixture of fear and excitement. I tried not to think about the hundreds and hundreds of case reporters, the thousand and thousands of cases, that might give me insight into the free exercise and establishment clauses. I couldn't worry about missing something significant; I had to follow my nose and assume everything important would eventually turn up. If I looked long enough, a clear picture would have to emerge . . . wouldn't it?

I searched for the cases Kahn had cited in the handout, and some of them were actually on the shelves. I ran into Michelle and asked if she had found the missing cases, and that proved a stroke of luck; ever diligent, she had already made photocopies and offered to pass them on after she had finished transferring case holdings and quotations onto index cards. I figured Michelle would regret giving up her copies as soon as she had to double-check something, but I didn't volunteer to return them.

I read the copies and underlined like crazy. I studied them in no particular order, beginning about eight in the evening and ending sometime after 1 A.M. I didn't speak with anyone that night besides Michelle, and with her only that one time.

The cases weren't long, averaging about twenty-five pages, and they weren't difficult reading, unlike the older cases we had studied — all had been handed down within the last twenty-five years. But they were troublesome nonetheless, for the Supreme Court seemed to be all over the map in the free exercise/establishment clause area. Each of the cases seemed at an odd angle to the others, like features in a cubist portrait, and I couldn't spot the principle linking them together.

In *Sherbert v. Verner,* a 1963 case, the court said — found? held? ruled? decided? the legal jargon continued to elude me — that a Seventh-Day Adventist fired because she believed she could not work on her sabbath, Saturday, was entitled to unemployment benefits. The court said that her right to free exercise of religion was substantially infringed by a state law denying her those benefits, and that its decision did not foster the establishment of Seventh-Day Adventism.

Then there was *Thomas v. Review Board,* from 1981, in which a Jehovah's Witness quit his job after being transferred to a new position in a weapons factory. Although Thomas believed he could in good conscience work with materials that might later be used to make armaments, he didn't think his religion permitted him to help directly in weapons production, as did his new position. The court again held that the employee's First Amendment rights had been violated and that the state could not deny him unemployment benefits.

Things looked good for the fundamentalists — at least if the reasoning in these job-related cases could be applied to educational issues. I assumed that was a proper gloss on the decisions, but I wondered how the lawyer was supposed to determine the broadness with which a case should be read; only later did I learn that narrowness was prized above all (except by judges when broadness suits their goals). Did *Sherbert* and *Thomas,* for instance, say that a state could not impose its will on someone if the imposition interfered with the individual's religious practices? That was the central idea behind the free exercise clause, after all, so why shouldn't holdings in these cases apply to other situations?

Because of *United States v. Lee,* among other reasons. Here, in 1982, the Supreme Court decided that the federal government could force an Amish farmer to pay social security taxes even though he understood his religion to prohibit the acceptance of social assistance from, or paying it to, anyone outside the Amish community. *Lee* seemed to be to *Sherbert* and *Thomas* what *Bowers* was to *Roe* — the end of the slippery slope, a notice that the Supreme Court would go no farther in making exceptions to an established principle. When push came to shove, the needs of the majority outweighed the rights of a minority — even if the "needs," as in *Bowers,* were imaginary.

And how did *Lee* relate to *Wisconsin v. Yoder?* A decade before it decided *Lee,* the court had permitted an Amish couple to pull their children out of school because they be-

lieved a public high school education went against the Amish
faith. The court, it seemed, could go either way with Amish
cases — though this particular case seemed more relevant to
Dove County, since it involved education. But there were
other aspects of *Yoder* to be considered as well. The author of
Lee and *Yoder*, Chief Justice Burger, had recently announced
his retirement; as a lawyer, did I need to take into account
the court's personnel change? It wouldn't make any difference at the trial court level, but *Yoder* was an excessively
personal opinion, a virtual paean to the unique qualities of
the Old Order Amish religion, and not very sturdy from a
legal viewpoint. Burger's departure seemed a factor worth
weighing, but I had no idea where my analysis was supposed
to end.

I attempted to draw up a scorecard for the four cases.
Three of them favored the religious minority, and that
seemed bad for my side. But I reminded myself that Kahn
had said constitutional litigation was almost always decided
on the facts of the case, not the law; if the law is clear, after
all, a case probably wouldn't advance past the trial court
stage. That thought didn't make me feel much better, however, because it forced me back into the very same problem
I had so often struggled with in journalism — determining
which facts are important to a situation, which irrelevant,
which diversionary, which just window-dressing. And all
those judgments were supposed to be made, of course, without contaminating the analysis with one's personal views,
whatever they might be.

Lee was in many ways an excellent case. It was not only the
most recent Supreme Court decision addressing this area of
the law, but unanimous as well — a majority opinion signed
by eight justices, plus a typically interesting, eccentric concurrence by Justice John Paul Stevens. *Lee* seemed to indicate

that the court was leaning in my direction, since it said quite plainly that a state "may justify a limitation on religious liberty by showing that it is essential to accomplish an overriding government interest." That was just the sort of reading I wanted, which meant that my main task was to make the incipient *Dove County* look like *Lee*. But how? Of the four cases, only *Yoder* involved education, the "overriding government interest" I needed to invoke, but it went against me. How could I claim my case was like *Lee* when *Yoder* looked even more similar?

I saw two hurdles to jump: first, making *Yoder* appear less relevant to the hypothetical than I thought it actually was, and second, finding a favorable lower-court case that seemed even more relevant. A solution to the first obstacle dawned on me after I had read *Lee* for the fifth or sixth time. Burger's opinion in *Lee* seemed curiously dispassionate when compared to his views in *Yoder,* and I eventually realized why; though both were brought by Amish plaintiffs, the chief justice downplayed the Amish aspects of *Lee* because he wanted the Amish to lose. By characterizing *Lee* as a social security case rather than an Amish case, he could make his ranking of the values involved appear principled rather than personal or arbitrary.

I saw the mistake I had made with *Yoder* — calling it an "education" case rather than an "Amish" case, a characterization that allowed me to "distinguish" it, in legal parlance, into irrelevancy. I saw what I had to do: read cases broadly or narrowly, depending on whether I wanted to place the hypothetical situation — in toto or just relevant parts — in a positive pigeonhole (*Lee*) or avoid slotting it into a negative one (*Sherbert, Thomas, Yoder*). It was a matter of selecting the "right" facts and issues and deemphasizing or ignoring the "wrong" ones. I could push *Yoder* away by overemphasizing its Amish dimension and draw *Lee* near by saying that education, like social security, was a system that brooked no exceptions. I would imply the law through the facts, just as Hazard had advised . . . though without admitting, of course, that my logic was reverse-engineered from *Lee* to mimic the way that decision had been reached.

I was quite pleased to have puzzled out this approach, for it made me feel I had cracked the nut of law. I had "unpacked" it in much the same way we "unpacked" cases in class — by reducing them to their component parts. Legal writing was simply the next step — the assembly of new, partisan structures from the various components discovered in the process of deconstructing relevant cases. It didn't matter, apparently, that these new structures were routinely built of blocks intended for entirely different purposes, that ill-fitting components were mangled or left out, that the completed structure often served the lawyer's purposes as much as his client's. The point was to create a building that looked better than one's opponents' . . . even if it was just a house of cards.

It took a few minutes before I realized the pride I felt was pride in cynicism, in being able to do battle with lawyers on their own turf. I had achieved the ability, basically, to impose a characterization on the Dove County case as disingenuous as Justice White's characterization of *Bowers*. I had thought myself the stalker, but sure enough, had become the ensnared; I had begun to read the world in legal terms, to believe it was not only right but necessary to impose my views on other people. If life is a jigsaw puzzle, the lawyer's job is to place a handful of pieces on the table and convince his viewers they saw a complete picture — even though the lawyer, more than anyone, knows the picture is fragmentary.

The strength drained out of me. I wanted to take a long

nap, and did, right there in the carrel with my head on *United States v. Lee.* It was one-thirty in the morning.

What was law? Animal, vegetable, mineral?

Animal. Blind Justice with her scales, human aspiration at its finest. A nice thought, but I had heard a lot more about "reason" and "logic" at law school (the lack of it, mostly) than justice and fairness. Lady Justice carries a scale that weighs not right against right but costs against benefits. (Is it significant that Themis, as she is properly called, is one of the least-known Greek gods?) The Amish are peaceable and picturesque, the blacks many and strong, we must do right by them. But polygamists? Homosexuals? If you don't *have* to recognize their rights, why bother?

Vegetable. Over the northeast entrance to the law school is inscribed the phrase "Law is a living growth: not a changeless code." Guido had spoken of William Blackstone's "tending the garden of the common law," plucking out weeds. If law inevitably changes, grows, advances, why should I follow decisions that are already outdated? Go along with a legal system that so often seems to choose between false pictures, presumes competing distortions will somehow reveal justice?

Mineral. Perhaps law is like this very building, an airy fortress, its strength obscured by ornamentation. Law as a sand dune shaped by the wind, a result of the world's forces rather than a force of its own. Then again, maybe law is a machine, stamping out judgments like the sayings on T-shirts. Or a *trompe l'oeil* painting, designed to fool through the false impression of depth.

I was overworked, underslept, and thoroughly confused.

For one thing, I had completely lost sight of the fact that the purpose of the Con Law memo was to advise the school board on existing law, not argue a yet-to-be-filed lawsuit.

But since most of what I had learned at law school had been presented through argument, it was hard to approach the case any other way.

For another, the more I read the less I seemed to know. Two new issues seemed to spring up for every one I appeared to solve. Yes, law was animal: a hydra.

Searching for elegance, I found only anarchy. But I couldn't surrender to anarchy, for that would kill something important in me — the belief that law had meaning beyond that manufactured in lawyers' heads. I still hoped to find a pattern, a reason to believe.

Before leaving the library that morning I stopped at another carrel. I had remembered seeing there, taped to one partition, a strange but apposite poem — the epigraph, I later learned, of *The Bramble Bush*, a book about law school written by a Yale Law graduate and one-time Yale Law professor, Karl Llewellyn. The rhyme went

> There was a man in our town
> and he was wondrous wise:
> he jumped into a BRAMBLE BUSH
> and scratched out both his eyes —
> and when he saw that he was blind,
> with all his might and main
> he jumped into another one
> and scratched them in again.

I had little choice, clearly, but to see the process through.

My desire to pulverize the fundamentalist parents in court eventually passed, a victim of the obliteration of my own convictions. I continued to conduct the research as I thought a lawyer would, however, seeking the second prong with which to make my case — a lower-level precedent that would counter the educational aspects of *Yoder*. Although Kahn had said we shouldn't spend much time with lower appellate cases, I felt I had better uncover whatever reinforcements I could.

I started with the cases cited in *Yoder*. In an annotated version I found the case parsed into twenty points, each of them cross-referenced to the publisher's *U.S. Supreme Court Digest*. Most of the points seemed relevant in some way to the issues in Dove County . . . so much so I was sorry I had considered using annotations at all. Should I find the *Digest* and track down the points that didn't relate specifically to the Amish?

I didn't. I glanced at a few of the cases in the *Digest* and decided there had to be a better way.

Below the publisher's summary of the annotated *Yoder* was a box with the heading "Total Client-Service Library® References." Listed were citations, as abbreviated in lawyer code, to *Am. Jur. 2d*, *A.L.R. Digests*, *L. Ed. Index to Anno*, *A.L.R. Quick Index*, *Federal Quick Index*, and *U.S. L. Ed. Digest*, to which I had just referred. This was both encouraging and depressing — encouraging because I was getting somewhere on a logistical level, and depressing because the research that lay ahead appeared to extend almost infinitely in time and space. This was even worse than the study of literature — fifty pages of commentary for every page of original writing.

I still feared missing something, however, so I dutifully found most of the books referred to. *Am. Jur. 2d* — *American Jurisprudence Second Series*, an eighty-two-volume legal encyclopedia — seemed the most useful, for it stated the law explicitly in actual situations. I found what I wanted under the "Schools" heading: sections entitled "Power to prescribe courses of instruction" and "Textbooks — Authority of school officers." Each gave citations to cases I had already run across, which was heartening. Better still was the book's use — albeit occasional — of unhedged, unshadowed sentences. Of compulsory school attendance laws, *Am. Jur. 2d* said, "Their constitutionality is beyond dispute."

Eventually I came to a section in *Am. Jur. 2d* concerning a school's use of the Bible as a textbook. It began, "While some authorities have held that the Bible's use as a textbook in the public schools is a violation of constitutional provisions against sectarianism or interference with religious liberty, other cases have held that the Bible's use as a reading book does not violate any constitutional rights."

I didn't know whether to laugh or cry. This wasn't my case, but close enough to push me even farther toward cynicism. Was I really expected to believe that "principled adjudication," as the saying goes, was at work when one judge decided the Bible could properly be used as a textbook, and another that it couldn't? I was willing to assume that the cases' facts were sufficiently different to justify different outcomes — but were they so different that they *alone* determined opposite results?

It seemed much more likely that the important difference, which went unacknowledged, was the fact that the presiding judges were different people. Their differences might be irrational and inarticulable — but that didn't mean they didn't exist, as the law likes to imply. I saw again the breadth of the chasm between trial and decision, how facts — messy, inconsistent, often downright ugly — were trimmed, highlighted, or ignored in order to make law work smoothly.

A new and better picture of Justice came to mind. She should still be blindfolded, and still bear her scales aloft, but she should also be shrugging her shoulders.

The secondary sources created more problems than they solved, just as Kahn had predicted. I tried another route, consequently, to the anti-*Yoder* holy grail; I went back to the four original cases and scanned their footnotes. I took heed of what Hazard had once said — that the next time he put a book together he would publish it upside down, since the footnotes always seemed more important than the formal opinion.

The cases I unearthed involved the teaching of evolution, school prayer, free busing of parochial school students, and similar church/state conflicts. I glanced at them, looked at their footnotes, and found citations to more cases. Then I looked up *those* cases, began reading . . . and realized I was getting nowhere. I had achieved a decent feel for the issues by this time, but the knowledge I gained seemed to take me farther and farther away from the facts of my case. The research was interesting, certainly, but practically useless.

I decided to cut my losses and start from scratch once more, this time with law reviews. At least they were written in something approaching standard English. I ran into Daryl from the small group and discovered he had already copied some of the articles I was looking for. He lent them to me, and after twenty minutes of photocopying I went home with an inch-thick pile of paper. The memo was due in five days and I was determined to get through the material in one sitting.

I did, and the articles were fairly interesting. All addressed the central dilemma — how do you accommodate minority views in a society where the majority makes the laws?

I assumed I would fall asleep immediately when I went to bed at 3 A.M., but I didn't. I couldn't get the ideas and entanglements out of my mind; every problem seemed connected to every other problem, and the more I tried to isolate those most pertinent to my hypothetical, the more futile the exercise seemed. The big picture I sought vanished in a mass of detail.

As I lay in bed I began to realize how much time I had wasted. Like most of the other law students, I had cast my net far too wide because I didn't know how to cast any differently. But that seemed to be half the point, maybe the whole point; our professors *wanted* us to get lost in the legal wasteland, apparently, so we would treasure lawyerly skills when mastery finally came. I saw no other explanation: law school was intended to confuse, to intimidate, ultimately to indoctrinate. Students were supposed to endure the same horrors their professors had . . . and if they couldn't, well, no lawyers they. We were to learn without benefit of the professors' experience — rather ironic, considering the U.S. legal system is *based* on precedent!

I eventually fell asleep, full of venom, and woke up the same way. From desk to bed the floor was littered with articles, cases, and yellow pages from my notepad, yet all that reading and scribbling had brought me no closer to an answer. I felt as if I had been sent in search of diamonds but found only glass — and then discovered that no one cared what stones I brought back so long as they seemed clear.

I had to get the job done however I could. I went back to the library without knowing my next step.

I turned to *U.S. Law Week*, a loose-leaf reference series that publishes important appellate decisions as soon as they are handed down. I was astounded to find, within a few seconds, exactly what I needed. The first sentence of *Grove v. Mead*, a 1985 case from Washington State, read, "At issue here is a school board's refusal to remove a book from a sophomore English literature curriculum based on plaintiff's religious objections to the book." Hallelujah!

Things only got better as I read on. The child had been given permission to leave the room while the book was discussed; she had been offered an alternative book, yet chose to remain in class; her mother complained to the school district, whereupon a school board committee read the book in question and decided it was "appropriate."

I was thrilled. How much closer could I get? Best of all, the school district won the case. The Ninth Circuit Court of Appeals found that the burden on the child's free exercise of religion was "minimal," and that assigning the textbook had not advanced, as the child's parents had argued, the religion of "secular humanism."

I felt rejuvenated, even slightly justified in my approach to legal research. I may have been slow as a turtle, but I ended up in the right place. *Grove* gave me a center, I thought, around which to build an argument.

The first thing I needed to know was what the Supreme Court had said, if anything, about *Grove*. I had to "Shephardize" the case to find out — "Shephard's" being a series of indexes that gives virtually every legal reference to virtually every written court decision in the United States. These "citators" are the most intimidating reference books in law school — there are hundreds of them, and every page is a cascade of page and volume numbers — but probably the most important as well. By the time he or she has finished Shephardizing, a legal researcher has a pretty good idea what a case, as lawyers often put it, is "worth."

I was disappointed to find that *Grove* wasn't worth very much. The Supreme Court had "denied certiorari"; that is, refused to hear the case. (A "petition for certiorari" is a form of appeal in which the attorney asks a court, usually the U.S. Supreme Court, to take a case it isn't required by law to hear.) The denial told me nothing about the Supreme Court's thoughts regarding *Grove,* but the court had let the opinion stand.

Both Audrey and Daryl, I learned, had consulted *Grove.* That was reassuring, as was the citation to *Grove* I subsequently found in the updating supplement to *Am. Jur. 2d,* having missed it on the previous go-round. Finally, I thought, I had tracked down some information I could depend on.

I began writing the following day. I wrote much more quickly than I had anticipated, mostly because — for the first time in my life — I had thought my ideas through before sitting down at the keyboard. It was almost a mechanical exercise. By showing the school board that it would probably win if it went to court, and then emphasizing the backlash the board would likely face should it choose to press the advantage, I tried to persuade my client that the conflict could be put to rest with only minor compromises.

Kurt gave back the memos a week after we handed them in. Some of the students were furious; I wasn't, for Kurt hadn't been too hard on me. He said I had done good research but tended to read cases much too broadly: I had lumped the children in *Grove* with those of the hypothetical Dove County parents, for example, while failing to discuss the different educational needs of secondary and elementary school children. Kurt made clear, too, that while it was conceivably appropriate for a lawyer to recommend in a memo that the client seek a particular result, I should stick more closely to its express desires. I was being paid (theoretically) to illuminate the direction in which the Supreme Court's collective mind was most likely to go, not the direction in which I believed justice should run. Having already placed many spokes in the free exercise/establishment clause wheel, the court wasn't likely to respond to arguments saying the wheel needed reshaping.

The writing of the final draft also went well. Talking with Kurt had helped me think of the issues in the discrete, specific language of the lawyer. This time I addressed the issues serially, logically, more neutrally, and, I thought, more persuasively. All in all, I was pleased with the memo when I turned it in, feeling I had played Solomon without even threatening to cut the baby in half.

Michelle and I celebrated the completion of the memo assignment by going to *Heartbreak House* at the Yale Rep. During the intermission I considered telling her how much Shaw's portrait of collapsing worlds reflected, upon occasion, my own state of mind, but I caught myself. No comment is innocent to law students, who leave few conversational gambits unpunished.

At the curtain Michelle said she loved the play and had had a nice evening. I could tell she was anxious to get back to the dorms, however, and as I walked her there realized that even the simplest of friendships could take an enormous amount of energy at law school. How could it be otherwise, when law students spend more time cultivating suspicion than overcoming it?

As for forming a "relationship" at law school . . . well, that seemed too much to ask. One of the first cases we studied in Contracts, after all, was *Balfour v. Balfour,* a 1919 decision in which an English court determined that a husband wasn't obliged to pay the allowance he once promised his estranged, now-crippled wife. "Agreements such as these are outside the realm of contracts altogether," the judge wrote, adding with apparent regret that "natural love and affection . . . counts for so little in these cold Courts." Law students seemed almost embarrassed to have succumbed to distractions like love and companionship: Sam and Kate each became engaged (to other people) during the school year, yet I never met Kate's fiancé and Sam's only once, by chance. Life outside law school was presumed to be of secondary importance.

Going back to my apartment with the bars on the windows and the single bed, I asked myself whether I really wanted to stay in law school. Michelle had previously told me about a first-year student who had dropped out of Yale Law a few weeks earlier, leaving a note for his roommate saying something like "This is horrible; I'm going home." Perhaps he had the right impulse — to get out while he still felt like himself, thought in his own language. Stuck all day in classes or the library, thinking of every event and belief in legal terms, I had forgotten how many things couldn't be captured in law's terms. In the theater Shaw found a way to make his voice heard; law school seemed to be suppressing mine.

No doubt about it — two months of law school had helped me speak better, analyze more deeply, think more logically. But I had a nagging feeling that my outward appearance had become disconnected from my inner self, that my new ability to put a rational veneer on anything had made me a stranger to myself. I felt a consistent low-level pain, at times a sense of being overstuffed to the point of bursting and at others of being achingly hollow, as if life fluids had been drained from me. The contradictory images reminded me of the description I had once heard of the

lawyer's mind: it was a bathtub, either filled to the brim
with the current task or empty awaiting the next. All or
nothing; the lawyer's job is to resist middle ground.

I consoled myself with the memory of an event that had
occurred the previous weekend. Yale Law had put on a sym-
posium concerning freedom of the press, and the highlight
was a discussion by judges, reporters, and law professors of
Reckless Disregard, the book by journalist and Yale Law graduate Renata Adler (who had taken the full J.D. program, not
the M.S.L.) about the libel cases *Westmoreland v. CBS et al.*
and *Sharon v. Time.* It was fascinating to watch allegiances
break down and realign themselves as the speakers at the core
session sought to convince each other that only their profession was really interested in truth. For me, however, the
best moment came at the close of a seminar when I saw, just
a few feet away, sparkling blue eyes in a round, beaming
face. It had completely slipped my mind that Shelly, an old
college friend and now a lawyer herself, was living in New
Haven while her husband finished Yale Law. I hadn't seen,
and certainly hadn't given, a smile that wide in months, and
we spent the next couple hours rejuvenating an old friendship.

I kept Shelly's moving, expressive face in mind. I was
soon to return to California for fall break, and I didn't want
to forget the good things to be said about life in the law. Yes,
it was possible to survive law school, to like being a
lawyer — Shelly did, especially when she got the chance to
work as a public defender — and to do so without losing
your friends or humanity. As long as I remembered moments
like that I knew I could withstand law school's fundamental
message, written in bold letters across the student brain:
Surrender, Dorothy!

Act II: Anesthesia

[The first year of law school] aims, in the old phrase, to get you to "thinking like a lawyer." The hardest job of the first year is to lop off your common sense, to knock your ethics into temporary anesthesia. Your view of social policy, your sense of justice — to knock these out of you along with woozy thinking, along with ideas all fuzzed along the edges. You are to acquire ability to think precisely, to analyze coldly, to see, and see only, and manipulate, the machinery of law. It is not easy thus to turn human beings into lawyers. Neither is it safe. . . . None the less, it is an almost impossible process to achieve the technique without sacrificing some humanity first.

KARL LLEWELLYN
The Bramble Bush

Six

Pandora's Box

[One type of law student] builds a "private self" as a counter-
model to the "public self." As this type's public self becomes more
and more controlled and aggressive, often more and more dishonest
and in any case less and less emotionally satisfying, his private life is
invested with vast quantities of intense feeling, sentimentality,
idealism, and exaggerated protectiveness. There is something
truly pathetic about his terror of talking about these "private
matters" in any context which, no matter how appropriate in
other ways, has even a whiff of the "legal" about it. . . .
[This] division of life into hermetically sealed "private" (emotional)
and "public" (effectiveness) compartments must lead to
deformations in both. . . . [It also creates] a model of private
life in direct opposition to public life as a lawyer [that] may
make it possible to accept conduct in the public area which
would otherwise be intolerable.

DUNCAN KENNEDY
Yale Law 1970
"How the Law School Fails: A Polemic"
Yale Review of Law & Social Action
1970

My feelings about returning to the West Coast were more
than a little ambivalent. My interest in the M.S.L. program
was genuine, but I had also applied to Yale Law because I was
desperate to leave town. My life in the Bay Area had become

a mess; I was struggling professionally, since the freelance work I hoped to get after quitting *California Lawyer* never materialized, and I was devastated personally, my wife having packed up and left some eight months earlier. To top it off, just before leaving for New Haven I had been doing four-days-a-week psychoanalysis, trying to figure out what had gone so terribly wrong in my life, and had broken up, painfully, my first postmarriage relationship. The West didn't mean sun and fun to me; it meant doom and gloom, and the fantasy of returning one day in triumph.

I stayed with Terri — the very woman I had left before going to Yale Law. At the time it seemed the right thing to do; she had gotten a raw deal from me, and I felt obliged to give the relationship another chance. Terri had helped me recover from my wife's departure, always seemed to be there when I fell into some wild careen, was even willing to pick up stakes and move to New Haven with me. I wouldn't let her, seeing the chance to jump-start my adult life unencumbered, but while at Yale I wondered if I had been too hasty. I didn't think I loved Terri when I left the Bay Area, but now I wasn't so sure. Law school, ironically, seemed to give me the reasons, and to some extent the tools, with which to understand personal relationships . . . even as it said, in effect, they weren't worth having.

Terri and I had a wonderful three days. Halloween in San Francisco, the weekend in Mendocino, much talk and laughter. We made love with a freedom and intensity I hadn't experienced before, as if recapturing an ancient innocence. How strange it was, I found myself thinking one evening, that when my landlord in New Haven had asked me if I wanted a double bed, I said no, without a moment's hesitation. There was a certain emptiness to my time with Terri, a feeling of insufficiency, but after the too-muchness of law school it seemed a respite. I was so happy to be listened to, paid attention to, that my lingering reservations were easy to ignore.

I didn't waste any vacation time contemplating whether law school had changed me. But I felt it had; I was more assertive and skeptical in my daily doings, from conversing with strangers to analyzing events in the morning paper. It never crossed my mind, however, that the new emphasis I put on my own views, beliefs, and preferences was anything but positive; I thought I had become more interesting and admirable, not more selfish and domineering. The indifference I began to show toward others' thoughts and feelings seemed a necessary part of thinking concisely, clearly, and efficiently. I was simply overcoming ordinary human frailty, and thought everyone else should be doing the same.

I didn't comprehend the extent to which law had influenced my private self until Alice and Mark invited me to dinner the day before I flew back to New York. I didn't even consider asking Terri to join us, a gesture that would have been automatic, I think, in the past. "If Terri wants to come along," I told myself, "she can say so, and shouldn't be hurt if I don't let her." She didn't ask, and I didn't feel mean-spirited; politeness had simply begun to feel unnecessary.

It was good to see Alice and Mark again. But our relationship, now, was qualitatively different from what it had been before; this time around I found myself attempting to establish a pecking order right off the bat. Mark and I talked football, as we had always done during our regular Sunday brunches, but I soon decided the conversation was trivial and insufficiently challenging. I didn't want to share a moment or a friendship; I wanted to lock horns, to show my stuff, even to intimidate. At one point, when Mark asked a question, I pretended to be distracted and simply walked away, as if to say his presence held little meaning for me. I headed into the kitchen to talk shop — law — with Alice.

She was her usual effusive self, saying again how great it was to get together. I soon turned the conversation toward legal topics, however, and then launched into a five-minute disquisition on tort law according to Guido. Alice said her experience with that particular class was much less interesting than mine, and I immediately attributed the response not to Alice's self-effacing graciousness but to the fact that she hadn't attended one of the best law schools — San Francisco's Hastings College of the Law might have been in the top twenty, but barely. A law school that didn't force every student to internalize law's methods to the point that they were second nature, I reasoned, couldn't produce very effective lawyers.

I told Alice that her cooking reminded me of another issue that had come up in the Torts — the different levels of care someone owes to social guests, business visitors, and trespassers. Did Alice recall what standard applied should I hit my head on an open kitchen cabinet? She didn't. Could Mark's barbecuing be classified as an "attractive nuisance," I asked, if those wonderful aromas drifting across the road caused a passing driver to crash? And what if Alice's flank steak killed me? Could I recover — not literally, ha ha, one of Guido's standard jokes — and how much? I would have died earning very little income, true, but the M.S.L. program was significantly increasing my skills and marketability. Should my estate be penalized because I had invested a few months now for future earnings later? Time is money — that's the American way, right?

Alice just laughed. She hadn't really been listening; Mark had brought in their baby moments earlier, and Alice's mind was on Katy. I began thinking that even now I might be a better lawyer than Alice, although she had practiced for four years; she was too willing to pass up a chance to learn more about law, too easily distracted by other things.

I too looked at Katy, held by Mark far over his head. I thought of the first time I had seen her, in Alta Bates Hospital in Berkeley — the same hospital in which I was born — and of the photo Alice had sent — me holding the baby in her swaddling — stuck on my refrigerator in New Haven. That was . . . when? August?

Just ten weeks ago. I suddenly felt cynical and cruel.

Why was I here with these old, old friends if not to enjoy, and participate in, their choices, their hopes, their triumphs and disappointments? I loved them because I was *like* them, because I understood them; so why did I insist, now, on making myself feel different, superior? It was a new habit of mind, one I had picked up since going to Yale Law, and for a long time I was willing to blame its appearance solely on law school. Ultimately, however, I couldn't; this newfound arrogance, this willingness to judge and condemn, was part of my own personality.

Law school hadn't created this unpleasant characteristic. But in emphatically fostering students' intellectual selves, law school gives them — me, in this case — license to ignore the more problematic, uncontrollable, emotional aspects of life. And that side of me had in fact withered away from disuse, to the point that I was willing to lose friends over the single-minded pursuit of psychological dominance. Law school hadn't turned me into a jerk, but it told me that if I felt the need to be a jerk, I should be a first-rate jerk . . . and not feel guilty about it.

I remembered how law school had, for a time, changed Alice. One summer she twisted her ankle during a raft trip sponsored by the law firm for which she was clerking, and Alice was furious beyond belief when the firm wouldn't pay her medical expenses. The firm was being stupidly tight-fisted, of course, but when Alice said she was seriously think-ing about suing, I was startled. The situation seemed a paradigm of what was wrong with law: the knee-jerk polar-ization, the instantaneous tactical maneuvering, the prefer-ence for battle over negotiation. I considered reminding Alice that she had gone on the trip voluntarily, but she was already reeling off the theory she would put to the court:

Law firms are corporate cultures. A summer associate isn't considered a team player if she — especially "she" — doesn't take part in firm events. That was doubly true for events like white-water rafting, which are arranged specifically for sum-mer associates and intended, arguably, to weed out the less competitive. If a summer associate doesn't go along, she greatly increases the chance that she won't be offered a full-time position upon law school graduation. No, Alice hadn't simply agreed to go on the rafting trip; the law firm had forced her to participate in a hazardous activity, and should pay for the injury she subsequently incurred — richly, in fact, because such a cheap, exploitive firm deserved a taste of its own medicine.

Alice, in the end, didn't sue. When push came to shove, she couldn't justify doing so . . . and five years later seemed to have come to the same conclusion about the practice of law as a whole. She didn't go back to her old firm (not the raft-trip firm, which didn't offer her a position) after her maternity leave ended, and indeed, at this writing, has yet to return to law. Alice fled, in short, what I now actively embraced — a frightening prospect, considering that I seemed, at times, to have a natural facility for law. I wondered — could I find my way back, or had I lost something forever?

Terri drove me to the airport the following morning. My chief memory is of sitting so far down in the seat that I could barely look over the dashboard, sensing the knots in my knees and ankles, arms pressed tightly against sides so as not to feel the chilling sweat rolling from my armpits. I said as little as possible, for I no longer trusted my ability to distinguish truth from self-interest.

What could I say? That I had somehow become the sort of person I generally despised, a person able to turn his feelings on and off as the occasion demanded? That I had learned how to mask emotions when they were inconvenient, mimic them when useful — and unconsciously, to boot? That I, this time around, had coldly exploited Terri — a woman who cared for me largely because I seemed to value relationships? For days I had seen nothing wrong with taking only what I wanted from Terri, giving her little or nothing in return, and making no attempt to ascertain her desires. Had I not seen Alice and Mark and Katy, I might well have returned to New Haven harboring the delusion that such behavior is acceptable.

Terri asked me if I was all right. I said yes, pleading temporary nausea. She tried to be cheerful and I tried to match her mood, but in my head I cursed myself for blindness.

I felt addicted to law. Law was so thrillingly empowering; how could I help but revel in its benefits? Free of its grip for a few days, however, and law felt like an artificial high to me. Law had made me less human, asked that I dismiss my moral center as a dangerous, incomprehensible Pandora's box. Lord Hale: "The Law will admit no rival."

Stephen Carter, my Contracts professor, had complained the previous month that fall break came at exactly the wrong time. First-year students, he said, went on vacation just at the point that they were able to "carry on a conversation" in the law, just when the lessons of law had begun to take root. Carter was absolutely right, perhaps more than he knew; my exposure to real life during the break had certainly broken law's spell over me. It reminded me how much I loved another form of conversation, another language, that law school seemed intent on eradicating.

Within a week of returning to New Haven I determined to write a book about legal education. I needed to understand how law school had succeeded, if only temporarily, in stealing my soul. I would write, first, to understand how law school had affected my values without my conscious knowledge, and second, to try to determine how law school training shaped society as a whole. The late Yale Law professor Grant Gilmore — a co-author of my Contracts casebook — had written fifteen years earlier that "[W]hat is taught in the law schools in one generation will be widely believed by the bar in the following generation," and I suspected his observation was as applicable to the spiritual subtext of the law as to its letter.

But was I really capable of the task I had set myself? Law school had showed me, and on a very personal level, that the way *in which* one learns greatly affects *what* one learns, that means are inseparable from ends. But that also meant I could never see law purely, for I had been trained as a journalist; I, too, had an agenda, whether I knew it or not. I seemed to face a variation on Heisenberg's uncertainty principle: not only would my observation of law school be altered by my presence, but law school would simultaneously, and continuously, alter me. Law school and I would revolve around one another in a state of fluidity, each defined mainly in terms of the other. That was a frightening thought; it meant, among other things, that my book on law school would not only have to admit such relativity but stress it, because it represented so well the kind of ambiguity upon which law thrives.

I immediately ran out and bought a copy of Scott Turow's *One L*, which I had been told was the nonfiction equivalent of *The Paper Chase*. I liked the book, and was relieved to see my thoughts about legal education had not been preempted; *One L* well described the Harvard law student's life but contained little analysis of legal education and its effects. Turow seemed generally to go along with the goals of legal education, if not its methods, and that was something upon which we would never agree. Indeed, when Turow wrote a new afterword to *One L* — which was republished following the success of his bestselling novel *Presumed Innocent* — he criticized legal training not because it changed students' understanding of the world — and thus their notions about justice — but because it didn't prepare them to operate within the existing legal system.

The decision to write about law school was liberating. It gave me a perspective, acted as an inoculation against law's darker powers — or at least its powers over my own dark side. I now had a good, healthy reason to be in law school — I could become, to some degree, an observer again — and soon found time to do social, healthy things. I drove to New Hampshire with an acquaintance to visit mutual friends, I chatted with Shelly on the telephone, I began to see a psychotherapist again. I even gave blood for the first time in ten years — though immediately passed out. When I came to I wasn't alone; Sam and Michelle, who had arrived independently to donate blood, were hovering over me, looking worried. I would later go to the infirmary and find I was suffering from a lung infection — not an uncommon complaint among law students, I learned in the spring on yet another, more serious trip to the infirmary. Two of the least healthy populations at Yale University, a doctor told me that time, were law students and graduate students in English.

I also tried to get better acquainted with some of the other students. Knowing Denise's interest in theater, I suggested we see a play, but she countered with lunch; we agreed on Naples, a favorite undergraduate hangout. The pizza there isn't so good as at New Haven's famous pizza places — Pepe's, The Spot, or Sally's, my personal favorite — but Naples is in some ways as historic as Mory's. It too boasts wooden tables carved with tangles of initials, names, numbers, and hearts.

Denise was already one of the most recognizable students, largely because of her devotion to the New York Mets. She talked about the team incessantly and intelligently, and the consensus at the law school was that given the chance, she would have compiled an even better managerial record than Davey Johnson. Denise was untypically tentative and nervous when we met up, so I came straight out and asked whether things were okay with her. She was completely nonplussed, and I immediately regretted breaking the law-student tradition of ignoring personal lives.

Denise quickly regained her composure. I don't remember what we ended up talking about, but I had a feeling it didn't much matter: each of us just wanted to connect with a fellow student outside the law school environment. After lunch, with an hour to kill before a make-up class in Contracts, we decided to take a walk in the Grove Street Cemetery. There was a late-fall chill in the air and a couple of inches of early snow on the ground.

I told Denise some of the Sturm und Drang that had begun to define my life. She was sympathetic, and I regretted I hadn't mentioned such things to her before. I asked, though not in so many words, how she managed to maintain equilibrium at law school when many around her were losing theirs.

Denise didn't reply directly, but I thought I learned the answer later in our walk. Her father, she said, was a Yale Law graduate who hadn't practiced law in many years; he had formed, and continued to run, a small company in the financial industry. It made sense that Denise would have absorbed the notion that law is only a means to an end, nothing more, and that law school, consequently, shouldn't be taken too seriously. Although Denise obviously delighted in the ideas and skills legal education provided, she also kept them in perspective.

The fact that Denise's father didn't practice law, like many law school graduates, reminded me of a lecture given by a Yale Law professor a couple days earlier. Anthony Kronman argued in "Living in the Law" that life in the law had "intrinsic worth" because it demanded the cultivation of good judgment and the practice of high ideals. That much I might have conceded if Kronman — the third and last co-author, along with Gilmore and Friedrich Kessler, of my Contracts casebook — hadn't gone on to say that becoming a lawyer necessarily meant the adoption of a certain character. The lawyer, he said, must experience a "turning about of the soul," in Socrates' terminology — or more precisely, "the development of a professional persona."

I told Denise I had found the speech unsettling. How could Kronman talk so cavalierly — so it seemed to me — about what he called "a transformation of one's own self"? Especially when few law students realize such a change is required when they apply to law school? Kronman admitted that such a transformation occurred, at least, and unlike Hazard, didn't joke about it; but he said nothing about the tendency of the new lawyerly "persona" to take over a student's life, nor its dangerous side effects. Kronman's understanding of the law seemed a far cry from that of former Chief Justice Earl Warren, who referred to law as a "teacher."

Denise wasn't much impressed by my analysis. I felt she didn't understand, and probably didn't want to understand, my central point: that while law provides its practitioners with many useful masks — counselor, advocate, cross-examiner, coach, bully, sympathetic ear, voice of reason, and so on — it presupposes the adoption of a more basic mask — that of the neutral, lawyer persona, a mask that was difficult, once affixed, to remove. Kronman himself had hinted at the Faustian bargain: in order to practice the law's ideals, he said, the lawyer must "submit to its discipline."

Denise and I agreed to disagree. I had realized, by this time, I'd be unlikely to find anyone connected with the legal profession who saw much truth in my views; they threatened the existing legal culture, and could never be expressed in the positivistic law-speak lawyers had endured so much to master.

It was this sense of an unbridgeable gap between Denise and myself that drove me, I think, to try and show her the grave of Elizur Goodrich, law professor. I couldn't locate the family burial area, as it turned out, but that was just as well. Elizur would have been equally skeptical of my views on legal education, no doubt, and at the very moment was probably spinning in his grave.

Kahn handed back our memos the following day.

He had said upon receiving them that our first drafts —

which we didn't know he had read — were unimpressive, so we were at least somewhat prepared for negative comments. We did not expect, however, the wholesale condemnation we got. Kahn said he wanted to spend ten minutes outlining some common failings, but almost an hour passed before he was finished.

We should have cited cases only for very narrow propositions: it was "frankly useless" to cite them broadly because "cases stand for too many things." For those of us who had used *Am. Jr. 2d* and other legal encyclopedias, Kahn had one bit of advice: "Don't cite them, don't use them — they're kid stuff." We "mouthed words without thinking very hard," wasted time on "trivial issues" and other "fluff," cited cases that "aren't good law anymore, even though they haven't been overruled." And, oh yes; we should purge the words *clear, certain,* and *compels* from our vocabulary because "nothing is clear, nothing is certain, and the court doesn't have to do anything."

I felt like an idiot. But I was furious, too. How could we be held to standards Kahn had neither defined nor brought within our compass? How could we be expected to follow the rules of the game without being told what those rules were? The situation reeked of the ex post facto (a form of lawmaking, prohibited, I now knew, by Article I, section 10 of the Constitution).

The small group left class that day in cowed silence. Denise and a few other students stayed behind to read Kahn's comments in the isolation of the seminar room; others, like me, didn't want to do so amid the other students, knowing how our faces would betray embarrassment and hurt. Liz stormed out of the room, her eyes filled with a genuine hate.

At lunch some of the anger came out. Scattered at tables around the dining hall, the members of the small group —

students who had their hopes pinned on the practice of law, many of whom had never experienced authentic failure before — denounced Kahn or listened numbly. Sam seemed particularly stunned; I thought Kate was about to cry. No student seriously claimed that Kahn's criticisms were wrong; the invective, surprisingly subdued, centered on the feeling that no professor had the right to attack student work so callously. Kahn had expected us, apparently, to be far more capable than we actually were.

Bill, as usual, wasn't at lunch, having gone to the gym for some exercise. His expression was naturally grim, even when he told jokes, but when I ran into him in the main hallway before our next class he had the look of a killer. We exchanged a couple of sentences, but I could barely understand what he was saying through his tight-lipped rage; every adjective that came out of his mouth was "fucking." I hoped Bill would turn those laser-beam eyes on Kahn . . . but for his own sake, keep his trap shut.

Kahn's comments on my memo were devastating. It was needlessly long, he said, frequently fuzzy, insufficiently analytic, often insupportable, and much too speculative and unspecific. My establishment clause section was weak, I hadn't spent enough time thinking about the issues, I "avoided detail in a disturbing way." Kahn didn't see how *Grove* related to the situation in *Dove County*; *Grove* turned on censorship, which made negligible the many factual similarities I had cited. Worst of all, like many students in the small group, I seemed to think principles would emerge from my research of their own accord. Didn't I know I had to impose a structure upon the material I developed?

Legally speaking, Kahn's comments were on target, although it took me a few weeks to admit it. But on a personal level I remained angry for days. Where was Kahn's common humanity? Why had he deliberately chosen not to sympathize with his students' struggles with the law? To say, as he had in one class quite explicitly, "Your views don't matter"? I got the message: the law student must think, talk, and act like a lawyer twenty-four hours a day if he or she hopes to "make it." At this point, at least, students were expected to obey the needs of legal education, not to try to put it in perspective.

Kahn happened to be giving the traditional small-group party the following Sunday. He was among the last professors to do so, and I was incredulous at his timing. Did he really believe we could slough off his to-the-bone criticism so easily? Apparently so — we had assumed Kahn wasn't going to give a party at all. Why would he lower himself to socialize with students who couldn't be taught, whose work was so obviously worthless?

The party, to my surprise, was quite nice. Kahn and his wife — Cathy Iino, the editor of the Yale Law alumni magazine — had packed their kitchen with rich desserts and made everyone feel welcome. Kahn, I sensed, was well aware of the awkwardness of his relationship with his students, and was willing (unlike many law teachers) to drop his professorial role if it conflicted with his role as host. Doting fatherhood seemed to be the role Kahn ranked highest; he rushed to the kitchen, or upstairs, whenever he heard his baby daughter squeaking over the intercom. I was among the last to leave when the party broke up, and Kahn bestowed on stragglers pounds of uneaten desserts. I had had a good time in spite of myself.

I still didn't understand Kahn. I now had an inkling, however, that his ideas about law and legal education weren't nearly so complete as he would have us believe. He seemed much more sensitive, more attuned to the tension between real life and law life than I had imagined; he, for one, had no intention of living in the law. At some level, I realized, he was probably wrestling with the same questions as I. How could he avoid seeing the contradiction between treating a person one way at a certain moment, and in an almost diametrically opposite way a few minutes later? Between living by one standard in professional life, by another in personal life? As Senator Joe McCarthy did, famously, by lambasting a witness before Congress and then, at the end of the day, throwing an arm around his shoulder and asking, "How'd I do?" Integration — we both sought it, I suspected, and disagreed mainly on the methods through which it was achieved.

Seven

"Pigs in Space"

Far more than money, law is capable of intervening between man
and his humanity. . . . [L]aw gets into the individual's mind and
substitutes its external standards, whatever they may be, for the
individual's own standards. We are taught that it is our moral and
civic duty to substitute the law's standards for our own. It is a virtue
to obey the law, a sin to ignore it in favor of one's own personal
desires. That doctrine serves a community well
as long as law is formed in a human image.

CHARLES A. REICH
former Yale Law professor
Yale Law 1952
The Greening of America
1971

First-year law students, myself included, considered fall
break to be a timely vacation. For second- and third-years,
however, it's "fly-back week," so called because they spend
it visiting corporate law firms all over the country. Wined
and dined within an inch of their lives, they return with tales
of fancy hotels, good interviews, not-so-good interviews,
and jet lag. It's difficult, given the nature of law school, to
begrudge the upper-class students their brief orgy of con-
spicuous consumption, but it's equally difficult to sympathize with their complaints of physical exhaustion.

It was while listening to such stories — usually, by eaves-dropping on nearby tables in the dining hall — that I real-ized November brought a shift in the law school's atmosphere. It had become more pragmatic, more compet-itive, more controlled, more cynical. The change wasn't the result of the shortening days, the midsemester blahs, or even my new, postbreak perspective on law school; it seemed specifically related to fly-back week itself, when upper-class law students discovered themselves to be valuable, fawned-over commodities. Ideas and cases no longer seemed a major topic of discussion; from now until Christmas and beyond, a favorite theme was budding employment opportunities.

The talk of jobs and career planning had actually started months earlier, during the first week of classes. That sur-prised me: Yale Law is proud, justifiably, of its reputation for academic excellence and independence, so why should it allow employment issues to surface early and prominently? Its graduates are virtually assured of landing good, well-paid jobs; they seemed to have much less need for career planning than most people. At first you'd think that reading so many cases about loss, disagreement, and real suffering would make students glad just to be alive and healthy, but almost the opposite was true; empathy was one trait sure to impair a lawyer's effectiveness.

Carter only scratched the surface when he said fall break came at a bad time, pedagogically speaking. Indeed, it exists solely for employment reasons, the school having concluded there is little point in holding classes when half the student body is scattered across the country being sold the pleasures of a hardworking, high-paying legal career. The term *fall recess* is a misnomer, and but one example of the ways in which corporate law has come to dominate legal education in recent years. The pressures students feel to take jobs with corporate firms are so high, in fact, that Yale Law spends a significant amount of time trying to persuade students they don't *have* to spend their lives helping reshuffle American corporate wealth.

I had been interested in the connection between legal education and law practice since 1982, when Derek Bok, the president of Harvard University and former dean of its law school, publicly castigated law schools for becoming captive to the legal profession. "The capacity to think like a lawyer has produced many triumphs," Bok told New York City's bar association in a speech that drew national attention, "but it has also helped to produce a legal system that is among the most expensive and least efficient in the world." For articulating such truisms Bok was roundly criticized by lawyers and judges as "anti-intellectual" and "unprofessional" — an odd reaction, I thought, considering that the legal community is supposed to enjoy a good argument. My employer at the time, the State Bar of California, reacted to this and similar criticisms by starting a public relations campaign to "improve lawyer image." As we joked cynically around the office, the bar's action was — in lawyer parlance — "nonresponsive."

When Cathy Iino asked the M.S.L.s in October whether any of us would be interested in writing a story about the legal employment process for Yale Law's alumni magazine, I immediately volunteered. Writing about job placement, I thought, would not only broaden my understanding of law school but also allow me, occasionally, to escape both its physical and intellectual confines. The article wasn't due until January, so I would have plenty of time to get inside, and think about, the world of career planning and recruitment; I would get a sneak preview of the mountaintop toward which my fellow students were marching.

I began my research straightaway, by investigating the annual three-week "Job Fair" (Cathy referred to it as "the meat market") that commenced the first week of October. I already knew something important was happening off campus from seeing upper-class students changing from jeans into suits in the men's room at school, but I had no idea they were participating in a major autumn ritual at law schools across the nation. This year, 424 law firms and twenty-four government and public interest groups had signed up to interview second- and third-years at New Haven's downtown Park Plaza Hotel, which worked out to well over one employer per Yale Law student.

I started going to the hotel whenever I had the chance, often between classes. The law school provided a shuttle bus even though the Park Plaza was only a few blocks away — a concession, I assumed, to high heels and bad weather. Most students walked, however, and I always encountered familiar faces on my way over. Those returning usually looked relieved; those going, nothing but tense. I imagine the sight was amusing, perhaps even a little scary, to unwitting hotel guests whose rooms overlooked the Green. Those stern-faced, pinstriped people commuting to and fro on that well-worn trail through the grass — what's going on, is someone filming another remake of *Invasion of the Body Snatchers?*

It was humid on my first visit to the hotel, and the students were suffering in their formal wear. As I walked into the lobby, a young woman emerged carrying a brown grocery bag in which I could see a black velvet dress with a white lace collar. She was wearing shorts, sneakers, a sport shirt, and a double string of pearls.

The job fair seemed to have taken over much of the hotel. Women from Yale Law's career-planning office handed out information and literature from tables set up across from the spiral stairway in the center of the lobby. Charts on two easels by the elevator bank gave the names of the law firms interviewing that day. In the corner café a couple of recruiters — lawyers themselves, as always — conducted unscheduled interviews. One student etched his Styrofoam coffee cup with a thumbnail while the interviewer hooked an arm over the back of the chair next to him. He wrote with the other hand on a notepad invisible in his lap.

Two floors of the hotel, consisting of suites without beds, were devoted to recruitment. I felt quite out of place after I got off the elevator on the eleventh floor. Wearing corduroys, a polo shirt, and a backpack, I was the only person around who couldn't have gone straight from the Park Plaza to the Metropolitan Opera.

The air was stifling, the closeness only heightened by the halls' heavy carpeting and dim lighting. A handful of students paced up and down the corridors or simply stood and stared, more intense, I thought, than nervous. Occasionally one would lean forward to examine the sheet of paper posted on a door near him. The students rarely spoke with each other, and I didn't see any take advantage of the silver tea service by the elevators.

A door opened soon after my eyes adjusted to the hallway light. I busied myself by rummaging in my backpack, pretending to be a messenger.

"James Canady?" inquired the room's occupant, a man in his middle thirties in rolled-up shirt sleeves.

Canady, who a moment earlier had struck me as looking like a convict awaiting sentencing, smiled and said hello. He stuck out his hand to grasp the one offered. "Welcome to the sauna," the man said. "The air-conditioning isn't working." The door closed smoothly behind them.

I toured the floor. The sheets of paper were interview schedules, with students' names penned in at half-hour intervals. If the interviewer liked what he saw in that time, as well as the student's law school transcript, he would invite the student to a second interview on the firm's home turf during fly-back week. Thirty minutes didn't seem like much time in which to judge a student, but I later learned that at most law schools these interviews lasted just twenty minutes. Yale Law was proud of its insistence on the longer time period, and also that recruiters interview all comers; a law firm that saw one student had to see all who signed up. Yale was one of the few law schools, it seemed, that could impose some of its own rules on the recruitment process.

I saw Barbara, one of the few second-years I had gotten to know, close a door behind her. A pale blonde, she seemed almost translucent when she passed beneath a ceiling light fixture. I didn't have the chance to say hello; she was rushing for the elevator, late, apparently, for an interview on the twelfth floor. Barbara nodded to the person the elevator delivered, and when he greeted her I realized I hadn't heard a word spoken between students in ten minutes.

Barbara told me a few days later that she had signed up for about thirty interviews. When my jaw dropped, she explained that students could sign up for as many as twenty interviews a week, or sixty in the course of the job fair — which meant that some students end up all but skipping

classes in October. Needless to say, most law professors abhor
this result, one — tax professor Michael Graetz — going so
far as to write in the alumni magazine that "Teaching law
students in the fall of their second year has largely become an
exercise in remote control." He also created a term for the
students who regard fly-back week as a junket, calling them,
with some justification, "pigs in space."

I began studying the schedules. Many had empty slots,
though most of the better-known firms in New York, and
virtually all the firms from California, were booked solid. I
decided to knock on doors showing some white space and try
to interview the interviewers.

A young lawyer from a large Philadelphia firm, a fairly
recent Yale Law graduate, had interviewed four people that
day. He was disappointed; at Harvard Law, he said, his
schedule had been completely full, and the firm had consistently hired students from other top ten law schools like
Virginia, Michigan, and Stanford.

"But we don't get our share from Yale. It's like people
aren't aware of Philadelphia or that the practice here is really
taking off," he said. "There's a lot of peer pressure to go to
New York — it's got the sizzle. I tell people we do the same
kind of work as the New York firms but we may not do so
much of it, which is why we see our families more. And there
are a lot of other advantages to Philadelphia that people just
don't know about. Even a second-year associate can afford to
buy a townhouse."

I walked to the end of the hall. A student and an interviewer shook hands in a doorway. As the student strode past
me, looking pleased, the interviewer, coatless and in a white
shirt with cuff links, stepped into the adjoining room. I was
about to knock on the open door, thinking I might be able

to talk with two interviewers at once, when I heard conversation.

"I liked this guy," said the man I had seen, his back
toward me. He was stooped over a small table where another
man sat in an armchair. The first man was gesturing at a
piece of paper. "But what the hell is 'Tragic Choices'?"

"Oh, that's Guido's, Calabresi's course," said the other
man, also dressed in a pressed white shirt and dark slacks. He
had a manila folder open on his lap and a thick stack of paper
that looked like a court document. "It's pretty much Torts
Two, really theoretical. Great course — I took it, really interesting."

"Look at these. 'Myth, Law, and History'? 'Power, Freedom, and Community'? 'Law and War,' for chrissake! Does
everything here have 'and' in the middle?"

"Hey, the best classes I took had the weirdest names."

" 'Images of the Law,' two credits? The guy said it was
basically a literature course. Corporations, Tax, but look,
nothing in antitrust, no estate work, no employment, no
secured transactions."

The seated man reached for the piece of paper and studied
it for a moment.

"I never took a U.C.C. course myself — I don't think
they even offered one.

"Well, maybe," he continued after a pause. "These can be
hard to decipher — he's got 'Law, Economics, and Organization,' that could be antitrust . . . 'Organization Theory,'
that could be something, it's taught by a good professor . . .
a course on nonprofits. . . . Look, maybe you're right, but
if he's . . ."

The phone rang and I backed around the corner. I headed
down another hall, stopping when I heard what sounded like
a party. The noise came from a corner suite occupied by a

small but well-known Los Angeles law firm, and I saw from the schedule on the door that an interview was supposed to be in progress. The firm was very popular for summer placement, and specialized, appropriately enough, in entertainment law.

Backtracking, I passed by a number of rooms occupied by major New York law firms before finding one with an empty slot. A man in his shirtsleeves — tall, tanned, wearing a Harvard Law tie — agreed to speak with me.

I asked what impressions he had of Yale Law students.

"Most of the people we see here are really quite interesting," he said slowly and paternally. "It's not always that way. The smallness of the school comes through; you do sense the truth in Yale's reputation for being contemplative, that the students are interested in the big picture. A Yale Law graduate may take a little longer to create a corporation — 'Oh yeah, we covered that, now what are you supposed to do. . . ?' But in the long run I think the sort of training you get is quite beneficial. The students have the intellectual curiosity and creativity that can make a real difference."

I asked him about the place of women and minorities in a profession that by tradition has been extremely white and extremely male.

"For women I think it continues to look very good. I've interviewed a lot of women this year, in fact we'll probably make offers to two of the women I talked with this morning. Last year, I believe, we had as many women summer associates as men, a handful from Yale alone.

"It may be different for minorities. My firm has at least as many minority partners as any firm in the city, but things may be getting more difficult for them in the profession as a whole. Some firms may be less willing to take chances with these high salaries. If you've got two equally qualified students, some firms may take what appears to be the safer route."

In a suite down the hall a woman in her forties, also from New York, said she wished she had more time to spend with students.

"Your people manage to give subtle and complicated ideas — they don't talk in clichés, they're willing to make conversations that are not run-of-the-mill. But they don't feel the need to assault me with the idea that their views are different, either, and that's nice.

"I've been kidding around with some of the students, saying I should wear jeans if they're going to wear suits. I do wish I could come up and kick the leaves a bit at the ivory tower, see the animals in their habitat instead of at the hotel. This room could be in Cambridge or Chicago. I'd like to go to class or teach a class or go to a dinner party — it's always so pleasant to come here."

I didn't encounter a recruiter from the public arena until I made my way up to the next floor. Like the major corporate firms, the New York district attorney's office had filled most of its time slots. The interviewer, gray-haired but youthful and vigorous, was recruiting at Yale for the first time. He gave his pitch with enthusiasm.

"How do we compete with the firms? Salary-wise, we can't, obviously. I tell them we're looking for idealists: public service, commitment, social good, the public trust. I can offer them responsible work right out of law school — they could be trying major felony cases, murders, homicides, in three to five years. This is where it's at if you want to be a trial attorney and mix it up, do the things people think lawyers do. We have some of the hottest cases in the country.

"We've never had a recruitment problem anyway —

there's never a shortage of qualified applicants. I'm finding that the people who interview really do want to do this. They may balk a little at having to stay at the job for three years, but that hasn't been a major concern. They know working for the D.A. is an incredible, exciting experience and you learn things there you can't learn anywhere else.

"Yalies? Yale is one of the places where the people we want are. I have nothing against recruiting people who are a little philosophical. We can use them. People sometimes forget what the big picture is."

Over the course of a dozen or so interviews I heard the phrase *the big picture* at least three times, always in reference to the idea that it was something Yale Law graduates tended not to forget. Each time I suppressed the desire to reply that it wasn't from lack of trying.

Before leaving the hotel that day I stopped at the literature tables in the lobby. A short stack of reprints on ivory bond stood out among the glaringly colorful photocopies, and it turned out to be a letter from Yale Law's director of career planning asking law firms to help fund a program that increased the stipend for students working in public service jobs over the summer to $250 a week. Without the program, law students interested in public law might well not be able to afford to take such positions; the New York County district attorney's office, for example, paid its law interns just $100 a week.

The figure from the career-planning center astounded me. Two hundred and fifty dollars a week — less than one-quarter the salary paid to summer associates at top law firms, comparable to the *hourly* billing rate of partners in those firms — and it would represent a major *increase* in pay! Was public sector work — sending criminals to prison, attempting to serve the general public, and otherwise trying to enforce the law — really valued so much less than corporate work? Of the hundreds of law firms that showed up at the Park Plaza to hire Yale Law students, the letter listed nineteen as having donated to the public service fund the previous year.

Back at my apartment I picked up the placement office's extensive annual guide to law firms. I looked up the firm that was supposed to have at least as many minority partners as any firm in New York City. The minority associates must have been elevated to partnership quite recently, for the guide listed the firm as having zero partners from minority groups.

When I told Kurt I was researching a story on recruitment, he said I should take his place in a couple of law firm interviews he had scheduled but was planning to cancel. The idea hung in the air like a Christmas ornament; what better way to understand what really went on behind those doors? I didn't take Kurt up on his offer, however, feeling it was well over the ethical line in both of our professions, and settled for a straightforward interview with my T.A. As it turned out, Kurt provided more insight into the recruitment process in a single long talk than I could have gotten in days on my own.

We talked in Kurt's dorm room because he was expecting a phone call from Holland concerning a judicial clerkship. It was a typical Yale student room, defined primarily by dark varnished wood and leaded glass, but it looked singularly unlived-in. That was, in fact, the case; like a surprisingly large number of third-years, Kurt lived mainly in New York City — where his wife worked — and stayed over in New

Haven only a few nights a week. (His half-time roommate, a graduate student from abroad, apparently spent most of his time in the library of international law.) Kurt's frequent absence annoyed some students in the small group, but I came to think of it as a major reason he managed to keep a sense of humor about law school.

When I asked Kurt to give me his sense of the recruitment process, he said "It's theater."

Kurt often spoke in terms that were evocative yet simultaneously mysterious. He was very much aware of the power of words, and careful not to pretend that they fully carried his meaning: his manner always implied that answers can never be given, only unfolded.

"There's a front stage and a backstage for both the lawyers and the students; there are entrances and exits and costumes and sightlines at the hotel. Everyone knows the game and how things are going to play out."

The metaphor, I noted, was of dissembling, not fidelity.

"There are a lot of implied understandings but very little outright lying. The closest thing is the firms saying, as they do, 'Yeah, we're always looking for people who will make partner.' "

Law school recruitment, I said, sounded as bad as Big Eight football.

"It's exactly like that. And you have to wonder why. Why are there so many buyers? The law firms know we don't know anything, since Yale doesn't teach law."

That was a standard joke at Yale Law. The other standard joke, this one applying to all law schools, was that the only job for which a newly hatched lawyer is qualified is associate justice of the U.S. Supreme Court.

"At real law schools the situation is probably different,

the recruiters have a better sense of what they're getting. The firms say they like Yale Law students because they're open and trainable, but I think it's mostly the credentials — they want gilt-edged résumés. There are plenty of people who didn't go to Harvard or Yale who could do the job just as well, but they want someone from Harvard or Yale or Boalt across the table from the guy with the Harvard M.B.A.

"The big firms want people who look like their idea of a big-firm lawyer — they want you to dress a certain way, look a certain way. The message is, 'Rebels need not apply.' You don't see overweight people in those places, for instance, though that's a somewhat different issue. That may well be the most pervasive prejudice, against overweight people, because it goes so directly against the image these firms want to project."

I asked Kurt how he decided which firms to apply to.

"There's a tier mentality among the major law firms: they're very conscious about maintaining or improving their position. The students become very conscious of the status issues, so they interview with the 'best' firms — and with halfway decent grades, will get at least a few offers. It's the tall building theory; you start as high as you can and eventually jump to a lower building where you have your own practice and can actually make partner."

Isn't that a rather cynical view of corporate law?

"Sure, but the firms encourage it. They go out of their way to say the sky's the limit, to the point where you know it's just a game, an unbelievable game. I got pneumonia on a fly-back last year and I planned to leave town early because I couldn't afford the hotel bill. When I told the firms that they said, 'Hey, don't worry, get room service, take a limo to the airport when you're better.' "

No wonder, I thought, law firms spend up to ten thousand dollars and more to land a single full-time associate.

"Last summer I worked for a firm with an office in Australia. The firm paid the round-trip airfare for me and Helen [his wife] even though I was splitting the summer with another firm and would be there only six weeks. It was great. Everyone knows the game. Plenty of people fly to the West Coast at the firms' expense — that's plural, the firms in one city pool the costs — with no intention of working there. Seattle and San Francisco are the classics. But sometimes it works — a couple of the recruiters I met ended up staying with firms they became interested in only because of fly-backs.

"The whole process gets surreal. Two guys with callbacks in New York went to dinner at some incredibly expensive restaurant like the Four Seasons — the works, the bill ran six hundred dollars or something outrageous. And they actually put it on the law firms' tab! They had already decided not to work for those firms so they figured, what the hell. They got the bill in the mail a few weeks later with a note from the firms saying, 'Hope you liked your dinner.' Fortunately, they could afford to pay it."

Pretty cynical all around, if you ask me.

"The firms really do ask for it. On fly-backs they show you this lifestyle out of *GQ,* and it's literally incredible. You're supposed to 'get to know' the firm, but even after you've been there for a summer you don't have any sense of what it's really like to work for the firm — it's parties, baseball tickets, concerts, shows, horseback riding, everything they can think of. The reality, once you're hired, is that you're squirreled away in some warren churning out memo after memo. And everyone knows it."

But if everyone knows it, why do students continue to feel such competition to get as many offers as possible? Rather than figuring out, say, what sort of law they'd really like to practice?

"The fact that Yale Law doesn't give much in the way of grades, doesn't rank students academically, must have something to do with it. Yale supposedly discourages students from competing, but everyone here is used to competing — it's almost automatic. And one of the few avenues left to compete is by stacking up offers. You notice the competition especially with judicial clerkships, but it happens with firms, too.

"For first-years it's tough, because they get left out. No one wants them; you can send out fifty, sixty letters and get one offer because employers know you're a bad investment, that you won't come back when you graduate. It's the second-years they want, and believe me, after the summer drought it feels great to be wanted. Last year they had to clear out an entryway at three A.M. when a first-year set off the fire alarm burning his 'ding' letters, the rejections.

"And obviously, money will always be an attraction. The firms do pay ungodly sums — it's sometimes hard to believe you may be offered sixty-five thousand dollars to start. But it's important to remember that when you're working for these firms you're putting in at least seventy, eighty hours a week. You're really holding down two jobs, and then the pay doesn't seem so spectacular."

Kurt suggested I also talk to Roberta, a third-year who had interviewed with thirty-five or forty employers the previous year but received no summer offers whatsoever. We met up in the dining hall for coffee a few weeks later, and I was surprised to discover that Roberta blamed herself for not landing a job. Her failure, she guessed, was mostly due to being overweight and for having participated in many left-leaning causes before and during law school.

"The firms saw me as a New York Jew with a public-interest person's résumé, a union supporter, a member of the National Lawyers Guild. And I admit, I may unconsciously have given the firms a bad message, but I really wanted an offer, some sort of alternative to think about. But it was really negative stereotyping on their part, and I just don't believe people should be allowed to make employment decisions on that basis. I wasn't one of 'them,' so I was incrementally pushed out.

"This wasn't a new thing for me, but the law school didn't do anything to prepare students for rejection. The biggest problem we'd face, people said, was juggling fly-backs, and I simply didn't expect to have *none*. After a while, for me, it was hell, because I couldn't come into the dining hall without hearing people talk about their fly-backs, the five cities they're going to.

"Students get so hyper about jobs that the people in the placement office want to reassure them. I don't blame them for that, but they end up using these absolute terms; they say, 'Don't worry, it'll happen, this is Yale.' Everyone says, 'Grades don't matter' — but they do, and so do the kinds of courses you take. No one makes it clear that the farther you are from the mainstream, the more trouble you have."

I barely needed to ask questions: I had obviously opened a still-fresh wound.

"If you're older, minority, have a doctorate, handicapped, the law firms are going to give you a harder time. And people get fed up. One firm asked Emily West, she's an older second-year, about this gap on her résumé when she was home raising her family, and she felt the way they asked the question was pretty insulting. She got mad and told them she was in prison.

"From the first day of law school, with all those idealistic speeches, it's like there's no acknowledgment of reality. My issue with Yale and the placement process is that you're not prepared for not succeeding. The process is so nice and rational that you can't object to it, and then you can't talk about rejection when it happens because it's not *supposed* to happen. When people throw ding-letter-burning parties, it's because they've had their share of offers. There's this mythology that everything is easier at Yale Law than other schools, and that's probably true, but I don't think I should be forced to believe it was easier for me when I know it wasn't.

"Sometimes I get down on myself, thinking I blew all the interviews, that I wasn't charming enough. It's funny, but I may have failed because I tried to play the game a little bit, to try to get at least some corporate offers. Some people just gave the acceptable stereotypes, and a lot have simply internalized the game — they've become the image. But obviously, I couldn't do that."

For one of the few times at law school I found I didn't have anything to say. Roberta understood some things in a way I never could.

Some time later I interviewed another third-year, Andy, who voiced similar views despite the fact that he was a "successful" law student with excellent job prospects. What haunted him, however, wasn't a sense of personal failure but a feeling that the recruitment process had a deleterious effect on students' views of law and even of themselves. We talked in his office at the *Yale Law Journal,* where he was an editor.

"This big on-campus job fair definitely skews people's

views," he said. "It's unlikely you'll pursue a law firm, even if you're very interested in it, if it doesn't show up on campus. And there are employers you never hear about that may do just the sort of law you'd like to practice, if only you knew, or if only it seemed like an acceptable option. Generations of Yale Law students have worked at Paul, Weiss and Cravath, Swaine in New York, so that's where a lot more end up.

"The job process is full of profoundly mixed signals. The placement office tells the first-years, 'Don't worry, don't worry, you'll have plenty of time,' and then you're suddenly told, 'It's time!' and all hell breaks loose. And by the third year you're making these major decisions months, more than a year ahead of time. It's never been clear to me why the system works this way.

"I was deeply confused and hurt that first year, practically volunteering my time but still finding it hard to get work. I ended up at a law firm rather than in public interest because I needed the money. And like most people, I found corporate work to be more interesting than I thought it would be, that firms aren't populated by ogres."

The phone rang. Andy talked with another editor about the cite-checking for an article. When he hung up Andy looked slightly agitated, as if simultaneously surprised, thrilled, and worried to be talking in a personal vein.

"I've known a lot of third-years who suddenly have these existential crises. They come to Yale telling themselves they want to do public-interest work, but deep down, they know they won't. They haven't given much thought to what they'd really like to do, and all they seem to hear about is law firms, and who got in where. Look at the casebooks, listen to the anecdotes, the 'Oh yeah, that's a good firm' responses —

corporate law is always the point of reference. And even though the faculty make snide comments about corporate work, you know that's usually what they mean when they call the practice of law 'intellectually challenging.'

"The money makes a big difference. If you've got major loans, corporate law may seem the only way out. The debt traps you a lot more than you ever think it will. And the loan-forgiveness program is really skimpy; I may start out in the private sector to pull myself out of debt a little. Besides, like you said, it may well be easier for a student here to get a law job paying fifty thousand dollars than one paying twenty-five thousand." (I later learned from Yale Law's placement manual that the school's graduates carry an average educational loan debt of $25,000, with 10 percent carrying debts of more than $37,000. And while I was writing this book Yale Law instituted a new program that cancels educational loans made to graduates who earn less than $28,000 a year, whether in the public-interest sector or not.)

One question that had been lurking in the background for weeks finally rose to the surface. Why, I asked, are law students so concerned about getting the best possible job when every time they walk to the Park Plaza they see scores of people earning half, a quarter, a fifth of what the typical Yale Law graduate earns? Why, in short, did they routinely look to and envy the 0.1 percent of the population that seem to have "better" opportunities in life rather than the 99.9 percent who had worse?

"I don't really know," Andy said. "I guess we don't expect to compare ourselves to the rest of the population."

In an effort to make the introduction to law less traumatic and conflicted, most of the major law schools prohibit employers from recruiting first-years before December 15. For many students, however, the prohibition only makes job offers seem that much more important; after hearing second-years' constant boasting about places visited and offers received, many first-years become restive and nervous. First-years showed up at the placement office with such regularity during the job fair, from which they were officially excluded, that the director sent around a memo saying that "it is not necessary for a first-year student to be doing *anything* about a summer job at this time."

The law firms, for their part, only increased the pressure. Skadden, Arps, Slate, Meagher & Flom, a high-flying firm since the explosion of its mergers-and-acquisition practice, invited only Yale's second- and third-years to a cocktail party at Mory's . . . but first-years and graduate students received notices in their mailboxes as well. A few of them decided to crash the party, as did I.

Mory's is less than a block from the law school, so it was no surprise that the party was well attended. I had dressed up a little, a jacket and slacks but no tie, yet found myself even more out of place than at the Park Plaza. Mory's reminded me of companionship, bad food, and killer drinking — mostly Red Cups, if memory serves — but the mood at the Skadden party was quite different. The grayness of the professional dress and banter seemed all wrong in this informal, clapboard clubhouse. I left after making a single circuit of the downstairs rooms.

During the next week I talked to other students who had stayed longer at the party, and their impressions were not dissimilar.

"I finally met someone I hate," said Barbara, the second-year I had seen at the hotel elevator. "They were so full of themselves. I was talking with a couple of lawyers about the firm and one of them said to his pal, 'Let's us men get a drink,' and off they went, just like that. Jerks."

"It was kind of disturbing," said Margie, a first-year. "The way the students changed, trying to impress everyone. It's a totally different world from the one at school. You get the sense there's something rotten in the state of Denmark."

Margie had also gone to another party recently given by a Skadden competitor and also officially closed to first-years. "They had a checklist at the door," Margie said, "and that made me wonder: did the second-years who didn't go to the party not get call-backs? I know I was being paranoid, but you get like that because the placement office always seems to keep the first-years in the dark."

The law firms weren't the only party-givers, either. In recent years the investment bankers had discovered (rediscovered, some say) that law schools are a rich recruiting ground for smart, articulate, aggressive employees. Some twenty law students signed up to interview with Morgan Stanley when that firm came to town, and a third-year subsequently explained its appeal to the *Yale Daily News*. "After five years, you can be making $150,000 to $200,000 a year," she said. "If you're in a law firm, you'll still be in the $70,000 range."

It was clear that the job-placement process could be reduced, for many students, to a question of money. Andy, it seemed, was right — thousands of law students enroll in law school every year filled with belief, idealism, and a sense of commitment, yet emerge three years later burdened with debt and anxious to take the highest-paying job available. Perhaps the students intended that result; perhaps law school gave them a push. The outcome was unfortunate, regardless of its genesis, for it amounted to what Derek Bok called, in the same speech quoted previously, "a massive diversion of exceptional talent into pursuits that often add little to the growth of the economy, the pursuit of culture, or the enhancement of the human spirit." One afternoon in the dining hall I mentioned that view to a few students from the small group, and they wholeheartedly agreed.

"I simply don't know how the choices I make now will affect what I do later," said Vicky, whose first interest still lay in public law. "I feel I'm being tracked before I want to be, that I'm being judged no matter what I do. It feels like it might be held against me if I work for a summer in Arizona or Texas, or even if I do public-interest law now. It's like there's a self-destructive situation in which you become this Yale Law image. And no matter how successful you are, it seems you're always going to wonder whether your choices have been limited by the experience here, and by others' perceptions of that experience."

Lois, the quietest woman in the small group: "You get this feeling you *should* be a member of the proper class."

"That it's shameful," said Liz, "to work someplace other than New York or Washington, or to take a job that's not on the 'approved' list."

It struck me that these three women — two of them from minority groups — might not be successful at Yale Law precisely because they understood it so well. They wanted to act, not be acted upon, and their reluctance to give up a part of their character to law had significantly limited their options within it. As Roberta had put it, such students faced the choice of "selling out or suffering," and selling out meant "internalizing the game" — welcoming law inside themselves. For many, it seemed, law was nothing less than a Trojan horse: a gift that came at a heavy price. Many other professions exact similar costs, no doubt, but those required for expertise in law seemed exceptionally personal and exceptionally high.

Eight

The Limitations of the Law

That lawyers have particularly pronounced intellectual habits
peculiar to them has often been noticed, especially by historians and
other students whose views differ sharply from those of the legal
profession. As one English lawyer has put it, "A lawyer is *bound*
by certain habits of belief. . . . A man who has had legal training
is never quite the same again. . . ."

. . .

The dislike of vague generalities, the preference for case-by-case
treatment of all social issues, the structuring of all possible human
relations into the form of claim and counter-claims — these combine
to make up legalism as a social outlook. When
it becomes self-conscious, when it challenges other views,
it is a full-blown ideology. . . . As law serves ideally to
promote the security of established expectations, so legalism
with its concentration on specific cases and rules is,
essentially, conservative.

JUDITH SHKLAR
Legalism
1964

The energy level at the law school fell off noticeably after fall
break. Intense devotion to the law was assumed, and given,
during the all-out sprint of September and October, but the
following weeks were fragmentary. Fall recess . . . two
weeks of classes . . . Thanksgiving break . . . three weeks of

classes . . . Christmas vacation . . . a few days of reading period . . . final examinations. The remainder of the semester was punctuated so frequently by time off in the real world that law school became harder to focus on and easier to question.

The thrill, in short, was gone. Once we learned law's philosophical framework, law school seemed largely an exercise in placing facts and arguments in the right places. Savoring gave way to digestion, contemplation to rote work, anticipation to impatience, anxiety to boredom. Hazard, having established his authority, stopped calling on students; Guido began to rush through cases, having covered less than half the course in two-thirds the time allotted; Kahn was less tense and demanding, perhaps knowing that he had earned some grudging respect. When students skipped class now it wasn't out of fear or lack of sleep but from ennui and displaced anger. Law school continued to fascinate at times, but it was the hypnotic fascination that flame induces in the moth.

The first-years became increasingly disengaged from their work. In October the dining hall had buzzed with animated conversation, but just a few weeks later it was dull and somnambulistic. Denise began to complain that the semester was passing much too slowly; she was anxious for the spring term, when she would work part-time in a legal services agency. Even Bill, who seemed less susceptible to the law school frame of mind than most students, showed its effects. About this time I disagreed, for some reason, with his theory of a case, and his response was to say, "If you don't agree, you can't have understood what I said," then walk away.

grammar of the law, regardless of content, and less tolerant of conversations employing any other. From this time onward the burden was on the speaker to make himself clear, even for thoughts that were beyond words; a breakdown in communication was now presumed to be a failure in the speaker's intelligence rather than a failure of language. The most one could expect in the way of help from a law-trained listener in the exploration of a new idea had become baiting, often diversionary questions. I began to understand the common criticism of law, sometimes attributed to Edmund Burke — that it "sharpens the mind by narrowing it."

I found myself spending more time with people who had nothing to do with law. I especially looked forward to the Sunday morning phone call from my two-year-old niece, Katherine, who invariably invited me to join her family for football and dinner. There, I knew, I would be immune from judgment; words still meant little to my niece and her younger brother, David Eli, both of whom preferred to communicate with looks, smiles, touches. These afternoons with my brother's family also helped salve the guilt I felt over my condescending behavior toward Terri, Mark, Alice, and Katy just days earlier.

Given my state of mind, it seemed serendipitous that Terri should call out of the blue one evening and suggest she fly out for the Thanksgiving holiday. I was noncommittal at first, no longer knowing what I wanted from Terri or she from me, but soon agreed; I saw, or at least imagined, one final chance to redeem my relationship with her. I called my brother and his wife, who had already invited me over for the day, and they said it was fine to bring a friend. Among family, I figured, in front of the kids, I would have to be true to my feelings.

The visit didn't start out well. I got lost in a heavy

rainstorm trying to get to JFK, the plane was late, and my heart didn't leap up when I finally spotted Terri; for some reason I wanted to criticize her new boots and hairstyle. Those danger signs dissipated, however, in airport hugs and later lovemaking, and for the rest of the long weekend I thought we got along well. We had fun baby-sitting the kids, shopping, touring, and visiting friends — or at least I did, not realizing for some time that I was paying only superficial attention to Terri.

I was caught off guard, consequently, by Terri's apparently sudden agitation the evening before she was to go back West. She asked quite bluntly whether we had a future. It was a reasonable question, one in normal circumstances I would have thought about at some length. As it was, I was completely unprepared — but thankful that in recent months I had learned to cope with such unpreparedness. I kept cool, and the analytical wheels began to turn, immediately and unbeckoned, in my mind. I made an argument that put Terri squarely on the defensive.

Yes, I have mentioned marriage, family, children, but you should have known better than to take me literally. I've been under a lot of pressure for more than a year, I've been seeing a shrink, I've talked about my general confusion since our first date. You had many good reasons not to believe me, yet you chose to disregard them and believe other signs, see other things. In any case, I made no promises.

These were protective excuses, of course, but it was now child's play to make them appear rational, worked-out explanations. Instead of being cold and saying we simply disagreed, or being harshly critical and calling her views mistaken, I created a situation in which Terri would most likely blame herself. I could make her feel she had misunderstood, had assumed too much, had even wronged me. And the result, I hoped at some preconscious level, would be that Terri concede I was right to relieve myself of all responsibility for the relationship.

Terri was stunned, then angry. She said almost nothing. I knew what she must be feeling.

How can you talk to me like that? And with such contempt, such pretense? How can you stay so far above it all, leave me no way to respond, no way to vent these feelings?

I was actually proud, at one level, to have produced this state of mind. I had controlled the situation so that expression went in only one direction; I had intellectualized the event, put Terri's feelings beyond the boundaries of the argument. I would listen if she ever decided to voice her emotions, perhaps even agree with her, but my own argument was complete. Terri's anger was a separate issue, one I could isolate and, if I saw fit, ignore. As one-time Yale Law professor Thomas Reed Powell said, "If you can think about a thing, inextricably attached to something else, without thinking of the thing it is attached to, then you have a legal mind."

If there is no "meeting of the minds," the law will not enforce an agreement — *Balfour v. Balfour* again. I was nervous and scared but ready to parry, for I knew I was untouchable. My strategy was not only effective but legitimate, for if the law sided with me I couldn't be wrong.

Right?

I pushed down the nagging dissent. I had acted similarly with Alice and Mark just three weeks earlier, true, but that was different — I was truly hypocritical then, thinking one thing while saying another. This time I was only withholding, and the failure to volunteer information couldn't be wrong.

Could it?

Yet this evening felt much worse. I had heightened the

pain of separation rather than mitigated it — more precisely, eliminated my own pain by adding it to Terri's. I had made my imperviousness to pain a source of pride.

Six months earlier I would have talked with Terri, tried to explain my need to break away, admitted to uncertainty and mixed feelings — anything to maintain some human connection. But meeting differences with reason, accusations with silence or surprise, was more practical, more efficient, so much safer! Terri could not expose my weaknesses if I hid them behind a seamless front, or exploit my ambivalence if I implied that internal conflicts had vanished. And who knew, maybe I could actually get tough by acting tough, like Ronald Reagan and John Wayne. Transform the image into reality; make my mind and heart truly invulnerable.

Terri shook in fury at the sink, washing dessert dishes, torn, I was sure, between crying and yelling.

I was suddenly very tired. I pushed the evening's trauma from my mind, got out my sleeping bag, laid it on the floor, and soon went to sleep. This wasn't tragedy, after all, like the Torts case in which the guy was run over by two trolley cars but the family couldn't collect damages because no one knew which trolley actually killed him. . . .

I had no nightmares. But as I showered the next morning I found myself imagining that the souvenir hunting knife Terri had given me a year earlier was plunging wildly through the shower curtain. As I dried off I told Terri, still in the single bed, of my hallucination. She replied, getting up, that if she killed anyone it would be herself.

I drove Terri to the bus stop an hour later and paid her fare to the airport. When the bus pulled out of sight, I put my head on the steering wheel and cried.

I was enveloped in numbness for the next few days. It

wasn't a sense of despair, or pointlessness, or even guilt; it was a sense of the impossibility of communicating fully and completely honestly with anyone else. The Sanskrit scholar Heinrich Zimmer, best known as the mentor of mythologist Joseph Campbell, once said, "The best things in life cannot be told, and the second best are misunderstood," and that Guidian-like koan summed up the state of my spirit. What do you do when you've come to the end of a verbal road, to the limit of your ability to express? You act: you have no other choice . . . unless you've been trained to believe that words are sufficient substitutes for action.

With Terri I had deliberately limited myself to creating an *arguendo* world that made perfect sense in its own terms, but bore little relation to the reality it supposedly captured. And now, with a few months of legal training under my belt, I could make such worlds at the drop of a hat — a marvelous skill, no doubt, but an extraordinarily dangerous one. Artificial worlds are much neater than real ones, and thus all the more seductive.

I had liked Guido's approach to the law from the first day of Torts, but as the semester progressed it became virtually the only one that didn't madden me. Guido seemed the only professor willing to acknowledge that legal education had a powerful influence over student values, that it could cause students to lose their humanity. Yes, he said, we want a legal system based on rules, on order — but not at the cost of eliminating the fanciful and quixotic, the unexpected, the unfathomable mysteries that make life worth living.

Guido constantly reminded us that law was a tool of limited uses. Law oversimplified the world, he seemed to say, because it allowed lawyers to replace personal experience with rules, subjective values with legal certainty. The law decided that euthanasia is wrong, polygamy is wrong, homosexuality is less worthy than heterosexuality — and that was supposed to put an end to the discussion. Why? Because law's value system — based on efficiency, rationality, orderliness — couldn't imagine any other conclusion. Guido recognized that the lawyer's value system, though apparently impartial, tilted the legal playing field, and ultimately society at large, in a lawyerly direction. And that frightened him — not because lawyers' values are necessarily bad, but because lawyers foster changes in society without its knowledge or assent.

The dean tried to instill in future lawyers the idea that they must understand law's choices. He taught that the conversion of love into contract, responsibility into rule, idea into word, is invariably a diminishment; that taking law beyond its proper role — to shape life rather than outline it — is to displace other ways of thinking, other values, that are equally valid but far more fragile. The lawyer himself will likely come to prefer the elegance of law to the anarchy of life, but if that lawyerly division means compromising the diversity of life, he must look to his conscience.

Guido expressed these ideas best in his lecture on the Gift of the Evil Deity, which came midway through the semester.

"Suppose an Evil Deity were to appear before you, as head of your country, and offer a boon, a gift, that would make life more pleasant, more enjoyable, in any way you wish. The gift can be anything you want — greedy, obscene, idealistic, it doesn't matter — but it cannot, at least for the moment, do one thing; it cannot save lives.

" 'In exchange for this gift,' the Deity says, 'all I ask is the lives of one thousand young men and women, every year, picked at random. They will die quite horrible deaths. All you have to do is agree.' "

It was the myth of Theseus and Athens' tribute to the Minotaur.

"Do you accept the offer?"

We say nothing for a moment, though a few students shake their heads. Guido has laid a trap, and we all know it.

A voice from the back says, "Sure." The class laughs — someone had to get Guido's ball rolling.

"You accept?"

Pause.

"So, what's the difference between the gift and the automobile?"

Silence.

"The automobile kills fifty-five thousand people a year, not one thousand. Is that the only difference?"

A woman raises her hand. Guido motions to her.

"We make automobiles safer all the time," she says. "Seat belts, air bags, and so on?"

"We believe we can, yes. And often think we do. There is an element of perfectibility that we like to have fool us.

"Well, this Evil Deity is pretty clever, he can make his boon perfect, too. He says, 'You want perfectibility? Okay, we'll make a game of it, let's call it "Guido's Roulette." I'll give you the boon, but instead of costing a thousand lives every year it will cost as many as two thousand some years, and in others, at least in theory, could go down to zero. But the number will vary inversely with the pleasures of the gift. Driving carefully will save lives but it won't be as much fun.' "

I become a little nervous. Guido was a major player in the ground-breaking field known as "law and economics" (and one of its few liberal voices); if he starts to play number games, this could be awful.

Guido looks down at his notes, palms on the desk.

"Let me tell you a story about perfectibility."

Guido said he had attended a conference some years before in which a doctor promoting a definition of death based on flat electroencephalograms was asked how often the definition would result in patients being buried alive. The doctor cited a very low figure, whereupon Guido asked whether the older definition of death was more accurate. It was, the doctor replied, in theory but not in practice; the "vital signs" tests — heartbeat, breath in the mirror, and the like — were better indicators of life as long as they were employed carefully, but often, in the rush of hospital work, they weren't.

"We ate of the tree of knowledge that day," Guido said. "We faced a new definition that ensured a specific number of people would be declared dead when they shouldn't have been, and another, perfectible definition which in fact led to a greater number of deaths."

This was going to be a good class.

"So the Evil Deity made the gift perfectible. Do you still think it's any different from the automobile?"

Silence.

"Come on, anyone, there are lots of differences."

"We've chosen the car as a society," says one man directly behind me. "When I buy a car I'm just going along with a choice that's already been made — the gift has already been accepted, whether I like it or not."

"You mean there was a vote for the automobile?" Guido bellows. "And you voted against it? Well, let's take another vote — it's perfectly possible for us to decide to ban them now, isn't it? Is that the difference you're talking about — choice?"

It didn't much matter what the student had in mind because Guido knew exactly where he wanted to go.

"Suppose the Evil Deity says, 'I see, you want people to

have a choice. You can have that as well; all I ask is that you don't forbid anyone from accepting this gift. Now if you personally accept it, your chances of being picked for death go up but are still trivial — it's only a thousand lives — and if you reject it, your chances remain very low.' The chance still exists, however, because cars kill pedestrians and passengers as well as drivers.

"So, do you accept the gift?"

Pause.

"Before you answer, think about what happens should you reject the gift. If you turn it down and most people accept the gift, you're actually much worse off than if it hadn't been offered at all. Will you still be able to walk to the market? Will there be good public transportation? Probably not. You've made a free choice, but it may not be as free as it looks. Indeed, I wonder how much our notion of free consent, on which we base so many of our decisions, is really a fig leaf."

Guido tells another story.

His brother, an oncologist, was treating several inoperable cancer patients with an experimental drug when he realized that the drug, given its make-up and previous tests, might also be useful in treating viral diseases. If he could expose the patients to cowpox — which is to say, vaccinate them against smallpox — and the vaccination did not take, it was likely the experimental drug was indeed a pox-killer; if he vaccinated them when they were off the drug (which was administered only a week a month) and the vaccination did take, it was even more likely that the drug was effective against viruses. The vaccination, in other words, wouldn't aid the patients, could hurt them, but might well help many other patients in the future. The doctor promised he would continue to treat the patients with the experimental drug regardless of their decision about participating in the doctor's virus research.

"I told my brother it wasn't much of a choice if the patient believed there was one chance in a thousand that they would die of pox, and one chance in a hundred that he was lying about continuing to treat them if they didn't go along. My brother said, 'That may be, but the experiment was worth doing, and I did the best I could to give them a true choice.'

"Was there a choice? We like to think there was, but really the experiment was done because it was worth doing, not because the patients chose it. But my brother did give as much choice as possible, and that's important.

"It's so crucial to say we may choose, even though it's not much of a choice, and even though we may want to hide from the idea that we're choosing, in the case of the automobile, 'this much' safety. In the Temple of Truth — and if this isn't the Temple of Truth, I don't know what is — the impression of having a choice may be as important as having the choice itself."

Another story. "This one," Guido said, "goes the other way.

"As you know, during the war Nazi doctors, so called, performed abominable experiments on people in prison camps. One survivor testified against these doctors at the Nuremberg trials, and I've always had tremendous admiration for this woman. When one of the doctors' lawyers asked whether she had consented to the experiments, she said, 'Yes.' Then this lawyer, who like so many didn't know when to shut up, asked — with a leer on his face, I've always suspected — 'Why did you consent?' And she looked at him and said, 'Better eternity in a brothel than one night in Buchenwald.'

"You could say she had a free choice. Yet that did not

allow the doctors to duck the moral responsibility for going along. They were convicted."

Pause.

"Do you still accept the gift?"

Silence.

"Okay. The Evil Deity says, 'You wanted to feel you're in control, so I gave you choices. You wanted perfectibility, so I gave you roulette, a game you could win. Now here's something else you may like, another variable. The more expensive the roulette wheel, the easier it is to play well.'

"Money becomes a factor. Safer cars can be built: it's perfectly possible to build very fast cars with frames and padding that protect only the driver, like racing cars, though they might cost a hundred thousand dollars. And you can build cars with bumpers filled with feathers that tickle people instead of hurting them and go only fifteen miles an hour. If people drive only feather-bumper cars, everyone's chances of being picked for death are lower; but if some people drive the fast, driver-padded cars, they have lowered their own chances of being picked while increasing the chances of everyone else.

"The Evil Deity says, 'I know you like this game because, in theory, the game can be played perfectly and nobody gets killed. It's so appealing — you can blame the people who are killed for not measuring up rather than yourself for accepting the boon. The game allows you to accept the gift you originally said you would not, and to blame the gift's drawbacks on those who play the game badly.'

"We create a subterfuge," Guido says, *sotto voce*, hands together, "and we make scapegoats."

This was getting a little frightening.

"Another story. Friedrich Dürrenmatt wrote a play, *The Visit*, about a very poor village in Austria and a woman who returns many years later after getting very rich, in America of course. A rumor starts that she will give a lot of money to the village if a certain man is killed, and it eventually becomes clear that she is behind the rumor. The man in question is elderly, no better and no worse than most of the others, but in his youth had seduced and abandoned this woman, which is why she left. Everyone in the village knew the story, and while nobody thought that what the man had done was good, they hadn't worried much about it. But the villagers, at first appalled that the woman has asked for this man's death, slowly decide that his sin is keeping them from their just deserts. And they kill him.

"As I say, we like scapegoats, and the Evil Deity is perfectly willing to let you have them, too. Scapegoating is a way of avoiding responsibility for our choices.

"We make decisions all the time about how much of the gift of the Evil Deity to accept, but we don't like to admit it. The trick, often, is to put ourselves in the position where we don't see a choice, don't have to ask the question. But can we duck the responsibility, even though it seems possible to get rid of it? We foster the illusion that we're on the side of life when we may be choosing dramatically against it.

"The question isn't really whether we accept the gift but when, and how much, and who makes the decision. We can't be cynical about looking into dark corners and seeing the choices we make. What you must think about is how to structure those choices in ways that allow us to choose as humanely as possible, and not make the mistake of trivializing the cost into dollars. The rules you make shape the people you are; they affect what you want in the future, your valuations, your tastes, your ideas.

"And of course," Guido adds jokingly with an almost

apologetic smile, "you must do so in the cheapest way possible."

Guido gave the Evil Deity lecture on Friday, the day before
the annual Torts picnic at Guido's hundred-acre farm, near
Woodbridge. The scheduling was no doubt coincidental,
but it supercharged my anticipation; I looked forward to
seeing the dean in an informal situation. Who was he, really,
and where did he get these extraordinary ideas?

I drove out to Guidacre — so the dean referred to the
farm, playing on the tradition of identifying litigating land-
owners as Blackacre and Whiteacre — with Vicky, from the
small group, and Allen, a graduate student from Spain.

Allen had just finished a five-year law program in Bar-
celona and had come to Yale in part to study with Guido. He
was particularly interested in toxic torts, a major concern in
his country since hundreds of people were killed by contam-
inated cooking oil a few years earlier. (The trial would com-
mence the following August.) Allen remarked that Guido
seemed to be much better known in Europe than in the
United States.

"Guido is like Harvard in Europe," he said. "Everyone
knows Harvard, not so many Yale." Allen's comment stuck
with me.

I hadn't driven the route in close to ten years but it came
back to me quickly. Little had changed: barnlike white
houses, narrow-shouldered roads, yellow leaves skittering
across wet black pavement. I had forgotten how easy it was
to leave the city behind.

We were among the first to arrive at the farm, formally
known as Sunnyside. I pulled off the graveled-dirt driveway
and parked on the edge of a grassy slope twenty yards below

a clapboard house. Beyond it we could see the barn where we were to gather if the weather turned bad, but the day was clear and brisk.

The house seemed empty. We headed up the road, toward the barn.

Guido appeared to have at least two of every sort of animal — horses, cows, geese, chickens, dogs — and they roamed around more or less at will. I first thought "ark," then "tort laboratory." The barn: Guido introduced the insurance issue by telling us how his claim was handled when it burned down. The apple trees: produce destined for the hypothetical "Guido's Fruit Stand," regularly demolished by bad drivers. The cows: they "escape with monotonous regularity," leading Guido to a lecture on tort law's use of categories. It's the movie *Shane,* Guido had said: in the 1870s, much depended on whether cows or crops were labeled as "trespassers" in court cases between farmers and ranchers over who should bear the expense of fencing the land.

The dean stepped from the barn and greeted us cheerily, arms outspread. I was very nervous, which is probably why a stream of far-out legal questions came to mind. Who was going to pay for the torts that were certain to happen today — students trampled by horses, consumed by pigs, beaned by bales of hay? We were invitees, not trespassers; as host, what standard of care was Guido required to show us . . . or had we assumed the risk of farm accidents? Could injured students argue, as Alice had about her raft trip, that although we appeared to have come to the Guidacre picnic voluntarily, the invitation was in fact coercive?

I bit my tongue. Seeing that Guido was already deep in conversation with Vicky, Allen and I walked on.

The driveway divided past the barn and one branch dou-

bled back and climbed a large, hay-strewn hill. We were
drawn upward, hoping to get a view of Long Island Sound
in the distance and fall color in the surrounding woods. The
crickets, jumping energetically before us, kept my eyes to
the ground, so when I looked up I was startled to see a table
standing in the middle of a level stretch of cut grass. It was
furnished with a red-checkered tablecloth, a few chairs, and
a corked bottle of red wine.

The tableau was too perfect to be believed — an Italian
farm scene, straight from Hollywood. And yet is was perfect
homage, however posed, to a country left behind; Guido, I
knew, had fled fascist Italy with his family in 1939. No
wonder Guido had ended up teaching torts, the one area of
law that forces a constant wrestling with loss. Guidacre,
surely, was the dean's new Tuscany (not Calabria, despite the
family name), his modern ark, a place to dream about the
end of loss, about the best of all possible worlds.

Every other spring Guido teaches a course called "Tragic
Choices," described in the catalogue as "A consideration of
those choices which a society cannot avoid making . . .
[that] undermine fundamental values of that society." Guido
provided a preview of the course in the Gift of the Evil Deity
lecture, and again toward the end of the semester while
discussing how tort systems often discriminate, perhaps unintentionally, against minority viewpoints. As always,
Guido asked questions that focused on the ways in which law
shapes society. If someone must suffer, how do we decide
who it is? Who, indeed, is "we"? And why should the
burden be placed, as is so frequently the case, on the unusual, the unpopular, the unconforming?

Guido started off with *Lange v. Hoyt*, a 1932 case in which
an eight-year-old girl named Minelda was injured in some

unspecified accident. Minelda's mother, a Christian Scientist, delayed taking her to the hospital, which made the injury far worse. A jury found the defendant had caused the accident and awarded damages to Minelda and her mother; the defendant appealed on the grounds that he or she — the casebook didn't say which — shouldn't be liable for the extra expenses resulting from the mother's failure to mitigate her daughter's injury, even if that failure was due to religious belief.

"The jury found negligence. The mother didn't take Minelda to a doctor as early as other people would have, and that resulted in more severe damage to the daughter. For our purposes, the central question is this: as a matter of law, can we say the mother was negligent in not going to a doctor when people who are not Christian Scientists would have been found negligent if they had likewise failed to mitigate damages? Is this a 'thin skull' case?"

Guido reminds us of the cases in which a plaintiff's unusual physical weakness — a thin skull, bad leg, weak heart — is found to be irrelevant to the establishment of liability. It doesn't matter that an ordinary person would have been uninjured by a slight rap on the head; if harm is done, the harm-doer must pay. The idea is commonly expressed by the phrase "You take your plaintiff as you find him."

"In other words, are there 'thin religions'? Or is it different when you're dealing with someone's belief? This court says the jury may take into account the fact that Christian Science is a widely held belief in deciding whether Minelda's mother acted reasonably. Now that seems a very strange thing for the judge to do — to let the jury determine, in effect, how many people have to subscribe to a view before it becomes reasonable.

"Does that make truth a popularity contest? Since Minelda won, that issue doesn't really come up. But if she had lost she could have argued on appeal, 'What does it matter whether it's widely held or not — it's *my belief!*'

"What do you think? Decided correctly or not?"

A student brings up Guido's "violinist in the steel mill" hypothetical from a few classes earlier. A musical prodigy mangles his hands in an extrusion machine while conducting research on the great working-class opera. The violinist can't recover, we decided, even though his performing career is over, because he consciously assumed the risk of injury; he was in a sense responsible for his mutilation.

"If the violinist is writing this opera for religious reasons," says the student, attempting to synchronize this situation with Minelda's, "we can say that while he followed his beliefs in doing this activity, he shouldn't recover damages because his beliefs aren't sufficiently pervasive to —"

Guido, who has edged to the corner of the podium nearest the student, almost leaps off it.

" 'Sufficiently pervasive'? Are thin skulls sufficiently pervasive? Is that the distinction? Remember, the violinist recovers if he's mangled by a car — the negligent defendant must pay his losses, which may be enormous if he's the only person with this great musical talent. It's only in the steel mill that he doesn't recover for his injury.

"What do you think? Somebody else."

"But shouldn't the 'reasonable person' standard apply to everyone?" asks another student. "I mean, beliefs aren't supposed to matter."

"Reasonableness and beliefs are different, beliefs aren't something we take into account — is that what you're saying?"

"Umm, I'm not sure this is right, but when you — "

"Well," says Guido, "I'm asking. Is this case right? Should a defendant pay because the plaintiff has an odd belief? Or is that outrageous?"

The class murmurs. It does seem outrageous, if you're the defendant. Guido is laying the groundwork for something we can't yet grasp.

A woman in the third row says, "It is outrageous. The mother refused to go to a doctor because her belief says, 'Leave things in God's hands,' let God decide on death, or cure, whatever. So why should the defendant pay the extra damages for God's decision?"

Much laughter.

"How many of you agree?"

A few students nod.

"Disagree?"

Most don't respond at all. It's too close to call.

"Let me give you another case. *Friedman v. New York*, 282 New York Supp. 2d 858, 1967."

Guido returns to the desk on the podium and reads from a newspaper article atop his pile of tattered, yellow, legal-tablet notes. " 'A Jewish girl from Brooklyn jumped twenty-five feet from a chair lift at a ski area rather than disobey a dictate of her religion and sit stranded for the night with a male escort, according to court testimony.' "

Expectant giggling.

Guido gives the rest of the case from memory. "It was summer, and the young woman went up a ski lift in the Catskills with a man named Jack Katz. At six or seven o'clock, around nightfall, the State of New York negligently closed the ski lift while they were still out there. Now Ms. Friedman had been taught — mistaught, as it turned out — there was an absolute rule that Orthodox women could not be with a man, after dark, in a place where no one else could reach them.

"So as the sun set romantically in the distance, Ms. Friedman jumped — or dove, apparently, because most of the injuries were to her face. And she sued the state, saying, 'Maybe for somebody else it might have been reasonable to stay there, but for me it wasn't.' Now, it doesn't matter whether she got the religion wrong, because she reasonably believed she had it right. And if you're thinking that she should have sued the rabbi, she didn't, because like most teachers, he had no money."

A sly look appears on Guido's face.

"I wonder . . . why didn't Jack Katz jump?"

Silence, then scattered snickering.

"Something deep inside me suggests that maybe today, she would have pushed him, and that wouldn't have been such an unreasonable thing to do. Why should she be the one who has to jump?

"In any case, the New York court says, 'Of course she can recover,' as the jury did in Minelda's case. So — do you think that's right?"

We nod, playing along.

"Okay, let me give you the Catholic case."

The class laughs freely even though we know — perhaps because we know — Guido will eventually arrive in each of our backyards.

"It's very interesting — I hypothesized this case for years before I found it in Australia. A woman's pelvis was damaged in an accident and bearing children has become catastrophically dangerous for her. She is a devout Catholic, and takes more seriously than most Catholics the Pope's encyclical against artificial birth control. She uses the rhythm method . . . or, as it is sometimes called, Roman Roulette."

Laughter.

"Of course, the only reason I can say such things is that I'm a devout Catholic myself."

Guido walks in front of the desk and stops, leaning against it. He is no more than five feet away and I see that his khaki trousers still show the extensive ink stain (right-hand pocket) I first noticed the previous day. The faded color indicates that the trousers have been washed, but I can't help believing Guido never knew the stain existed.

"Her choices are three. She can abstain from lovemaking, and the law will give her very sizable damages for abstention. Or she can violate her conscience and use artificial birth control — but what, in that case, are her damages? How much are the pains of hell worth, the price of a soul? Or she can follow her conscience and continue to use the rhythm method.

"Suppose she chooses the last option, and though very careful, becomes pregnant. She now faces another choice: to violate her conscience at this point and have an abortion, or to try and have the child. But if she does carry the child to term, catastrophic death. Catastrophic death.

"So she sues the person who shattered her pelvis and replies, 'I have behaved reasonably.' The defendant says, 'Hah! You didn't — someone who wasn't a Catholic would have chosen another method of birth control, and you would not be pregnant. If you want to have this kooky belief, have your kooky belief, but don't make me pay for it.'

"But our Constitution says something about having no establishment of religion. I don't mean this is a constitutional issue — that's a different question — but surely constitutional notions affect what tort law will do. 'Law is a seamless web,' as they used to say, or to use a modern metaphor, has a 'gravitational field.' And if the notion of reasonableness ends up protecting what I call 'banquet religions,' those beliefs represented by our leading religious practitioners — rabbis, ministers, priests, what have you — at civic gatherings. We are in danger of having what amounts to a state religion, one based on the 'widely heldness' of certain beliefs.

"So doesn't the gravitational pull of the establishment clause mean that if we protect these ordinary religions, we must also protect the odd ones? And doesn't that make beliefs a gift of the Evil Deity? If we're going to accept all religions, mustn't we pay the costs associated with them? For Minelda's crippling, even if it was caused by her peculiar religion?"

Guido pauses and a student interrupts.

"Does this apply only in contributory negligence cases, or are you saying —"

Guido cuts him short. "We'll have to come back to that. So is she" — he gestures to the woman who made the joke about God's will — "right? Thin skulls, physical problems are one thing, but beliefs, moralisms, religions, values are another? Reasonable men don't have beliefs — they are scientists? People should do what's reasonable to mitigate damages, they must bear the burden of unreasonable beliefs?"

He addressed the woman directly.

"Is that what you're saying? 'I think Christian Science is a kooky belief, and Orthodox Judaism is a kooky belief, but I don't think Catholicism is and therefore this woman ought to recover'? Or at least in Connecticut, where Catholicism is a widely held belief, though not perhaps in South Carolina, where it isn't?"

The woman has no intention of replying, since Guido has altered her comment to suit his teaching purposes. And in any case, he doesn't give her the chance.

"That gets you into some significant difficulties. What's a reasonable belief? How do we decide what's reasonable? We can say, of course, 'Beliefs are out of the equation, we won't take them into account.' Do you agree with that? Anyone?"

A male voice from the right side of the room. "No. In Minelda's case the court is saying that widely heldness is to be used as evidence to show that —"

"But where do you draw the line? The line breaks down between 'no establishment of religion'/'all religions are all right.' It could be that if a court just doesn't like a religion, and belief in it isn't widely held, they'll just call it a 'cult,' a 'sect.' They'll use different words to get around what we say we consider a very basic American value, the freedom to worship as we choose.

"The court may say, 'We're not prohibiting this religion, we're prohibiting only *acts* under the religion.' But the distinction makes no sense. It'll say, 'We're not doing anything to Mormonism by prohibiting bigamy,' as in *Reynolds,* but they are, and more. It's a little like saying 'Free speech is absolute,' and then barring some speech not by saying it's too dangerous, not by balancing speech against the harm it may cause, but by saying it isn't speech."

Pause, to let the idea sink in.

"If you admit that you're deciding whether something is a 'reasonable' religion, you're doing something very different than if you say, 'It's a cult, it's a sect.' For when you call a religion a 'cult,' you've in effect said, 'Change your beliefs or you're out.' You've made outlaws of those who believe in kooky religions.

"And that, of course, is exactly what happened to those Mormons who wouldn't go along with the prohibition of polygamy. They became outlaws and began to behave as outlaws behave, because we pushed them outside the Constitution."

How ironic, I thought — law not just naming outlaws but causing them. But could it be any other way? As philosophers frequently remind us, defining "x" invariably defines "not x" as well. Is that the deepest tyranny of a majority — the fact that it often achieves a sense of identity not through the building of a community but through the invention of minorities, followed by discrimination against them?

"The most difficult cases are those like *Roe v. Wade,* where you've got beliefs on both sides. That's the stuff of which tragic choices are made."

Guido moves to the other side of the podium.

"Well, what about these other beliefs? Why isn't the solution just to say, 'You've got to behave reasonably apart from beliefs.' Anybody think that's a good idea?"

"Yeah," says an older student to my left, "if you think of 'reasonable' in terms of ordinary experience. Like the woman who knew that she might get hit by a foul ball at the ballpark, but went anyway. . . ."

"Yes, knowledge, knowledge, is . . . well, let me give my White Anglo-Saxon Protestant case. I don't know whether the parties are White Anglo-Saxon Protestants or not, but they might as well be. It's called *Troppi v. Scarf,* 31 Michigan Appellate Division 240, 1971. Actually, it's in the book, page 535."

Guido hadn't assigned the case. He didn't want to reveal the punchline prematurely.

"A couple decided they couldn't afford to have any more children. They got a prescription for birth control pills, but the pharmacist negligently gave them tranquilizers instead."

Pause, until the giggles subsided.

"Well, they made love, as calmly as could be" — a new wave of laughter — "and she became pregnant. The couple sued the pharmacist, saying, 'We can't afford this child,' and there was very strong evidence that expense was indeed the reason they decided not to have more children.

"Now there were all sorts of fascinating issues at the frontiers of tort law in this case — wrongful life, whether the benefits of having a child always outweigh the costs of having it. But before reaching those questions the court faced the argument that the plaintiff had failed to act reasonably to mitigate damages. The pharmacist's attorney said the couple could have had an abortion, which was legal in Michigan, or put the child up for adoption, and didn't only because the parents had some kind of belief that they shouldn't.

"Well, the court got mad and said, 'As a matter of law, *as a matter of law,* a reasonable person has the right to decide not to have an abortion, and after the child is born, not to put it up for adoption.' The person can decide the other way, of course, but the law won't let someone else impose that pressure on a person's beliefs. A reasonable person can have these beliefs.

"As you may expect, that can cause a lot of trouble. You can try to escape the difficulty by saying that 'reasonable' beliefs are 'secular' and thus deserving of protection we won't grant to religious beliefs, but it's hard to draw the line between religious and secular, and most of our secular beliefs are really part of older, accepted religions anyway. They became part of our secular thinking because they were held by the first settlers — because they were widely held then. Or you can protect all religious beliefs, both common and idiosyncratic.

"And if you're going to play the game this way, what happens to *Vaughn v. Menlove,* which of course you all reread last night? The whole notion of 'reasonableness'? Do you end up giving a benefit to religions, saying that all religious beliefs are okay because we don't want to distinguish between popular and unpopular beliefs, while saying that nonreligious beliefs are only okay if they're widely held?"

Pause.

"It's a problem, it's a problem."

The class is supposed to be over but no one is fidgeting.

"Suppose there is somebody who believes in progress. He believes you must always move forward, never back. He gets out of a trolley car — this is *Bence v. Teddy's Taxi* — and sees a cab trying to squeeze through between him and the curb. Now someone who doesn't have this belief in progress would stop, or go backward, but this man goes forward and gets hit.

"Does anyone doubt that he would lose? That he would be found contributorily negligent, probably as a matter of law? But that if enough people had the same belief, religious or not, it would be considered a reasonable act?

"There's a gift of the Evil Deity here. Our unwillingness, in principle, to distinguish among religious beliefs costs something. It creates more accidents, and somebody's got to pay. Who? A negligent defendant, or someone who did something for which we feel he ought to be liable. It's a cheap, easy way of maintaining this society's set of values, complex though it is."

Silence.

"Okay, next time we'll do . . ."

Guido's recital of two or three case names came through clearly, for once not nearly drowned out by the sound of heavy books slamming shut and chairs skidding on linoleum.

*   *   *

A few months later I came across a paper by another Yale Law professor, also a specialist in tort law, in which he discussed the rise of law and economics. "Calabresi views complexity itself as a virtue," the professor wrote. "The style of *The Costs of Accidents* [Guido's first book] can be explained in no other way."

I smiled, for he was exactly right. But I didn't agree with this professor's humoring tone, for by this time I understood Guido's love of complexity and contradiction. He refused to compromise life in the name of law, knowing that since life was complicated, law must be so as well; he saw that the drive for simplicity closes the doors to wisdom as often as it opens them. It's convenient to assume that the earth is the center of the universe, but the assumption precludes a deeper understanding of the heavens.

Nine

Slam-Dancing in a Corset

[There is a] paradox of form and substance in the law. In form its
growth is logical. The official theory is that each new decision
follows syllogistically from existing precedents. But . . . precedents
survive in the law long after the use they once served is at an end and
the reason for them has been forgotten. The result of following them
must often be failure and confusion
from the merely logical point of view.
OLIVER WENDELL HOLMES, JR.
The Common Law

Guido aside, the one thing that made law school tolerable in
the last weeks of the semester was working on an appellate
brief for Con Law. Kahn handed out the assignment before
fall break, but it languished at the bottom of my suitcase
while I was in California. I didn't read it until the flight back
east.

I was surprised to find that the brief, like the memo,
focused on the First Amendment. That seemed odd, at first;
why should we cover that ground again when we knew nothing about so many other areas of constitutional law? I eventually realized, however, that Kahn had his reasons for asking
us to continue our investigation of First Amendment issues.
His primary job, after all, was to teach legal skills, not
substantive law; whatever law the students picked up along

the way was gravy. More important, however, using the
same area for both brief and memo assignments demonstrated starkly the difference between the two principal
forms of legal writing. The lawyer must look at the facts and
law quite differently when his role changes from that of
counsel to that of advocate before a judge.

The brief assignment was based on an actual case, *Board
of Airport Commissioners of Los Angeles v. Jews for Jesus, Inc.* The
U.S. Supreme Court had recently agreed to hear Los Angeles's appeal of a ruling that its airport could not prevent the
religious group Jews for Jesus from conducting activities
generally protected by the First Amendment, such as talking
to people and distributing information, within the airport's
central terminal area. The issue, stated in purely legal terms,
was twofold: first, whether the central terminal area (or
"CTA") was a "public forum" and thus open to all First
Amendment activities, and second, if not, whether the airport's regulation of such activities was reasonable. The parties had agreed to a "stipulation of facts" in order to expedite
the lawsuit, and it was available on reserve in the library.

This description of the issues took up only half a page but
I had to read it a few times before making sense of it. The
case was basically a turf battle, and my gut reaction was that
the airport deserved to win, but wouldn't. You had to have
a pretty good reason to infringe somebody's First Amendment rights, and this case looked like infringement in
spades; it's difficult to defend any case involving speech infringement, but especially so when the plaintiff is a religious
group. The reference to the "public forum" doctrine, moreover, only seemed to make matters worse for the airport. I
had no idea what the doctrine was, and couldn't imagine how
airport CTAs could be "public forums," but the phrase in-

dicated that the case had been couched — that it "sounded," in legal parlance — in free-speech law.

Kahn divided the small group into eight two-person "law firms," four pairs representing Los Angeles and four pairs Jews for Jesus. One partner in each pair was to address the public forum issue, and the other, whether the airport's regulation of speech was "reasonable." Since there was an odd number of people in the small group, I volunteered to do the brief on my own. Kahn agreed to that proposal but added a nice twist: he made me counsel (at his wife's suggestion) to the fictional American Association of Airports, for which I was to submit a friend-of-the-court brief arguing that CTAs are not public forums.

I was glad Kahn asked me to address this issue rather than the one concerning reasonableness. Appellate attorneys are supposed to argue the law, not the facts (since the relevant facts have been established, at least theoretically, at the trial-court level), but the stipulated facts looked terrible for a "reasonable regulation" argument on behalf of the airport. Its board had passed a resolution saying that the CTA was "not open for First Amendment activities by any individual and/or entity," and even a nonlawyer could understand such a blanket ban was probably unconstitutional. If anyone in the small group could make a good, effective argument for that regulation, she'd deserve a diploma then and there.

The briefs were due in three weeks. Writing them was only half the assignment, however, for we were also required to present and defend them in "moot court." Kahn, Kurt, and a third person — perhaps another student, perhaps a real-life judge — would preside over two evenings of oral argument at the end of the term. The judges would not, however, render verdicts; they would assess, instead, the quality of the arguments presented and the students' ability to respond to tough questioning. It was a frightening prospect, but we looked forward to moot court nonetheless, for it promised to be a break from recent lethargy and a chance to act like bona fide lawyers. We were anxious to try out our new legal wings, even if the result was public humiliation.

The case was considerably less complex than the one in the memo-writing assignment. A few hours in the library told me that every appellate court to address the airport-as-public-forum question had decided that CTAs were indeed public forums. My side, in other words, was a major, big-time loser; it was hard to understand why the Supreme Court had bothered to take the case . . . unless, of course, it intended to abandon the public forum doctrine or make airports an exception to it, neither of which seemed likely. Strangely, though, the lopsided nature of the case proved more invigorating than depressing. If I couldn't prevail under the existing rules, maybe I could politick for new, better rules. . . .

That was not the tack the other students took, however. The brief assignment became a major topic of conversation among students in the small group, and the net result was homogenization — purgation — of the most interesting arguments for both sides. At the time these group discussions seemed useful, allowing students to try out new approaches, winnow bad arguments, and isolate the weak spots of good ones, but they only encouraged students to repeat the most conservative points of view. Again and again I heard students argue over technical legal points and side issues while the heart of the matter — the limits a government should be allowed to place on the right to speak — was ignored. Some of the arguments seemed deliberately diversionary, designed to induce listeners to challenge the fringe elements of an argument and thus leave its center unchallenged. Before long I began to think the brief assignment did more to mold student minds than any other aspect of law school.

I was probably less susceptible than most students to a conventional reading of *Jews for Jesus* because I already knew that however wonderful in theory, in practice the First Amendment is often invoked as a cover for questionable doings. I was naturally sympathetic to the idea of unencumbered free speech, but at the same time couldn't think of a less appropriate place for it than airports. The vast majority of air travelers are interested only in confirming plans and quelling fears; alternately rushed, apprehensive, testy, fatigued, and bored, they want above all to be left alone. Groups like Jews for Jesus canvassed at airports not so much to communicate, I thought, as to exploit; airports are simply the easiest place to catch a high percentage of affluent people with their guard down. At some point the right of free speech inevitably results in the imposition of invasive speech, and Jews for Jesus had crossed that line.

Although my intuitive view of the case was straightforward, its translation into legal terms proved difficult. I found a series of cases on the "right to be let alone," but it was of limited use; its greatest supporter, Justice William O. Douglas, was dead, and its leading case, *Lehman v. City of Shaker Heights,* concerned advertisements in city buses. The case described bus passengers as a "captive audience," just the sort of characterization the airport association needed, but I doubted I could convince a judge that buses and airport terminals were similar — especially since another public forum case involving a bus terminal had gone against the airports' position. How could I argue with a straight face that bus terminals and airport terminals are substantially dissimilar? I could make distinctions, to be sure, but they would likely be distinctions without differences.

Clearly, I wouldn't get the expansive reading of the right to be let alone I needed. My next thought was to jettison the public forum doctrine altogether, but since the case had been framed in those terms, I felt constrained to work within them. I did so with reluctance; why should I have to shoehorn my ideas into a futile form when another, yet-to-be-articulated framework might work far better? I didn't seem to have much choice in the matter. The only way I could win the case was to challenge directly the Supreme Court's analysis of this area of the law, but that would mean challenging the law itself, and ultimately, the legal profession. And that was something no lawyer could afford to do.

I grew almost sentimental recalling the memo assignment. It had been muddled, to be sure, but there at least I could choose the doctrines with which to work. Brief writing seemed liberating, at first, but became confining as soon as one tried to put an idea into action, understood that arguments are guided not by logic but by the requirements of precedent. No wonder Kurt called brief writing "slam-dancing in a corset."

I began, grudgingly, to survey the various inflections of the public forum doctrine.

It had emerged, I discovered, as one of many attempts to get around the absolute wording of the First Amendment. The amendment says Congress shall make "no law" abridging freedom of speech, but it has long been interpreted to mean that government authorities can't restrict speech without extremely good reason. Some laws abridging freedom of speech make perfect sense, like a prohibition against the false shouting of "Fire!" in a theater (to use Oliver Wendell Holmes, Jr.'s classic example), but such laws are exceptionally difficult to formulate; it's obviously difficult to defend a law that contravenes the Constitution's plain language. How, then, do lawyers manage to convince people that our most basic legal document doesn't always mean what it says?

One way is by approaching such problems through the back door. Lawyers and judges discovered they could control speech through the First Amendment by regulating *where* something was said rather than *what* was said. This geographically based regulation frequently amounted to censorship because it prevented speakers from reaching the audiences they sought, but its apparent reasonableness and neutrality allowed courts to gloss over the fact that they restricted First Amendment rights at all. Instead of saying "This idea can't be spoken" and finding himself impeached, a judge could say, "Sure, this idea can be spoken — just not here."

Justice Owen Roberts set the groundwork for this form of regulation in 1939. In *Hague v. CIO* he held unconstitutional a Jersey City ordinance requiring any group, in this case a union, to apply for a permit before gathering in local "streets and parks." Intent on making a strong stand in favor of First Amendment rights at a socially intolerant moment, Roberts failed to foresee that the phrase "streets and parks," which he lifted directly from the ordinance he struck down, would be taken by many as a complete inventory of the places in which free speech could not be regulated. But so it was.

In the 1960s, however, civil rights attorneys began to argue that Roberts's phrase was too restrictive. Wasn't the phrase "streets and parks" arbitrary? If people could express themselves freely in those places, why not in libraries, on statehouse grounds — indeed, any public place? Since civil rights protestors seemed able to get their message across only by communicating in untraditional places, and on the whole seemed to represent a cause that went to the heart of American democracy, courts often agreed with them. "Street and parks" soon seemed to misrepresent Roberts's analysis, becoming in some ways a court's worst nightmare — a rule evolving from a key phrase borrowed from a law being condemned.

Roberts's rule broke down irretrievably in 1976, when the Supreme Court considered a case in which Dr. Benjamin Spock was prevented from giving out flyers on the *streets* of an army base, Fort Dix — just fifty miles from where *Hague* took place. The court could have tried to regain control of the old doctrine by creating a narrow "military installation" or broad "national security" exception to "streets and parks," but it must have been evident that Roberts's theory was too vague and misleading to survive. So in *Greer v. Spock,* Justice Potter Stewart, a Yale Law graduate, created a new rule. He said that the correct analysis — which had been floating around in law review articles and a handful of Supreme Court decisions for a decade — examined whether Fort Dix should be classified as a public forum. He concluded, unsurprisingly, that it was not.

Although *Greer* itself restricted First Amendment rights, its institutionalization of the public forum doctrine created a golden opportunity for expanding the boundaries of free speech. A lawyer could catalogue the similarities between a street (or park) and the place in which his client had been arrested for conducting a First Amendment activity, and then argue that it was *this particular* bundle of characteristics that constituted a public forum. And since no one could clearly define a "public forum," what opposing lawyer or judge could prove him wrong? Most plaintiffs eventually lost nonetheless, but for years to come the Supreme Court would have to deal with a line of troublesome cases of its own making.

It seemed a ridiculously self-defeating sequence of events. Roberts's phrase, intended to celebrate the protections of the First Amendment, when taken literally secured only a narrow understanding of free speech; Stewart, seeing a misuse of the phrase and an ossification of the theory that lay behind it, utilized a new phrase that was even more vague and ended up protecting many activities, like fund-raising, that seemed to have nothing to do with the First Amendment. It was easy to see how the language of the law took on a life of its own.

When we discussed *Marbury v. Madison* in September I had thought John Marshall's opinion devious and intellectually dishonest. But I realized now that he was responding to a legal system so controlled by categories, linear thinking, and the need for certainty that the inflexible mass could be moved only by distortion and indirection. Law had almost been forced to assimilate subversion; it was the one way law could adapt to changing circumstances without losing the appearance of rationality and inevitability from which its authority derived. What irony — to learn in law school that nothing in law is certain, but that to admit to uncertainty is to court social collapse! Anarchy and elegance: law was defined by these polarities, immersed in one but always longing for the other.

Jews for Jesus seemed to confirm these abstracted thoughts. It marked the fourth time in six years that the Supreme Court had dealt with the public forum doctrine, which was aging so poorly that it had begun to encompass arguments over "forums" lacking even geographical locations. The doctrine, not real-life issues, had become the focus of discussion; even as it complained of overwork, the Supreme Court heard three cases in which the central question was whether a letter box, a mail system, and a workplace charity drive, respectively, were public forums. The judges' interest in the cases seemed to emerge not from the requirements of justice but the desire to hone a judicial tool to perfection.

I couldn't help but think that law often operated for the benefit of its adherents rather than for the community it served. It was becoming increasingly easy for me to regard law as Frankenstein's monster or the computer HAL — a wonderful, inspiring, romantic creation . . . until it escaped its master's control. I too had bit of the legal apple, and was either on the edge of true knowledge or about to be expelled from the garden of innocence, perhaps both. Unless, of course, I had simply gone off the deep end, a possibility upon which I preferred not to dwell.

These ideas circled hazily in my mind as I thought about my brief, and in the end I reconsidered arguing along standard public forum lines. Guido often said in Torts, "You know more than you think you know!" — and what I knew most deeply was that the public forum doctrine was a crock, an excuse, a glaring example of expediency. I decided I would rather risk the wrath of Kahn than go against my own beliefs, as legally laughable and inarticulate as they might be.

I ultimately settled on a two-pronged compromise. I would write the brief using the public forum doctrine and bring up the important issues only indirectly, as the law's conventions dictated. At oral argument, however, I would take a different tack: I would drag in everything I thought the law left out, using the public forum argument only as a springboard from which to discuss the deeper issues. The moot-court approach was risky because it amounted to relitigating the case, but the legal record with which I had to

work had proved much too constricting; it couldn't accommodate the policy arguments I thought paramount. It was
likely I'd go down in flames, but I did hope to get across my
sense that the rules of the game were fixed.

The final draft of the brief was good, I thought. Having
already decided to disown its substance in moot court, I tried
to think of its composition as a practical exercise in form. An
airport CTA, I wrote, is not (1) a traditional public forum
like a street or park, (2) a designated public forum opened
up for general expressive activities, like a school, nor (3) a
limited public forum opened up for certain expressive activities, like a state fair. And so on; the arguments were technical, boring, and seemingly endless. In the end, I adopted
the approach Justice John Paul Stevens had taken while dis-
senting in the most recent public forum case to go to the
Supreme Court. The doctrine might be clumsy and distracting, he said in more judicious language, but if his fellow
justices insisted on using it, he felt obliged to go along.

I was fairly happy with my intended approach to moot
court, too, until I realized who was on the other side of the
argument. One of the students addressing the public forum
issue on behalf of Jews for Jesus was Grant, the student
intellectually most like Kahn — and thus the most likely to
spot and annihilate a weak position. To make things worse,
he was rumored to be as proficient at making arguments as
he was at destroying others'. Grant's memo was said to be the
only one Kahn had liked; many of the students in the small
group had borrowed it to find out what they had done wrong.

My fear proved well founded. Every student was required
to give a copy of his or her brief to opposing counsel a few
days before moot court, and my perusal of Grant's told me
he had seen and shielded his client's Achilles' heel. Many of
the courts addressing the airport-as-public-forum question

had steadfastly maintained that central terminal areas "resembled" city streets, but Grant had recognized the absurdity of the argument. He tried to give the assertion some historical basis, consequently, by saying that airports drew crowds when they were first developed, had never lost their initial appeal as gathering places, and so continued to be traditional public forums like streets and parks. It was an ingenious approach (though rather outside the case record); I could see Grant telling the court that his parents had taken him to the airport on countless Sundays to watch the planes take off. The argument wasn't convincing . . . but it didn't need to be, for it was just one more rationale allowing a judge to go along with existing precedents.

Grant gave me a different kind of scare after reading my brief. At the end of Procedure one day I suddenly found a finger shaking in my face and Grant saying heatedly, "I have just one thing to say to you: Los Angeles isn't Athens and it isn't Rome!" After recovering from my shock — I was so startled by Grant's appearance I almost fell into the row of seats behind me — I figured out what he was referring to: the section of my brief in which I argued that airports need flexibility in regulating First Amendment activities because they are common targets of terrorism, and thus weren't so different from the military bases found *not* to be public forums in *Greer*. Grant seemed to be saying that the argument was easy to dispatch, but I reasoned that if it moved him to such outrage, it must be fairly effective.

Kahn gave us some pointers about moot court a few days before it took place. "The trick to answering questions," he said, "is to incorporate them into your argument. Don't let the judges get you off track — anticipate their questions and answer them in your own way. Hit on two or three points at most, and don't simply repeat your brief." Kahn reminded us of a legal truism about arguing before the Supreme Court: while you can't win your case at oral argument there, you can certainly lose it.

I had already attended three or four moot courts on campus, a couple of them staged as part of a national competition. One had proved especially helpful. After commending one student for responding directly and succinctly to questions from the bench, the judge — a professor in Yale Law's clinical program — praised the other for a very different approach. "Hammering away at one issue again and again is a good way to make your point," he said. "If you keep coming back to the same idea no matter what the judge says, you may be able to get him thinking, 'Gee, this guy really seems to believe what he's saying. Maybe there's something to it. . . .' "

Tension grew as the moot evenings approached. A number of foursomes put on mock arguments, hoping to kill opening-night jitters, but I didn't participate, with the idea of keeping my arguments fresh, intense, and under wraps. I watched others practice, however, and it was interesting to see how individual styles affected almost identical arguments.

Sam was nervous, and unconvincing because he often strayed from his role of advocate to make jokes. Phil, Michelle's partner and the third Californian in the small group, had the opposite problem: he argued with all his heart, and his all-American-cheerleader sincerity made him unbelievable. Daryl's presentation also elevated form over substance, for although he seemed very sure of his argument's correctness, it sounded canned, memorized. Michelle, her slight figure looking even slighter as she stood behind the lectern, spent much of her time laughing self-consciously and obviously wishing she were somewhere else. If she was this jittery before friends, I hated to think what a wreck she'd be doing the same thing for what Hazard called "those cats in black sheets."

The moots began on a mid-December Wednesday in Room 119. I had forgotten how the bench and jury box dominated the space. The room was overheated, as usual, and I began to sweat heavily even though I wasn't scheduled for oral argument until the following evening.

Kurt, who was to be a judge along with Kahn and another third-year named Jack, asked me to play bailiff. I agreed, and the three of us waited for Kahn outside the classroom door. Kurt hadn't found enough judicial robes — other small groups were mooting that night, apparently — and when Kahn arrived Kurt suggested we go ahead without them. Kahn said no, and a third robe was eventually found in the Barristers' room across the hall.

"All right, let's get started," said Kahn to no one in particular.

I marched into the room and gave, as Kurt had instructed, the bailiff's cry. "Oyez, oyez, oyez, the Kahn Moot Court is now in session, Chief Justice Kahn presiding."

Students scrambled to their feet and watched us parade onto the bench. I sat in the witness box, where I found time cards with which to show speakers how much time they had left. Each student was allotted fifteen minutes.

The first group to argue was Michelle's. She and Phil went first because they represented the losing party at the lower court level. I was all ears; Phil was arguing the same issue as I, though from the perspective of the Los Angeles airport rather than airports in general.

Phil began by outlining the facts of the case, which the first speaker in every foursome was obliged to do. Kahn launched into him almost immediately for giving a selective account of the facts. Hadn't the airport invited any number of organizations to put up informational displays? Hadn't it allowed newscasts about the '84 Olympic Games to originate at the airport? Hadn't a Christian Science Reading Room been in operation for years? Even if the CTA had once been a private forum, in the light of these facts how could it claim that status now?

The onslaught knocked Phil off balance, and it took him a few seconds to regain his composure. He recovered fairly well, however, disposing of most of Kahn's challenges in a sentence or two. The closest he came to losing his poise was while citing the case *Clark v. Community for Creative Non-Violence*. He got as far as saying, "In *Clark versus Community for Non-Creative* . . ." before stopping himself. I caught Denise's eye, and we barely avoided breaking up.

The arguments given for the remainder of the evening were familiar and, thankfully, resembled those in my brief. It was the judges' questions, consequently, that proved most provocative, for they occasionally cut to the heart of the matter. But just as often they impeded arguments, for the students frequently got tangled up in the defense of irrelevancies.

Steve, who kicked off oral arguments for the second foursome, was barely able to get to his argument because Kahn pushed him so hard on the facts. At first I assumed Kahn constantly interrupted the first student in each group just to establish his authority over the court, but he later explained he had done so because neither Phil nor Steve had made a tight connection between the facts of the case and the legal issues being argued. To Steve he eventually said, too late to help, "Don't let the judge push you around."

Kahn eased up as the evening wore on. Sam, who lost his

color as soon as he stood up to speak, never quite got control of his argument. Steve's air of exasperation with Kahn had given him an odd credibility, as if he couldn't believe the judges failed to buy his position; by contrast, and equally strangely, Sam's willingness to accept the judges' skepticism seemed almost to justify their badgering.

The revelation of the evening was Michelle. She spoke clearly and confidently, as if she had argued before a court many times. She had one distracting tic: whenever a judge asked a difficult question she physically retreated from the counsel's lectern. Instead of responding instantly with strong words, she shrugged her shoulders, smiled broadly, and looked charming while awaiting, apparently, further elaboration from the bench. At first I thought Michelle's body language had betrayed her, but then it occurred to me that judges might find it refreshing to encounter a lawyer who didn't pretend to know everything.

Kahn, in his general comments at the conclusion of the evening, told the advocates they had done "surprisingly well." It was faint praise, but more than we were accustomed to.

I mooted — a verb form probably unique to law school — the following evening.

I didn't commit many thoughts to paper until a few hours before court. I hoped that by letting my ideas percolate on their own until the last possible moment, unchanneled by the requirements of law, the pressure to speak the truth as I saw it would naturally bring forth the right words. To some extent, the approach worked; when I finally jotted down some key points with which to discredit the public forum doctrine, I saw all over again how it obscured the most important issues. The central dilemma the court faced was if and when the security of a vulnerable public facility can impinge upon First Amendment guarantees, yet that question was buried so deeply in abstract doctrinal arguments that it seemed virtually ignored. This was the question I wanted to drag back into the spotlight, whether or not it was answered in my client's favor.

I gave myself a pep talk as I walked to the law school. The air was invigoratingly cool and I breathed deeply. Seize the initiative; frame the issues cleanly. Don't let Kahn change the subject; stay cool when he disparages, disagrees, denies, turns an argument on its head. Listen politely, don't wince, and above all hang in there. Confidence is all; my arguments would be dismissed as foolish only if I implied — admitted? — they were foolish.

When I got to the law school, however, panic set in. Most of the other male students were wearing ties, and they seemed more professional, more lawyerly, than I. *Shit — I bet they're much better prepared, too.* I began to sweat profusely and wished I had just taken a shower.

I tried to defuse my anxiety by bantering with Liz and Orin, counsel for the Los Angeles airport — and thus allies — at my trial. Grant and Kate, opposing co-counsels, were seated at the petitioner's table and seemed relatively placid; both were generally high-strung, but tonight they seemed calm and ready. We glanced as a unit at the door whenever it opened, and the room's closeness increased every time it was someone other than Luke, the evening's bailiff. If he didn't show up soon, I was going to explode.

Luke eventually appeared and led in the judges. The panel was different this night; Jack had been replaced by a gray-haired, kindly-looking man. Someone said his name was Frankfurt, and I assumed he was a real-life judge.

I didn't pay much attention to Orin's argument, which was scheduled right before mine. He spoke softly, without conviction, and barely touched the issues on which I focused. I was glad for the virgin territory.

I didn't wait for Kahn's prompting to rise from the petitioner's table. I took a single long stride to the lectern and placed my one sheet of notes, written on nonglare yellow paper, upon it. I set my shoulders straight, paused, tried to look each judge in the eye, glanced at my notes once more, and began to speak.

"May it please the court, my name is Chris Goodrich and I represent the American Association of Airports, which has entered this case as amicus curiae on behalf of the Board of Airport Commissioners of the City of Los Angeles. Our position is that this case is not really about the First Amendment; the central issue is whether a government agency can retain control of its facilities. Should this court hold that an airport terminal is a public forum . . ."

It was a ridiculous gambit, to claim that the case didn't really concern the First Amendment, but it got the court's attention. As Kurt told me later, "We were stunned to hear something that was so obviously untrue."

"Counsel," said Kahn, half in surprise and half in frustration, "how can you say this isn't a First Amendment case? That's exactly what it is, isn't it?"

I let go of the lectern, which I had been clutching hard with both hands, in relief. Kahn had risen to the bait! I wanted him to underestimate me, to regard me, if need be, as a law-impaired idiot. Only by knocking *him* off balance first, preemptively, did I feel I had a chance to realign the legal playing field. I wanted Kahn to know, too, if he cared to read between the lines, that I understood law was really about power — the ability to dictate the outcome of a legal dispute by arguing from the right starting point, within the right form.

"No, Your Honor. I'm not denying that the First Amendment plays a significant role in this case. But what's been overlooked is the concrete and compelling need of the government, in this case the airport commission, to run essential facilities. If this court allows terminal access to every group claiming its activities are protected by the First Amendment, airport security will be severely compromised. Sending a signal of that nature will —"

Kahn interrupted. "Counsel, on what basis do you make that assertion? Is it anything more than speculation?"

"In Europe and the Middle East, Your Honor, airports have long been targets of terrorism. To a degree the danger is speculative, but —"

"Are these incidents in the record of this case?" Kahn asked.

The answer, of course, was no. Stupidly, I hadn't thought my argument would be brought to a halt so quickly. A way of getting around Kahn's objection, however, suddenly came to mind.

"I would like to ask the court to take judicial notice of the fact that terrorist incidents have occurred at airports in Europe and in other parts of the world."

Kahn smiled slightly, but I don't think he nodded.

Now what? I knew I'd have to wing my argument eventually, but not at this early juncture. Fortunately, Kahn asked more questions; he poked a few more holes in my position, to be sure, but the fact that he was willing to engage with it at all conferred a certain validity.

Responding to his questions was distracting, yet I found the interaction actually bolstered my confidence. I knew what I was doing, from a strategic point of view . . . even if no one else did, and even if I didn't do it particularly well. This must be the thrill of litigation. Sensing your control of the situation, drawing judges and opposing counsel down certain thoughtways, setting the tempo and tone of the debate. . . .

I returned to the main body of the terrorism argument. I spoke uninterrupted for a couple of minutes before Kahn suggested I move on, which I did, to the "right to be let alone" argument. I talked about "captive audiences" and "enclosed spaces" and the isolation of airports, trying to convince the court that this line of analysis made more sense.

"Finding that an airport's central terminal area is a public forum," I said, "will open the floodgates to every conceivable group. These facilities are already strained by increased traffic, by —"

"Isn't that just more speculation, counsel?"

The question came from Kurt, and I realized I was making no headway with the court. The judges wanted to hear nuts-and-bolts law, arguments taken directly from public forum cases; policy, value issues did not interest them. I tried to oblige, knowing I had no choice.

"Our position, Your Honors, is that airport CTAs are *sui generis*. They are by no stretch of the imagination 'public forums.' While it is true that a few circuit courts have rejected that position, we believe that to call these places 'spacious common areas,' to say they resemble 'public thoroughfares' — as the Seventh Circuit did in *Chicago Area Military Project v. City of Chicago* — defies logic. Airport terminals have never been gathering areas and were never intended to be gathering areas, as counsel for the respondent has argued."

I felt Grant's eyes upon me.

"People go to airports for transport and nothing else. Whatever First Amendment activities happen to occur there are purely tangential to the airport's function or are simply inflicted upon an unwilling population. An airport terminal cannot be properly analogized to a park or street."

I then gave the punchline, worked out days earlier and based on two descriptive phrases culled from the public forum literature.

"People go to airports to 'meet and greet,' not to 'gather and exchange information.' "

Kurt looked impassive. Frankfurt was frowning. Kahn wrote something down, then leaned back in his high-backed chair with a poker face.

My best line had absolutely no effect. Were these judges listening to anything I said? Was my presentation so far out it didn't seem worthy of response?

I looked over at Luke in the witness box, who had just turned over the card saying "Five minutes left." It suddenly occurred to me that fifteen minutes was a long stretch through which to maintain an air of forthrightness and conviction. Trouble was, having been discouraged from addressing policy issues any further, I had nothing left to be forthright and convinced about.

I turned back to the judges with a look, I'm sure, of wild-eyed fear. The one thing I wasn't prepared for was silence. Dammit, I thought, ask me a question, challenge me, give me an indication about where you want me to go — just don't leave me twisting!

I had totally screwed up. The judges and I were operating on completely different wavelengths; my approach had failed to resonate in the slightest way with any of them. I probably should have shut up, sat down, and cut my losses, but the thought never crossed my mind.

I glanced at my notes and saw the word *sidewalks*. I started talking, halfheartedly, about *United States v. Grace,* a recent decision in which the Supreme Court decided that the sidewalk in front of its very courthouse was a public forum.

"Even if all First Amendment activities were banned from CTAs," I said, "which of course we don't argue and don't desire, anyone is free to conduct such activities on airport sidewalks. To that we have no objection."

Frankfurt continued to frown. "Tell me, why is it okay to hand out leaflets outside the terminal and not inside?" he asked. "What difference does the roof make?"

I almost laughed, for it was simultaneously the most threatening and interesting question I had been asked. A roof made an enclosed space, and thus (in theory) a captive audience, but I could see Frankfurt setting the stage for asking whether I believed roofed places could never be public forums. I wanted to berate him for abstracting my argument instead of helping me clarify it, but I couldn't think fast enough to dispose of his red herring. I merely reiterated the principle of *Grace,* hoping that the sidewalk would continue to be a strong candidate for the boundary inside which the assertion of public forum status would be the exception rather than the rule.

I was done. I thanked the judges and sat down, flushed with adrenaline and relief but so tired that few details from the following presentations stayed with me. One of the few that did was Frankfurt's asking Audrey the same question he had asked me — why the roof? She replied, without missing a beat, "To hold up the walls."

Kahn critiqued our arguments one by one. He was surprisingly charitable, as if to say it was more important to survive moot court than succeed in it. Daryl was too stiff; Orin needed to speak up; Liz had "a deference problem" — she needed to get the superior tone out of her voice. Most of us suffered from one of two problems: we either tried to cover too much material or were sidetracked by questions and lost the thread of the argument.

This last comment certainly applied to me. Kahn didn't single me out, however, or say my approach to the case mystified him, or that it was hopeless; his major observation, an accurate one, was that instead of representing airports in general I had become too involved in defending the conduct of the Los Angeles airport.

At Denise's suggestion, Luke had held up a card from the bailiff's box saying "It's Miller Time!" when the last student concluded his presentation. Half the small group did indeed end up going to a local bar, and a feeling in the air suggested that the hardest part of law school was over. We had seen the game through; each of us had argued, sometimes strongly, about an issue we cared little about. Only in retrospect did that seem an extraordinary waste of time and talent.

The Supreme Court heard *Jews for Jesus,* the actual case, three months later. Some students in the small group went to Washington, D.C., to hear the arguments — I couldn't, being sick — and their experience was instructive. Our moot court stacked up pretty well against the real thing, Denise said; the lawyers didn't make any arguments we hadn't considered ourselves, and seemed, if anything, too agreeable.

"We got annoyed when they conceded points we didn't think they should have," Denise said. "We kept saying, 'No, no, that's a good one, keep after it!' " She brought me a souvenir from the trip — a Jews for Jesus pamphlet handed to her on the courthouse steps, courtesy of *United States v. Grace.*

Jews for Jesus was decided in June and played out much as

we had expected. Justice Sandra Day O'Connor wrote for a unanimous court that the airport's regulation of free speech was unconstitutionally "overbroad" because it banned all First Amendment activities from the airport's central terminal area. She reiterated that an airport was free to restrict such activities in a more limited way, but to this day it remains unclear what restrictions could pass constitutional muster.

The most interesting thing about the decision, to me at least, was that O'Connor wrote it without invoking the public forum doctrine. The court didn't have to decide whether a CTA was a public forum, she said, because the airport's regulation couldn't be justified even if a CTA were not a public forum. I smiled when I read that, thinking the court just might be coming around to my point of view — and prepared to let the public forum doctrine sink slowly into oblivion. It was a sign that the legal system did work . . . though so glacially slowly that its positive effects frequently went unseen. Justice delayed was rarely justice denied, but it was often justice unappreciated.

Act III: Coming To

Your commonsense has gone. It is time now to seek to regain it, to reshape it. It is time, too, to bring your ethics out from under ether. This time, however, in a better guise, a commonsense, a body of ethics no longer at war with law or preventing you from seeing the legal question, but informing law, helping you solve and criticize; no longer impeding your techniques, but furthering them.

KARL LLEWELYN
The Bramble Bush
on the second year of law school

Ten

Love in the Ruins

For the essence of bullshit is not that it is *false* but that it is *phony*. In order to appreciate this distinction, one must recognize that a fake or a phony need not be in any respect (apart from authenticity itself) inferior to the real thing. What is not genuine need not also be defective in some other way. It may be, after all, an exact copy. What is wrong with a counterfeit is not what it is like, but how it was made.

HARRY FRANKFURT
"On Bullshit"
Raritan
1986

Classes ended the day after moot court. I was exhilarated; only January's exams stood between me and the successful completion of the first semester of law school. I had stretched myself to the limit, both mentally and psychologically, and felt I had conquered something — my fear of failure, perhaps, or of professional schooling, maybe even of law itself. Whatever its cause, I enjoyed the sense of having picked my way through a mine field without serious injury.

I was ready to start a new chapter in my life, and did.

I had met Lisa — tall, slim, dark-haired — at a wedding of mutual friends the previous summer, when I was best man and she (as the bride put it) best woman. We kept in touch in part because of these friends — they gave us an excuse to drive to New Hampshire together — but also because of a shared interest in books. Lisa was an editor in New York, and I thought some of my literary friends in the Bay Area might be writing the sort of novels she'd like to publish. We had gotten together a couple of times during the semester, and I had already speculated aloud about writing a book on law school.

Lisa invited me to a fellow editor's Christmas party the evening of my final day of class. Literary agents would be there, she assured me, and I thought I was ready to start talking about a possible book on the legal frame of mind. When we met at Grand Central, Lisa was wearing one of the roses I had sent her — something I had done totally on impulse, hoping to break through her New York veneer.

We took the subway to Chelsea. As soon as I took off my coat, I realized I had no idea how to describe the book I wanted to write. I was convinced I had stumbled upon the key to lawyers' power, as others surely had before me . . . but who'd believe my understanding was special, having been experienced on a very personal level, not arrived at through scientific study? In my head I could hear publishing types asking what form the book would take — memoir? exposé? new journalism? conventional narrative? — and having to confess I had only the haziest idea because the book, at bottom, would be *about* form . . . how in law, at least, what one said was largely dictated by what the limited forms of law allowed one to say, anything left out automatically being considered second-rate or useless. I seemed to have thought myself into a corner and doubted many people would follow me there voluntarily.

Lisa and I stayed at the party for an hour or so, talking to hardly anyone else, before deciding to get some dinner. We walked to a local Thai restaurant, and within minutes I launched into a two-hour tirade about law — how terrible it was, how mesmerizing, how seductive. I was showing off and venting spleen, to be sure, but I also felt a dam had burst inside me. Until that evening I didn't know I held such strong opinions about legal education; it was as if I realized, for the first time in fourteen weeks, that my opinions were just as valid as anyone else's. My ideas might never be fully consistent, and they might take hours — days, years — to capture with any clarity, but that didn't mean law school had the right to dismiss them as "fuzzy" and "incomplete" — indeed, they might be important precisely because they *were* fuzzy and incomplete, because they didn't pretend to anything more than provisional truth. I didn't care about achieving the persuasiveness of the lawyer so much as feeling I had brushed up against some deeply rooted reality. The tragedy of law, from my point of view, was that lawyers often achieved that same sense — but too often, being paid to do so, looked away.

Lisa listened gamely to my rantings. She gave me permission to speak my mind and reacted as if she, too, believed I was onto something. Her natural tolerance was reassuring; it encouraged me to think I actually could find a vantage point from which to write, for unlike most of the people I had talked with in recent months, she didn't listen in order to seize on errors nor to set the groundwork for a response. She seemed to sense that the passion with which I expressed myself was significant in and of itself — that the chaos in my mind swirled around some fruitful kernel of wisdom.

I luxuriated in the chance to throw out a jumble of thoughts without having them instantly hammered down. Could I really prove that law school, in its ability to form in students a new, controlling habit of mind, was the source of lawyers' influence? Prove that it wasn't just the access to money and the decision-making process that gave lawyers power, but the way legal training caused them to think about the world, altered the range of values they considered necessary for inclusion in the concept of justice? Was *prove* the appropriate word, or was it *demonstrate, illuminate,* simply *argue?* Wasn't every professional school — medicine, architecture, business, journalism, you name it — in many ways designed to teach students how to empower themselves, to master at least some portion of the world?

A year later Lisa told me she actually had no idea what I was talking about, but found herself interested, engaged, nonetheless. At the time, that reaction was just what I needed, since I had endured the opposite response — much rational understanding, little trust — for months. At law school the burden of proof, and often even of belief, was on the student.

We took the subway uptown. I had planned to stay with a friend who lived some thirty blocks north of Lisa's apartment, but it was too late to call. I didn't want to call, either; I needed more time with Lisa to correct the lopsided impression I had made. What I sought was personal connection, but I had ended up keeping Lisa at bay with ideas; I couldn't find the words, ironically, to say that my speechifying was all prelude, that I was obsessed with law because it seemed to be used so often to excuse people from dealing with real, difficult, painful, conflicted feelings. I wanted Lisa to help me leave the law, and ultimately, perhaps, find a way to humanize it.

I asked Lisa whether I could spend the night on her couch. She agreed, and we walked the four flights up to her apartment. Lisa's cat appeared at the door when it opened, and vanished as soon as she saw me.

*   *   *

I returned to New Haven the next day. On the train up, with no studying to do, the world seemed to spin more slowly. I felt as if I had passed through the waist of an hourglass — that after being inexorably pressed down by the weight of sand above, and frightened simultaneously by the drop below, I had made the return leap, like Alice through the looking glass, into an earthier world. I felt I had escaped law's grip, had regained the ability to choose for myself.

It was the week before Christmas, and although I could hardly wait to see Lisa again, I still had many other things to do. I bought presents; I caught up on my nonlegal reading; I finished writing the job-placement story for the alumni magazine. The article still needed fact-checking, however, so on Christmas, after watching my niece and nephew dismantle their mountain of presents, I went over to the law library. It wasn't open for the first and only time in my experience. The law school was eerily desolate, yet its very emptiness made it seem all the more like a church. I still loved the place, but as an adolescent loves its parents: warily, resentful of an influence that can never be escaped.

I called Lisa, who had also spent Christmas in Connecticut with family, and asked whether I could visit her in New York during my week off. We arranged to meet on a train the following day, but couldn't find each other on the crowded cars. We caught up at the gate, and Lisa was as nervous as I.

For most of the day we talked, Lisa more this time, and I sensed more and more that we fit well together. Me, obviously angry, reckless, sentimental, fiercely attached to something I couldn't quite identify; she, angry in more subtle ways, loyal, shy and superficially distant, fearful of making mistakes. We were two sides of the same coin; we adjusted so easily to each other, in words and beyond words, that the only question seemed to be whether I could adjust to leaving California. I moved in with Lisa, psychologically at least, for good that night.

The following week was an idyll — at least in the evenings, when Lisa came home from work. We did the normal things romantic couples do — went to restaurants, museums, watched the late movies on television, made love as often as possible — but the events carried a new meaning for me. I had regained something law school had taken from me: the ability to operate on trust. I felt, even in New York City, that I could release the reins of control.

My daylight hours passed rather differently. I still had four exams to take, so I spent most of my time in Lisa's apartment going over class notes.

"The first thing I do when I begin studying for exams," Sam had told me a couple weeks earlier, "is take off my belt and lock up the sharp instruments." I couldn't take pass/fail exams that seriously, but every law student had felt the pressure mounting. The professors (Guido aside) did little to relieve it; Daryl had talked with Hazard in his office about exams, and his account of the meeting was already legendary. A workaholic, Daryl had hoped to hear he could spend at least a couple of days of Christmas vacation with his wife and child, law-free, but Hazard would have none of it.

"Married?" Hazard had asked. Daryl nodded. "Staying with relatives?" Yes. "Wife gets along with them?" Yes. "Good," Hazard concluded: "She'll have somebody to talk to."

We knew what the exams would be like. There would be two or three hypothetical situations, each going on for perhaps two pages of single-spaced text, followed by questions like "Who is liable to whom, and why?" or "What arguments would you make if you represented A? B?" Another question might be a court decision to reconsider in light of different facts, or an open-ended essay on a controversial legal theory. Having read some old exams in the library — bound just like any other book and placed on reserve — I didn't think four hours, the standard time allotted at most law schools, would be enough. It took me forty minutes just to read the questions with the necessary care.

This foreknowledge didn't make exam preparation any easier. Studying remained a matter of trying to winnow out every significant element from an intimidatingly massive amount of material. Class discussions focused less on rules than on the situations in which they were used, but by exam time it seemed impossible to separate a rule from its application, theory from practice. How could we understand when and where to invoke a rule if we didn't also understand its relationship to other, competing rules? Whether the rule was an exception to a more general doctrine, was shot through with exceptions of its own, or was expanding, contracting? It was, I suppose, predictable; the more I studied and learned, the more legally ignorant and uneducable I felt.

I could see why many law schools encourage students to form study groups, in which each member concentrates on just one course. By exam time, a participating student should be able not only to distill his particular course into a fifteen- or twenty-page outline but also to grasp how legal doctrines evolve. Group members pool their outlines, of course, so they can be fairly sure of handling whatever questions the professors throw at them.

Study groups at Yale Law were rare, however, deterred by the fact that the administration — if not many members of the faculty — frowned on anything that might foster competition among the first-years. What emerged instead were informal quiz sessions in which students asked each other all kinds of "What if . . ." questions. I had eliminated that study technique, of course, by opting to stay with Lisa before exams, so I concentrated on creating court synopses on my own. I started with my notes, and when I came to something I didn't fully understand — every three or four minutes, tops — I went back to the case being discussed or some other supporting material. I usually figured out where my difficulty lay, but on several occasions gave up in frustration and crossed my fingers.

During the day, books and notebooks lay scattered all over Lisa's living room. Her cat, Cocoa, liked the mess — so many papers to crackle and knead, so easy to become the center of attention — and after a while I rather liked it myself. I didn't know whether my approach to the material was efficient, but it felt organic, sovereign, authentic. And most important, it worked — many of the things I thought I learned in New Haven I actually learned in New York.

That was the best part about preparing for exams — the realization that law school cramming, unlike any other I had weathered, was genuinely educational. It did more than sharpen my understanding of a few theories; it collapsed time, allowing me to see the ebb and flow of law, the rise and fall of good and bad ideas. Connections appeared; doctrines revealed their origins; progress was implied and occasionally made. Some of these revelations were so basic I concluded that law professors don't teach so much as force students to teach themselves. I guessed that was the major reason for having high-pressure exams — to compel catalysis, to foment intellectual synthesis of a higher order.

The more I studied, the more reluctant I became to condemn law wholesale. It certainly encouraged people to accept the status quo, usually as defined by lawyers, but I had to admit, all things considered, that law did a creditable job of guiding society into the future. Many of the cases we studied were as manipulative as *Marbury v. Madison,* but at bottom they seemed to work toward growth and revitalization nonetheless. Though the legal system worked slowly and obliquely, it did tend to be self-correcting; and with the Constitution to rely on, law couldn't stray too far from its founding principles.

And yet . . . and yet I still couldn't love law. If law primarily curbed a culture's extremes, as Tocqueville had hinted, perhaps its hidden influence could be tolerated. But it did more than that; it encouraged people to be morally lazy, to hand over their social responsibilities to the legal class, who then reshaped society, to a large extent, in their image and interests. And I resented that shaping; law's apparent certainty, its maze of specialized words, obscured a soaring spirit rather than liberated it. From the outside law looked to be a fabulous mansion, but from the inside, it seemed a jury-rigged contraption. Elements and beliefs that didn't reinforce the mansion's imposing presence, and particularly those that undermined it, were squirreled invisibly away or cast off altogether. "A house divided against itself cannot stand," said Lincoln; but neither can a house whose surface is maintained at the expense of its foundation.

Studying for exams only solidified my impression that law was cousin to the Great Oz. I was triply skeptical of law, as Dorothy was of the Wizard, once unmasked by Toto: for promising more than it can deliver, for doing so with full and conscious knowledge, and for using others to implement its institutional desires. Both the law and the wizard had exploited a natural trust by failing to acknowledge their limitations.

*   *   *

I took a train back to New Haven a couple of days before my first exam, Procedure. My small-group friends hadn't killed themselves with study, I was glad to see, but they had been industrious in other ways; some had spent the break interviewing with law firms and a few had even lined up summer jobs. Their devotion to work made me feel shiftless.

The exam period was intense and boring by turns. The fifteen hours of tests were grueling, but unfolded in a manageable rhythm: exam, two study days, exam, three study days, exam, and so on. The major surprise was that we got no curve balls; the closest was Kahn's optional exercise, "Take a position we discussed in class and disagree with it." The question was actually a joke — Denise had said it should be on the exam because it captured the quintessential Kahn Law experience. I took Kahn's sly compliance as a subtle indication that he wished to get along better with his students, but the gesture didn't improve his standing with some. Liz left the exam session first, and as she exited slammed her Con Law notes into a trash can.

That was our last exam. I left for New York a few hours later, reveling in the week of freedom with Lisa before the next semester began. Law trailed me, however, in unexpected ways.

At Lisa's apartment I found a copy of the most recent *Harper's* magazine, and while leafing through it I ran across an article entitled "Reflections on Bullshit." I glanced at the author's byline and instantly felt the grip of synchronicity. The essay was by Harry Frankfurt, chairman of Yale's philosophy department, where I knew Kahn had received a doctorate before going on to Yale Law. It was the same person — the "judge" who had asked difficult, why- and off-the-wall questions at moot court.

I read Frankfurt's article with trepidation. Had he written

about serving on a moot court panel — was he writing about the small group's particular performance? Thankfully, no; the piece was adapted from a work published months earlier. But did Frankfurt have law in mind? The word *bullshit* had often entered my head in law school; it usually went unspoken, however, for I could never isolate the point at which law's truth-seeking aspect ended and its bullshit began. Perhaps Frankfurt's article would help me pin down that sea change, or at least understand law independently of legal thinking. . . .

The article was a serious examination of the differences among truth-tellers, liars, and bullshitters. In a nutshell, Frankfurt said that while truth-tellers and liars use truth as a reference point, bullshitters do not. Unlike the liar, the bullshitter may or may not intend to misinform his listeners, because the truthfulness of the information he imparts is irrelevant to him; he hopes to deceive not about particular facts but about the existence of his larger agenda. The liar doesn't want his listeners to know that he believes to be false what he claims to be true; the bullshitter, by contrast, doesn't want his listeners to know that his statements are cannon fodder, strategic pawns of no value to him. The liar and the truth-teller, in short, play a game from opposite ends of the field, while the bullshitter only pretends to play the game; he mimics familiar moves in order to obtain something — information, commitment, whatever — from the players, which he hopes to use to further his own hidden agenda.

Frankfurt's description of the principles of bullshitting seemed almost paradigmatic of law-think — the ability to play a game without caring who wins or loses, or even whether the game is completed. He went on to describe the ultimate bullshitter as someone who not only doesn't care about the truth of his statements but no longer believes it is possible to establish truth. And wasn't that the overriding message of legal education — that everything is relative, nothing sure? That the capacity to *show* conviction is more valuable than the capacity to *have* conviction? That justice, quite literally, is a matter of opinion?

"Reflections on Bullshit" gave me an entirely new perspective on law school. I read it a number of times, just like a case, and gradually understood why I found it so persuasive. Frankfurt wasn't bullshitting; he was trying to convince me he was right by doing exactly that — by convincing me he was right. He didn't use analogies or rhetoric; he didn't establish his readers' beliefs or disbeliefs in one area and then transfer those responses elsewhere. I found his logic compelling, not manipulative, because he was more interested in exploring issues than shaping them. His agenda was just what he proclaimed it to be — the giving of a "rough account" of bullshit.

It made more sense to me, now, why Kahn — a former student of Frankfurt? — seemed ambivalent toward law. He knew that the law's version of logic was no better than any other — and perhaps worse, because it pretended to be better. Surely he knew that many lawyers clung to law out of fear, not belief; that they grew to love law because it was the one thing they were allowed, indeed encouraged, to love without question. They found new faith — perhaps ironically, perhaps inevitably — in the very system that destroyed their native faith.

"Reflections on Bullshit" would have had a tremendous impact on me if Frankfurt had discussed only the conscious bullshitter. But he didn't; he concluded the piece by describing the unconscious bullshitter, a child of our relativistic age. The unconscious bullshitter, having come to understand there is no such thing as objective truth, attempts to redeem himself by putting his faith in subjective truth. He replaces the ideal of "correctness" with the ideal of "sincerity," realizing that if he can't be true to the facts he can at least be true to his personal understanding of the facts.

I winced as I read this analysis, for Frankfurt had captured nicely the approach I intended to take when writing about law school. But worse was to come; Frankfurt closed the piece by proclaiming that "sincerity itself is bullshit." Why? Because subjective truth is, if anything, even more difficult to establish than objective truth. Human nature is unstable and insubstantial, continually changing in response to happenstance, especially difficult to comprehend in oneself — so why should the *absence* of perspective make for a more accurate rendition of life? The photorealist painter appears to render life exactly, but he has merely hidden his choice of perception, sometimes even from himself, by working within a form that's apparently, superficially neutral. Inaccuracies aren't eliminated from the work, just buried within it.

I was caught in a familiar philosophical dilemma. How could I criticize the unacknowledged game-playing — the bullshit — in another form of belief unless I acknowledged the bullshit inherent in my own? The requirements of the writer's form would obviously affect what I wrote — a book needs characters, plot, conflicts, ideas, and so on — but what concerned me more was my journalistic perspective. How could I examine law's values without examining journalism's as well? I couldn't . . . not after having recognized that one of the values I most disliked in law was shared by journalism — the idea that if you can't establish truth, the next best thing is to provide an effective simulation.

It had to be a personal account of law school — that was the only way I could write with the certainty I felt while simultaneously conceding that my certainty was subjective. Admitting to fallibility, inconsistency, ambivalence; it seemed all wrong, but unavoidable, too. False certainty thrives in law and journalism because people prefer to be incorrectly sure than correctly unsure; yet perhaps the most basic point of my book would be that thoroughgoing uncertainty — the willingness always to listen in hopes of learning more — wasn't such a bad thing. This was a point of view — a point of view that made room for other points of view — I could live with.

Eleven

Truth Channels

Who ran the country then? I learned that there was an elite group, a
class that shared certain assumptions and values, and made basic
decisions without offering them to anyone as a choice. It was
sometimes called The Club. Its members held controlling positions
in government, in [law] firms like mine, in the courts, and in the
law schools. They were mostly male lawyers from Ivy League
schools — all top-notch achievers. Although they were fiercely
competitive, and gave the appearance of representing many different
sides of the issues of the day, it gradually dawned on me that the
values they shared, rather than those they debated, represented the
true decisions which governed the country.

CHARLES REICH
The Sorcerer of Bolinas Reef
1976

More than seventy courses were offered in the spring
semester — plenty, one would think, to satisfy even the
pickiest law student. They were not particularly diverse,
however, and often so narrowly focused I couldn't imagine
their holding anyone's interest for long. Some students were
no doubt anxious to spend three months studying administra-
tive law, corporate tax, banking regulation, estate planning, federal jurisdiction, international taxation, property,
and the like, but those courses sounded dull to me. The only

lecture classes I wanted to take were criminal law and intellectual property law — and of course Guido's "Tragic Choices," which I planned to audit.

There were some interesting-sounding classes, too, but almost all were limited-enrollment seminars bearing titles like "Adjudication, Interpretation, and Judicial Review," "Anarchy, Liberty, and Community," "Law, Culture, and Social Control," "Tolerance and Intolerance." They were very difficult to get into, however; students were admitted largely according to professorial whim. I found two seminars particularly appealing — "Images of the Law" and "Problems in First Amendment Theory." The latter was taught by Benno Schmidt and Floyd Abrams — a well-known First Amendment scholar who happened also to be the president of Yale University, and perhaps the foremost First Amendment practitioner in the country, respectively — so its appeal was obvious; this was the M.S.L.s' one chance to sit at the masters' feet and learn about the area of the law that most affects them. The M.S.L.s soon got word that if we listed the seminar first in our ranking of seminar choices, we were virtually guaranteed admission.

For all that, however, the course I was most attracted to was "Images of the Law." It consisted of readings in the portrayal of law and lawyers throughout history — from Aeschylus to Dickens to Camus to Martin Luther King, Jr. — and I thought it might help me think about law in a broader way. Furthermore, the professor, Paul Gewirtz, seemed to share my sense that law was reductive; in the catalogue he described the course as being inspired by Lionel Trilling's belief that liberalism, bent on organizing life in a rational, equitable way, tends to oversimplify it. Gewirtz quoted Trilling's comment that literature provides "the fullest and most precise account of variousness, possibility, complexity, and difficulty," and apparently hoped to use literature to remind students that fiction can capture ideas about justice and legitimacy that law itself cannot.

I was torn between making Images and the First Amendment course my first-choice seminar. I eventually decided to go with the First Amendment, reasoning that if I felt obliged to rank professional training over personal fulfillment, most law students would do the same. That strategy seemed justified a few weeks later, when the seminar acceptances were posted on the spring-course bulletin board. Although I had not been admitted to Images outright, I was well up on the waiting list. I felt even more encouraged when I heard a couple of students who had been accepted in the course call Images "classic 'fuzzy studies' " and wonder whether it was a good idea to have it on their résumés.

My sanguine mood vanished, however, as soon as I spotted the First Amendment listing. So many students had applied for the class, said a headnote, that the professors had decided to accept everyone who had given it a first-choice ranking. First Amendment theory, in short, was no longer a seminar but an impersonal lecture class.

I was livid. It was bad enough that I now faced the prospect of having zero seminars; dumb bad luck could have had the same effect. What infuriated me about the First Amendment class's change in format was that it was done so cavalierly. For months the law school had drilled into students the idea that justice was largely a product of even-handed procedures, but as soon as its own, presumptively neutral procedures created a problem, did it seek further advice, consult with those affected? No; it simply breached them. The president of the university — notably, a Yale Law graduate — had changed the rules in the middle of the game and effectively annulled my seminar ballot.

I had the law school dead to rights, but that, of course, made no difference. The registrar's office said complaints should be taken up with the professors; Schmidt was impossible to reach, Gewirtz reiterated that I could get into Images only if the waiting list cleared, and the dean in charge of the curriculum said he'd be happy to help me find "similar courses." No one, clearly, was going to admit that the law school had broken its own rules; the school would deal with my problem by hoping it would go away.

Fortuitously, it did. By the third week of class the attrition rate in Images was high enough to elevate me to permanent status. And First Amendment theory soon looked to be a dud in any form; before long the M.S.L.s referred to it as the "Floyd and Benno Show" because the class resembled nothing so much as an interview program on public television. The class was worthwhile regardless — both Schmidt and Abrams told entertaining war stories about First Amendment practice — but paradoxically, I think I learned more about law's impact on personal expression in Images.

Gewirtz had struck me as somewhat like Kahn when I first encountered him — authoritarian on the surface, ambivalent underneath. For a time I thought that mask would never come off, for he began the first few classes by lecturing rather than inviting discussion. That changed, however, in the fourth week, when Gewirtz assigned a 1949 *Harvard Law Review* article called "The Case of the Speluncean Explorers." It turned out to be an imaginary decision from the Supreme Court of a fictional country, and it was quite provocative: the author, Harvard Law professor Lon Fuller, was intent on demonstrating that many inconsistent legal conclusions, all legitimate, can be derived from the same set of facts.

The case concerned five explorers trapped in a cave by a

landslide. They had few provisions, and were advised by radio that some of them would almost surely die of starvation before they could be freed. The explorers were ultimately rescued more than a month later, but only four remained alive. The survivors admitted that the fifth man had been killed and eaten nine days earlier; he had been not only the first to suggest cannibalism, they said, but selected as the victim by his own pair of dice. The survivors were subsequently indicted and convicted of murder, though both the trial judge and jury petitioned the country's chief executive for clemency.

We gleaned these facts from the split decision rendered by the Supreme Court of the Commonwealth of Newgarth. Each justice filed a separate opinion. Chief Judge Truepenny affirmed the lower court's decision to convict while also advocating clemency; Judge Keen also affirmed, by reading literally the statute prohibiting the willful taking of a life; Judge Foster voted to overturn, holding that the court lacked jurisdiction because the explorers had been forced to adopt the law of the jungle; Judge Handy voted similarly, saying that the country's ultimate lawmakers, the people, had expressed in polls their overwhelming desire that the explorers be pardoned or let off lightly; Judge Tatting withdrew from the decision entirely, pleading overpowering moral confusion and declaring that the prosecutor should never have brought murder charges in the first place. Deadlocked two-to-two with one abstention, the death sentence stood.

"The case obviously illustrates the problem of living with uncertainty and ambiguity," said Gewirtz. "So how does a judge go about deciding on which side to come down in a case like this? Who, in your opinion, comes closest to doing justice? Or is it simply the judge's job to choose however he can?"

Gewirtz asked each student to cast a vote. All the judges save Keen, the irascible "strict constructionist," got at least one, but the ballot was grudging; the weaknesses in every opinion had been bared in the others. Truepenny, by attempting to defer to the chief executive, admitted that a legal system cannot always do justice on its own; Foster, by appealing to natural law, condoned a system without discernible standards; Tatting's abstention implied that a court can't deal with hard questions, the very things it was created to decide, while Keen's literalism put the integrity of the legal system above the actual dispensation of justice. Handy, appealing to mass opinion, suggested that the passions of the moment should dictate law's course.

When the question came around to me I tried to defend Foster's law-of-the-jungle argument. He, at least, valued life over law; he stretched the law to do so, certainly, but better that than convict these men, or fall prey to Tatting's paralysis or Handy's buck-passing. Foster recognized that "the law" meant "man's law," and that man's law was a subset of natural law. If man's law seemed incapable of doing justice to a situation, wasn't it "natural" to expand the definition of the applicable law in order to render judgment?

The argument, stated much less concisely at the time, provoked a defense of the abstainer, Tatting, from an intense first-year named Randy. At bottom, he asked, wasn't Tatting not only as realistic and reasonable as Foster, but more honest? Only he, after all, had encompassed within his opinion the views of all the other judges — that was precisely why his opinion ended in paralysis. And wasn't Tatting's paralysis also a microcosm of the paralysis produced by the court's evenly split vote? He was the one judge who refused to abolish uncertainty — which was, after all, the case's hallmark.

"For the other judges," Randy concluded, "the balance of reasoning is probably something like 51-to-49, but they end up writing their opinions like it's 95-to-5. That's coercive; it misrepresents the case. Tatting comes right out and says it's too close to call, and then refuses to call it."

Gewirtz had an interesting footnote. While Tatting's opinion might indeed be an unshifted, unmediated reflection of his innermost view, his refusal to break the court's tie vote upheld the explorers' convictions as surely as Keen's unsympathetic vote. The fact that a procedural rather than a substantive rule ended up validating the lower court's decision may protect Tatting's sense of personal integrity, but it also disguises the fact that legal analysis has real-life consequences. Tatting's dithering seems like inaction, but it amounts to action of a decisive, fatal kind.

Gewirtz didn't want to teach us to "think like lawyers" but to think for ourselves. If he had an agenda, it was to help students get in touch with their own values — or as he put it while defining the judge's task, "to forge meaning in the crucible of particulars."

In the next class the ideas unleashed in "Speluncean Explorers" came home to roost. Gewirtz had assigned *California v. Brown,* a case handed down less than a month earlier in which the U.S. Supreme Court had been asked to decide whether it was constitutional to allow a judge to instruct a jury, in determining a sentence for a convicted rapist-murderer, that it "must not be swayed by mere sentiment, conjecture, sympathy, passion, prejudice, public opinion, or public feeling." The California Supreme Court thought not, but in a 5–4 decision written by Chief Justice William Rehnquist, the U.S. Supreme Court reinstated the jury's sentence of death.

I found the majority opinion difficult to comprehend. By

upholding the jury instruction, the U.S. Supreme Court was insisting, essentially, that jurors act like lawyers — that it's perfectly acceptable to insist jurors be merciless logicians rather than who they are and should be: a defendant's peers. It seemed to have escaped the court that juries exist in the legal system expressly to retain the common human responses that legal thinking tends to eliminate. If the court didn't dare require that jurors actually be lawyers, it wasn't beyond attempting to eliminate from jurors' hearts and minds what Rehnquist called "extraneous emotional factors."

"I don't get it," said Wendy, an often tough-talking New Yorker, "this idea that 'When we depart from reason we depart from the rule of law.' How do you know when you're 'departing' from reason? Why should we assume there is only one kind of 'reason'? People always talk about law as if they're talking about math or physics — as if there are obvious, discrete categories. Everyone can tell an even number from an odd one, but I think it's destructive to pretend you can make that same kind of distinction in law."

Wendy spoke forcefully, as usual, and it struck me that few men in the class — only Gewirtz, most of the time — followed up on her comments. I wondered: was Wendy a conversation-stopper because her arguments were based on personal conviction more than abstract theory? Or because the men in class were accustomed to dominating discussions and found themselves unable, or unwilling, to deal with her strong opinions?

I wondered, too, whether Wendy was gay. As that thought crept into my head I realized I was indulging in exactly the sort of pigeonholing she criticized — the categorization that allows judges and lawyers (among others, of course) to stereotype certain people and thus devalue and

ignore them. Wendy didn't believe that judges should be
made solely of legal reason, and neither did I, yet I was ready
to believe that an assertive, challenging woman was
manlike — a lesbian, in short.

I was reminded of an attorney who had illuminated for me
years before some of the injustices brought about by legal
categorization. A client, a poor fifteen-year-old black girl,
had been arrested for prostitution and was likely to be sent
to a detention camp for delinquents. Why, the attorney
argued, should she be saddled with the label "hooker" or
"delinquent" when it was only a matter of chance that she
had been picked up in that role? The girl was also a runaway,
a foster child, and sexually abused; why didn't those labels
stick instead, especially since their underlying causes no
doubt precipitated, in part, her own illegal actions? If the
legal system truly believed in reason and efficiency, shouldn't
it emphasize crime prevention by helping those most likely
to commit crime in the future, those whose values have
already been crippled, rather than fulfill the immediate interests of individuals lucky enough to have escaped a similar
fate? Had the defendant in *Brown* met an attorney like this
much earlier in his life, there might have been no need for
a murder trial, let alone a death sentence.

Gewirtz got the discussion going again by turning to
Justice O'Connor's concurring opinion in *Brown*. O'Connor
argued that the sentencing stage of trial "should reflect a
reasoned *moral* response to the defendant's background, character, and crime rather than mere sympathy or emotion."
Gewirtz pointed out that her vote, like Tatting's, was decisive, for if she had gone the other way the defendant would
have faced life imprisonment instead of a death sentence.
What was O'Connor saying, Gewirtz asked, when she talked
about a "moral" response?

Carol, one of the more traditionally intellectual students in the class, usually waited for an exchange to get rolling before she added her thoughts. This time, however, she jumped right in.

"Methinks the lady doth protest too much," Carol said. "O'Connor is trying so hard to distinguish 'moral' from 'emotional.' It's what Wendy was saying — the categories aren't as distinct and unconnected as she makes out. It's when distinctions are *not* clear that people feel the need to make them. O'Connor seems to be trying to mitigate Rehnquist's opinion, if that's the right word, but she ends up in the same place. She doesn't want to recognize an emotional response either because it's beyond reason, it's outside the lawyer's role."

Wendy spoke directly to Carol across the table. "Emotions get pushed into a black box," she said. "They're just pushed aside."

"There's no willingness to deal intelligently with emotional responses," Carol continued. "O'Connor says, in effect, 'mere emotion.' She separates the emotional from the moral so she can pour reason into one and almost scorn the other. It's arrogant. It shows the system has no interest in dealing with emotions up front. And with this decision it seems the court doesn't even want to let them in through the back door, through the jury."

Carol and Wendy were talking about the law as a whole, I reflected, not just this particular case. Like me, they too felt emotionally repressed — and oppressed, and depressed — at law school. Images was one of the few places students could talk openly about feeling and belief, and I wondered what we would have done without the class; it seemed to have become a back door through which to reclaim legal education. If students couldn't feel a little less like lawyers here, a little more like ordinary people, they had probably already reached the point of emotional triage.

I had signed up for six classes in the spring semester: Images, First Amendment, Criminal Law, Intellectual Property, American Legal History, and a clinical course in which students try to obtain temporary restraining orders (TROs) against people who beat up their mates. Besides "Tragic Choices," I also hoped to audit a course on antidiscrimination law and another on broadcast law — taught, coincidentally, by the lawyer who represented the school board in the real-life version of the small group's Dove County memo case. It was a heavy schedule, two credits more than necessary for the M.S.L. degree and a lot of extra class time, but I didn't want to feel I had wasted my final chance to understand law from the inside.

My plans changed, however, one morning in late January, when I woke up with an exceptionally sore throat. I made it through the day's classes but by evening could barely speak. The nurse at the health clinic sent me home, saying I had probably caught strep throat, but the next morning it hurt so much to swallow I went back to the infirmary and insisted — mostly through hand gestures — on admittance. After being given a blood test I was put to bed with an IV dextrose bag and some aspirin. I got the bad news the following afternoon: mononucleosis.

Humiliation, relief, anger, amusement, frustration — a thirty-year-old law student with mono was a ridiculous concept, an archetype of bad timing, proof that God had a sense of humor. It was entirely possible I'd have to drop out of law school; it was likely I'd have to drop some courses, or fall so far behind I wouldn't know what was going on in class when I returned. Fortunately, I got my diagnosis on Friday, and Lisa was able to come up for the weekend.

She arrived an hour or so after visiting hours, but law school had prepared me for dealing with such problems. When Lisa called from the admittance desk saying the nurses wouldn't let her upstairs, I told her to say I was coming down to argue my case, IV pole and all. The nurses promptly decided to bend the rules — a flexibility that seemed appropriate to me this time around.

The strange thing about my case of mono, besides its unknown origins and attendant throat infection, was that it didn't make me particularly tired. As a result, after my brother and Lisa brought over my schoolbooks, I got an enormous amount of reading done; for five days, with no television to watch and no voice to speak with, there was little else to do. And when I could no longer bear to read, I thought. Perhaps because of my new relationship with Lisa, or because some of the women in Images had articulated ideas all but absent in other classes, I thought a lot about the role women played in the law.

The preoccupation first appeared when I read *Billy Budd* for Images. Melville's fictional account of the events leading to a sailor's execution seemed an eloquent expression of the law's tendency to be willful, insensitive, stoical, and unforgiving — to prefer the "macho," in a word, to the merciful. Budd, a young foretopman impressed on a British warship, had become a favorite with the rest of the crew for his good humor in the face of ill fortune, which included a stutter. His popularity maddens master-of-arms Claggart, however, who falsely tells the captain that Budd is fomenting mutiny. Called to answer the charge, Budd, infuriated, strikes Claggart and kills him.

Captain Vere convenes a court-martial, where Budd's only defense is his stutter. Slandered in the worst possible way in front of his captain, Budd says he was compelled to say something and "could only say it with a blow." Vere is sympathetic, but holds he is "not responsible" for the rigors of martial law and the Mutiny Act, which requires the death sentence for those striking a superior officer. Vere announces unhappily that Budd must hang.

Commentators have noted that while Melville may have understood the law correctly, he cited the wrong law — Britain's Mutiny Act governed the army, not the navy. It's a telling mistake and conceivably deliberate; Melville's father-in-law, Lemuel Shaw, was chief justice of Massachusetts, so he was likely to be familiar with such jurisdictional distinctions. The aspect of the novel that struck me most strongly, however, was Vere's belief, declared immediately after Budd's execution, that "With mankind, forms, measured forms are everything." Vere believed law had to be followed blindly; it could neither by rethought nor adjusted to fit the criminal, regardless of the injustice such ritual obedience might wreak. His concern for the preservation of authority outweighed his professed desire for individual justice.

Vere, I realized, viewed the law in much the same way as the fictional Judge Keen and the all-too-real Chief Justice Rehnquist. But there was one very significant difference: Vere didn't pretend his decision regarding Budd was reasonable, openly admitting that his court is "arbitrary," more a vehicle for maintaining order at sea than for establishing justice. While Vere refuses to question law because he believes it a divinely inspired imperative of royalty, Keen and Rehnquist do so for the opposite reason — because they know, all too well, that law is man-made. They feel threatened by the modern inclination to interpret law, because interpretation demonstrates law's uncertainty and unpredictability; that the legal system is fallible and may not deserve the respect and authority it presumes.

Law needed to be "feminized" — that was the word and the idea, at least, that sprang to mind. How else return to law the qualities I had long associated with women: empathy, sensitivity, trust, and the like? What seemed more important than the characterization, in any case, was the naming of a being, a group, capable of redeeming law. As a majority of citizens, and voters, women had the power to transform it — and the incentive to do so because their values, however they chose to define them, had been little reflected in law. Women seemed the one group in a position to make law adjust to its values rather than the reverse.

It dawned on me why the spring course called "Feminism" had become controversial. It was taught by Owen Fiss, and at first I assumed many women students were offended at a male professor's presumptuousness in offering such a course. That reaction made a certain amount of sense; Fiss taught Procedure, was best known for his work on injunctions, and seemed personally aloof . . . hardly the sort of background to make him sympathetic to what was often an angry, radical discipline. But now I saw the women's deeper fear — that Fiss would unconsciously misinterpret feminist theory until it became a watered-down, male-approved, unthreatening shadow of itself. Since feminist legal theory challenges not only existing law, not only entrenched approaches to law, but even the very idea of law, merely allowing Fiss to teach feminism was to invite cooptation.

What may have made the women especially annoyed about "Feminism" was that a course offered by a female professor in the same general area, "Women and the Law," wasn't likely to be any better. This professor seemed to have her finger on some important issues — the course would cover, for instance, the influence of legal education on the values upheld by law — but was extremely unpopular for being downright nasty at times toward her students. She apparently saw no irony in the fact that she used the powers of her law professorship to devalue students even while teaching that law devalued women.

The irony bypassed most law students as well, however, for they were far too busy reading cases to have time to think about such disjunctions. That was, perhaps, the ultimate irony of my stay in the infirmary — that I best understood law when I wasn't studying it.

I missed only one Images class while marooned in bed. That was fortunate, for the course became more interesting as it went along. Readings about law had dominated the first month of class, but Gewirtz soon weaned us away from the straight analysis of legal texts. Many of the ensuing readings focused not on what lawyers do with law but on what law does to lawyers.

For a class discussion called "Detachment and Commitment" Gewirtz assigned an excerpt from *The Sorcerer of Bolinas Reef*, a book in which former Yale Law professor Charles Reich described his early years practicing law. I was surprised to learn that this was the same Charles Reich who had written *The Greening of America*, a much-praised, much-derided countercultural bestseller of 1970. Law was mentioned only infrequently in that book, but Reich's denunciation of the impersonal, corporate values that had begun to dominate the United States was obviously informed by his experience in the legal profession. Modern law, he wrote in *Greening,* tells people it is "morally right to surrender" to law's control, "to deny their own inner values in favor of law which has become, unknown to them, corrupt, unjust, and antihuman. . . ."

Reich's first job after graduating from Yale Law School in 1952, he writes in *The Sorcerer,* was a joy. He worked as a law clerk for Justice Hugo Black, even lived in his house, and had breakfast, lunch, and dinner with him almost every day. He came to love Black because the justice "possessed the power of love," because he was "passionate about justice for each individual, no matter how inconsequential the person might seem to the world." Reich soon learned, however, that his clerkship was an anomaly in the practice of law. When it ended he took a job at a corporate law firm, as most Yale Law graduates do today, and for similar reasons: high pay, considerable prestige, and great expectations. Having clerked at the Supreme Court, Reich had many offers of employment to choose from, and he decided to work at a firm in Washington, D.C., that shared his interest in the New Deal and civil liberties. At such a firm, he thought, he could see firsthand how American democracy worked and master the skills with which to make it work better.

Reich was quickly disillusioned. He was active and busy, found his work stimulating and often valuable to clients, but that surface enjoyment masked a deep personal malaise. His life seemed to be meaningless, an artificial orchestration in which his time and soul were forced to memorize discordant parts. In order to play the lawyer's role, Reich saw, he was expected to give up every other.

At a conference with a high government official, Reich relates, the atmosphere was "inhuman" and the participants "spoke lines, they did not communicate." During meetings with clients and colleagues, detachment was necessary but not sufficient; those present must also "ring with seemingly true belief." Going out for meals, young corporate lawyers "listened only for the purpose of replying," regarding conversation as "an oratory contest" and "impatiently waiting their chance to earn an A in Lunch." Always on the spot, always on call, always presumed to have a good answer or at least a good argument, Reich spent so much time responding to others' expectations that he lost track of his own identity. Before long, he writes, "the public self became first the only visible self, then the only real self."

Reich's six years at the law firm made him financially comfortable, but the personal cost was immeasurable. He knew that the lawyer's life had "a fundamental lack of limits," but his firm, in typical legalistic fashion, turned that vice into a virtue; the ability to work hard at any hour of the day or night was considered a sign of being "tough," the lawyer's ultimate accolade. Other people envied Reich's ability to walk the corridors of power, to dress in expensive suits and work in fancy offices, but he knew he was a hired gun; like every newspaper and drink he bought on his business travels, "Every motion I made, every word I uttered, every thought I had was also not my own." Isolated from other people and his former self, Reich felt sick, frightened, stifled, deadened. "You cannot strike your head all day with a hammer," he writes, "and then expect that the person within will want to come out when you get home."

Reich's account of corporate law was appalling, especially since the law firm he described — Arnold & Porter, co-founded by former Yale Law professor Thurman Arnold — had a reputation as a haven for liberals. I was surprised, consequently, that Gewirtz didn't spend much time discussing Reich's portrayal; didn't he want to point out that the practice of law had become even more competitive, even more image-conscious, since Reich's time?

I wondered, too, whether Gewirtz felt implicitly criticized by Reich for maintaining any connection to law. Reich, at one point, describes a dam license proceeding as existing largely "to rationalize what was otherwise decided" and suggests that

> The person who contributed intellect to such a process was helping to create and perpetuate a lie about how things really happened; he was an unintentional conspirator in the cover-up of social truth.

Was Gewirtz a co-conspirator in a similarly deceptive process — the inculcation of artificial, soul-deadening legal values — merely by teaching law? I guessed Reich had come to the same conclusion himself, for he had quit his tenured professorship at Yale Law in 1974. (I subsequently learned that Reich's reasons for leaving New Haven had much less to do with law than I believed; after a few years away from law, he resumed teaching it at the University of San Francisco.)

As it turned out, I was overly suspicious about Gewirtz. He wasn't avoiding the issues brought up by Reich; he had just delayed them, wanting to talk about the effect of law on lawyers only after we had read *The Death of Ivan Ilych*. He said when we began discussing it, "I think this story is applicable to most of the students who pass through this place" — a startling comment, considering that Tolstoy's novella describes a man's conviction that he can escape death because, as a lawyer, his life has overflowed with "legality, correctitude, and propriety."

*   *   *

Ivan Ilych Golovin, a lawyer in the Ministry of Justice, has felt a constant pain in his gut ever since he fell while redecorating his new house, which he bought after receiving a major promotion. Though doctors have given many different diagnoses, for a time Ivan Ilych is content to believe his agony is caused by a problem in the appendix or kidneys. As the medicines fail and the pain grows worse, however, Ivan Ilych begins to think he is beyond help. He remains haunted by the sense that "he had put something aside — an important, intimate matter which he would revert to when his work was done."

Eventually, Ivan Ilych entertains the notion that his pain is a natural consequence of his way of life. After examining the thought, however, he dismisses it as without merit: "But how could that be," he asked rhetorically, "when I did everything properly?" Having always taken great pride in the ability to "separate his real life from the official side of affairs," Ivan Ilych is unable to comprehend that this very distinction is killing him. He doesn't understand that he has spent his life rationalizing rather than reasoning, that he should never have congratulated himself for

> reducing even the most complicated case to a form in which it would be presented on paper only in its externals, completely excluding his personal opinion of the matter, while above all observing every prescribed formality.

Trained to categorize, Ivan Ilych has fallen victim to the category "lawyer": instead of experiencing life firsthand, he followed to the letter the path his profession seemed to prescribe. He can die in peace only after coming to understand that he has poisoned himself, and his family, with his insatiable appetite for status, fashion, decorum. "I was going up in public opinion," Ivan Ilych finally admits on his death-bed, "but to the same extent life was ebbing away from me."

"One of the great skills we have as lawyers is being able to rationalize everything," Gewirtz said toward the end of the *Ivan Ilych* discussion. "We often look to convention for guidance, but it's convention that's killing Ivan. His illness is an acid eating away at the armor hiding Ivan from him-self." He wants to be a man of honor and principle, but in obeying "oughts" and "shoulds" rather than his own beliefs, following rules instead of trying to understand them, Ivan Ilych has ensured his soul's demise. "After reading this book," Gewirtz continued, "you have to ask yourself, 'How can I prevent this from happening to me?' And one way of doing that is reading — by cultivating the imagination, lis-tening to other voices, getting beyond the ordinary emphasis on the superficial. You just have to keep the truth channels open all the time."

Wendy hated *Ivan Ilych,* and the vehemence of her dislike put the class on edge. It wasn't until much later that I thought I understood her reaction. Tolstoy had explicitly linked the death of the soul with professionalism and chosen a lawyer to represent that idea; he came very close to saying that lawyers could not avoid Ivan Ilych's fate because their ties to tradition, rank, and formality prevented them from defining their lives in any other terms. That was an ex-tremely disturbing way to read the story — especially to a third-year law student with visions of transforming her pro-fession from within.

I could imagine the questions Wendy didn't dare ask, even of herself. Has law school changed me without my knowing it? Have I already started down Ivan Ilych's road, despite constant resistance? Is law incapable of real change — does it require not reform but revolution, over-throw? Those questions certainly coursed through my mind during law school, and at this writing, I can answer them no better than I did then.

Gewirtz, like most law professors, was more interested in characterizing problems than proposing solutions. In the last weeks of class, however, he assigned a very short work that incorporated an alternative, constructive philosophy of law. The reading was unusual in that its author, Martha Minow, saw a way in which law could transcend its structural lim-itations; she envisioned a system that avoided law's tendency to distance and formalize, refused to shoehorn real-life needs into existing legal forms. Two other facts made the reading even more unusual: it concerned the judgment of King Sol-omon, and was written by Minow as a Yale Law student.

Solomon, of course, settled a maternity dispute by or-dering that the baby in question be cut in half. One woman approved the king's ruling, content with equal treatment; the other relinquished her claim, putting the child's life ahead of her own desires. Solomon declared that the woman willing to give up the baby alive must be the true mother, for she had volunteered to suffer great injustice herself rather than cause an even greater injustice to another. By creating a situation in which the women had to rethink their posi-tions, the king caused one to adopt a wider view of justice: she showed, quite unintentionally, that she represented the culture's best values, and the law could not help but take her side. By dropping out of the litigation, ironically, the true mother ensured that justice was done.

Solomon's wisdom, Minow writes, lay in his providing disputants with the chance to "grow." He didn't see the judge's role as the proclamation of winners and losers; he saw it, instead, as an opportunity to transcend self-interest. While most law is a selective masking, the tailoring of facts and theories to legal form, Solomon's law was the reverse — an unmasking, the revelation of inmost wishes and motivations. Solomon didn't decide the truth but forced private selves to go public and face a tragic choice . . . and in their choosing, compel the judgment they deserved. The king didn't actively change the community, but the effect of his judgment was to encourage a search for overriding social values.

By asking for "more than the pleadings, more than the facts, more even than a choice of rules," Minow writes, Solomon invited his culture to expand to meet its declared ideals. By asking litigants to become "vulnerable," he allowed them to admit to flaws, hurts, and uncertainties, to share inevitable human failings. Making the reenvisionment of law an element of the judging process, Solomon simultaneously tested his people and himself; he shared the challenge of doing justice with those he judged. In the final analysis, his good judgment arose not from detachment but from commitment — his willingness to be a part of his community, not above it.

We didn't spend much time on Solomon, caught up in the end-of-semester rush. But Minow's analysis stayed with me, especially after I noticed her name coming up from time to time in the legal and mainstream press. Solomon's wisdom might yet make headway in modern law; Minow had gone on to become a professor at Harvard Law.

Twelve

Crime and Punishment

"Prisoner at the bar, you have been accused of the great crime of laboring under pulmonary consumption, and after an impartial trial before a jury of your countrymen, you have been found guilty. . . . You were convicted of aggravated bronchitis last year: and I find that though you are now only twenty-three years old, you have been imprisoned on no less than fourteen occasions for illnesses of a more or less hateful character. . . . [W]hether your being in a consumption is your fault or not, it is a fault in you, and it is my duty to see that against such faults as this the commonwealth shall be protected. You may say that it is your misfortune to be criminal; I answer that it is your crime to be unfortunate."

SAMUEL BUTLER
Erewhon
1872

I got my one and only real-life law client on my second day working for the student-run Temporary Restraining Order Project for Battered Women. Checking in with the woman's shelter, I was told that Gloria Astor (a pseudonym) had called its hotline the previous night to say that her husband, Jack, had become violent. She was unhurt but scared, and wanted to know how she could make Jack stay away from her. The hotline operator told Gloria about the TRO Project and said a law student would contact her in the morning.

Law school, finally, felt like a prelude to something important.

I called Gloria immediately. She was obviously upset, but not to the extent I expected; she was more angry than frightened as she described how Jack had come home drunk, knocked her down, smashed a few toys in the children's bedroom, and thrown a bottle that narrowly missed Gloria's head before shattering against the wall. Although Jack had eventually passed out and in the morning agreed to stay with friends for a couple of nights, Gloria didn't quite believe him; she thought he still might return to the house and hurt her. He was six foot two, she explained, and weighed well over two hundred pounds.

I told Gloria we needed to meet and talk about what we could do for her. When I suggested I make an appointment with an attorney that very afternoon, however, she balked; Jack had the car, she didn't want to take the bus with her two small children, and it wasn't worth the trouble for me to drive out and pick her up myself. The following morning was soon enough, Gloria said, for by then she'd be able to find a babysitter and a friend to drive her downtown. When I asked Gloria whether she was sure she'd be safe that evening, Gloria said yes; Jack was violent only when he drank, and she doubted he'd be drinking again so soon.

I went directly from the phone booth to Criminal Law, arriving fifteen minutes late. At first all I felt was relief; I had hours to reach an attorney from the TRO volunteer list willing to shepherd me through the process. Soon, however, I felt uneasy and distracted, for the very idea of being in class began to feel wrong. I had just gotten off the phone with a woman in legitimate fear of life and limb, yet I wasn't doing anything about it; I was listening, instead, to a bow-tied professor wondering aloud whether it was a criminal act for a nuclear power plant operator to fall asleep on the job. Part of me wanted to race out of the classroom and drive to Gloria's house, or read up on temporary restraining orders, or find out more about New Haven's family court judges . . . but another part of me was paralyzed.

For the first time in my life I felt totally responsible for somebody else's, and I didn't know if I was up to the assignment. Was my role, as the closest thing Gloria had to a lawyer, to do what she wanted? Aid her in figuring out what she wanted? Was I supposed to trust her judgment, probably impaired at the moment, or exercise my own? Gloria now trusted me to help her to the extent the law allowed, but I simply didn't know how much help that meant; and in any case, I had the feeling that even if I did manage to fulfill my professional obligations I would fall far short of giving Gloria what she needed. I knew where the lawyer's responsibility began, but not where it ended.

I had signed up for the section of Criminal Law taught by Joseph Goldstein partly because Alina, who had been in his small group, thought him a good professor. What most intrigued me, however, was the fact that he was a psychoanalyst — indeed, had written a number of books with Anna Freud. I had been in four-day-a-week analysis for a year after the breakup of my marriage, and was curious to see how Goldstein would fit law and psychology together. My psychoanalysis had convinced me it's better to explore the irrational rather than ignore, manipulate, or eradicate it, but law, it seemed to me, often did just that.

In Goldstein's class, however, the tension between law and psychology didn't seem irresolvable. Although he clearly relished using lawyerly arrogance to knock law students down a peg or two, he extended the analyst's compassion to those who actually needed it — those whose interests were scorned or undervalued by law. To some extent, Goldstein did for criminal law what Guido did for tort law (not really such different disciplines, a crime essentially being a tort deemed so offensive that the state steps in to punish the offender). He showed that a society's rules, as expressed in law, are better understood as crutches than pillars.

Goldstein made that point quickly and vividly by devoting the first two weeks of class to a case involving a pediatrician's apparent homosexual abuse of numerous young patients. "Be aware," Goldstein said as he introduced *State v. Martin* to the thirty-five or so students in the course, "that criminal law is culture-bound."

Dr. Daniel Martin — the name, as used in Goldstein's casebook, is fictitious — was arrested and charged in 1955 with violating Connecticut statutes forbidding "indecent assault" and "injury or risk of injury to children." Until his arrest, Martin had been considered something of a hero to local residents for his ability to instill self-confidence in children and help them overcome physical and psychological problems. The doctor's pederasty came to light after he asked the parents of a ten-year old boy with a severe stutter to allow his brothers to visit him for a few days at the doctor's camplike clinic; the brothers' presence, Martin explained, might help illuminate the stutter's origin. The parents agreed, but when the younger brother returned home he referred to Martin as a "pig." When the boy explained his meaning, his mother called the police.

Martin pled no contest to all charges, saying that the boys' health would suffer from a public trial. Since the doctor's plea of *nolo contendere* amounted to a guilty verdict, detailed evidence about his relationship with children did not emerge until the sentencing hearing. At that proceeding

Martin's attorney said that while the doctor's methods might appear unusual, they were rooted in the psychologically sound idea that psychic injuries received in childhood could be treated by inducing a patient to regress into a childlike state — a state created by the "permissive environment" of Martin's camp-clinic.

The homosexual acts between the doctor and the children, Martin's attorney argued, were thus not only natural but therapeutic. If a patient did indeed suffer from the "sex-guilt" Martin diagnosed, the doctor's temporary "spiritual-ization" of homosexual acts could guide him "out of sex perversion to a more socially acceptable sexuality." The doctor knew his actions were illegal, but the lawyer argued that just as killing was usually criminal in peacetime but often heroic during wartime, so could Martin's otherwise criminal acts be considered well intended and, under the circumstances, appropriate. Martin's peculiar form of therapy, however irregular, for some children might represent their only chance to become functioning members of society.

Like *Bowers v. Hardwick,* the case demonstrated that judges frequently make decisions based as much on cultural beliefs as on facts or law. For although Goldstein's textbook (written with his former student Alan Dershowitz and a third law professor) provided copious background material on the case — court transcripts, newspaper articles, letters to the editor, judicial and sentence review board decisions — it was still impossible to say whether Martin was a cynical fraud, a reckless pioneer, a self-deceiving fool, a combination of the three, or something else entirely. I was sure of only one thing after finishing the readings: that Martin showed good judgment exactly once, in his choice of counsel. The attorney actually made the therapy seem plausible — though one had to condemn Martin's actions regardless, for his goals didn't justify his means. For all that, however, it was hard to say where justice lay.

"Does it matter," Goldstein asked in his gravelly, professorial voice, "that Martin was a doctor, educated, a social worker? Is that a difference we want to account for or ignore?"

Account for, I thought. In tort law, a doctor is held accountable for whatever professional skills he has; he can't successfully defend himself by claiming he doesn't know something which, as a doctor, he should have known. Applied to criminal law, the standard would mean that Martin was presumed to be aware that his "therapy" could cause at least as much psychological harm as it cured.

"And does his being a doctor mitigate or worsen the offense?"

That was harder. Worsen, because Martin seemed to be breaking the Hippocratic oath; he may well have done harm, and had treated his patients, in effect, as guinea pigs. But mitigate, too; although his "therapy" was bizarre, it seemed to work for some patients — including (at least for a time) the stuttering youth who inadvertently caused Martin's downfall.

"His punishment?"

Much, much harder. Martin faced up to twenty years in prison; surely there was a better way to punish a talented doctor for a very serious mistake other than locking him up for a decade or more? Give him, perhaps, a choice among prison time, unpaid work in a hospital for adults, house arrest coupled with drug therapy and counseling? Even let him opt for chemical castration? Why not allow him to continue practicing medicine in some form, so long as his ability to do damage was eliminated?

"Should baseball players be treated differently when they

assault the police" — the reference was to New York Met Dwight Gooden, another "doctor," recently arrested for arguing with highway patrolmen — "or should all people who assault the police be treated like baseball players? What standards do we invoke? Community standards?"

Goldstein surveyed the room.

"How do we define the community? Do we let the judge define it? The legislature? Vocal proponents?"

Goldstein looked amused — but that was always the case, for a slight smile played perpetually on his lips. His wavy silver hair, which somehow managed to cascade upward, added to the effect.

"Should we have a national law of crimes? We do have a law prohibiting polygamy. Would Dr. Martin, or anyone, be justified in breaking that law if he could show good reason?"

Pause.

"Perhaps the family should be the baseline measure, if we can define 'family.' We may decide to exclude law from the family relationship; we may call spanking one's own child 'disciplining' while spanking another's, 'criminal assault.' It might be worth pointing out in this context that ritual circumcision, as practiced in a number of cultures, seems to fit comfortably within the statute under which Dr. Martin was convicted. A crime in one society, you see, may not be a crime in another."

Dr. Martin, however, was a convicted criminal. Although the trial judge recognized his "outstanding ability" as a physician and wished for a way to treat his "affliction," Martin received one to six years in state prison.

I read the TRO Project's manual the evening before my interview with Gloria. This was it — my chance to try to *do* justice instead of just think about it. I had volunteered for the project because it was the only one in which I felt I'd always be on the right side of an issue, but Criminal Law made that ideal seem unrealistic. Gloria remained a victim, true; but to what degree, and to what legal effect? The gap between legal theory and legal practice proved wider than I had anticipated.

My troubles began as soon as I tried to locate an attorney who had the time to supervise my handling of Gloria's problem. None of the four officially on call for *pro bono* TRO work was available when Gloria was, and I ended up having to make a dozen calls before reaching one able to take the case. Mary Basham — a pseudonym, to respect the attorney-client privilege and both women's privacy — said I could interview Gloria at her law firm the next morning.

I arrived at nine o'clock on the dot and introduced myself to the receptionist, who motioned to two women sitting stiffly in a cluster of nearby chairs. They were young, no older than twenty-three or twenty-four, and both had manes of blow-dried hair. I went over and introduced myself, regretting the TRO manual hadn't mentioned that at least in the first clinical encounter, the law student will probably feel like a complete fraud. I was wearing a jacket and tie and attempted to project an air of authority, but on the inside I was saying, "Please, God, don't let me screw this up!"

I asked Gloria and her friend Stephanie to wait for a few minutes while I talked with our attorney. I found her, and she showed me to an office I could use for the interview, adding she'd drop by after a while to see how we were doing. I went back to the reception area to collect Gloria, only slightly embarrassed at the fact that I had spent even less time in these offices than she. Stephanie followed us into the interview room, and I hoped I wasn't breaking any ethical rules by allowing her to stay. If Stephanie's presence made

Gloria more comfortable and forthcoming, I reasoned, so much the better.

I sat behind the desk, pulled a notepad out of my briefcase, and explained I was a law student working under Mary's supervision. Our first task, I said, was to draft a document in which we outlined evidence with which to persuade a judge that he should order Jack to stay away from Gloria and the home they shared — and solely on the basis of Gloria's version of the facts.

I asked Gloria if she still wanted to get a TRO against Jack. She nodded, but added that Jack would "kill her" if he learned she had gone to a lawyer, let alone to court; I gathered from Gloria's expression that she meant the phrase figuratively. Gloria said she still loved Jack, but planned to file for divorce despite his objections. When I asked whether he had ever hurt or threatened the children, she quickly replied that Jack loved the kids and would never do such a thing.

I asked Gloria to repeat once more the circumstances of their most recent fight. I felt like a cop on a stereotypical television show: "Ma'am, just tell us exactly what went on that night. . . ." While the detective asks the question seeking the final, overlooked piece to the puzzle, however, I did so to tailor the facts to the law. The relevant law, I had learned from the TRO manual, was Connecticut General Statute Section 46b-15, which offered legal protection to individuals over the age of sixteen "subjected to a continuous threat of physical pain or physical injury" by another household member. The key phrase, I knew, was "continuous threat"; a judge was almost sure to grant a TRO if I could show a pattern of abuse by Jack and a pattern of fear in Gloria.

Gloria recounted her story without further prompting. Jack had gone to the package store after work, she said, and was drunk when he got home. After Gloria remarked in anger that he spent too much money on beer and left hardly enough for household expenses, Jack "went crazy." He tore a poster off the wall in the elder child's room; he smashed a rocking horse and threatened to hit Gloria with it; he punched her in the leg, slapped her face, said he was going to punch her in the mouth, threw a cola bottle at her, bent her hand backward until her fingers almost broke.

I tried to retain a stone face — why, I don't know — as I took notes. I asked Gloria if there had been similar incidents.

"Remember, around Christmas last year?" Stephanie said to Gloria. To me: "He's beaten her up at least four times when I've been there."

They were living in Jack's hometown then, Gloria said, "a couple miles from here. He got upset because I was out with a girlfriend when he got home, you know, dinner wasn't on the table, and when I got home he just picked me up and threw me all over the house. He smashed glass everywhere and I really got cut up, there was blood all over the floor. The paramedics wanted to take me to the hospital — the neighbors must have called them, it wasn't like this was the only time it had happened.

"Anyway, the police came, and I heard one of them say, 'He's here, Astor's here!' — he's been in so much trouble, the cops know him by name. Thirteen came that time. I went to my parents' house, the cuts weren't deep or anything, and he spent the night in jail. But the Family Relations Department just slapped him on the wrist — they made him promise to go to a counselor at work, but he never did."

The third incident, like many of the others, started over money, but it was the only one in which Jack wasn't drunk. He began choking her, and threatened Stephanie when she tried to intervene. That time, Gloria said, the children were terrified; both howled, the four-year-old screaming at Jack that she loved him and begging him to leave Mommy alone. Gloria mentioned other incidents that were no more than family spats, but I listened attentively; as a reporter, I knew it was often impossible to tell what was relevant to a story until you tried to commit it to paper.

Three instances of major abuse over two years, two resulting in blood and calls to the police — surely that was enough at least to argue "continuous threat," especially since any number of friends, relatives, and policemen had been witnesses. We had already talked for forty minutes, but I questioned Gloria for another ten just to make sure I hadn't missed anything.

I told Gloria it would probably take me an hour to write up her statement in legal form, and suggested she and Stephanie take a walk or get a cup of coffee. When they left, I pulled out my portable computer and printer — I didn't know whether I'd be able to use the computers at Mary's office — and began writing. I had already started the document at home, over breakfast, so when I typed "astor.tro," up popped the word AFFIDAVIT, centered and in bold capitals. This was definitely the real thing.

Forty-five minutes later I had thirteen numbered paragraphs, two single-spaced pages' worth, on heavy bond stationery with the law firm's name running up the inside margin. It looked quite impressive. The writing had been easier than I expected, for composing an affidavit turned out to be much like writing a news story on deadline. The major difference was that I used fewer adjectives and someone else's voice — it was Gloria, after all, who would swear to the affidavit's truth.

I had just finished when Mary came into the office. I

handed her the document and fiddled anxiously with the computer while she read through it. I knew the writing was good, but was it good *law* writing? Mary made a few marks with a pencil, then looked up. Her expression told me nothing.

"Did you ask whether they had relations after the most recent incident?"

I must have looked mystified, because Mary rephrased the question.

"Do you know if they had sex that night?"

The question would not have occurred to me in a million years. It was obvious, however, in retrospect; what better way to elicit a sense of how threatened Gloria felt? Whatever answers she gave to that and related questions — Was she a willing partner in sex? Did Jack sleep in the same bed with her? Did she think about sleeping elsewhere herself? — would speak volumes about Gloria's frame of mind.

"No," I said, "I didn't think of that." I almost added "sorry," but refrained.

Mary read through the affidavit again. Finally she said, "This is good . . ."

A wave of relief washed over me — and then surprise and frustration.

". . . but I think we'll have a hard time getting a TRO on this one."

If the affidavit's good, how could it fail to work?

I agreed, however, once Mary explained her reasoning. The crux of the problem was that while Gloria might at times truly be in danger, she seemed to have done little, if anything, to mitigate it. Perhaps she was right to insist that Jack leave the house instead of leaving it herself, for example, but the fact that she had made the request, and that Jack had acquiesced to it, didn't fit very well under the governing statute. Gloria's actions and choices raised a lot of questions, and made her seem like something less, and more, than a battered wife.

The central problem seemed to be, ironically and appallingly, that Jack wasn't abusive enough. Most of the battered women Mary had worked with in the past had bruises, cracked ribs, and worse, so scared they had left their homes and sought refuge in the women's shelter. If the judge we drew had a similar impression of TRO petitioners, he might conclude that Gloria's situation didn't warrant the interference of the court, or at least that any decision should be delayed until Jack made his case.

Although Mary didn't say it aloud, she also seemed to think that Gloria might have provoked Jack. At first I thought the idea totally irrelevant; Jack had no right to turn to physical violence no matter what Gloria had said. But I think I understood what was on Mary's mind. If a TRO were granted and Jack fought it at the renewal hearing (which had to take place, by law, two weeks later), his testimony could cast serious doubt on the black-and-white account of events I had put down in the affidavit. The fact that I had allowed Gloria to depict herself as blameless opened the door for Jack's attorney to paint her as a spoiled, possibly lying nag.

Gloria herself had given me some evidence for such accusations, but I had rushed past them in my eagerness to help. For one thing, she had consistently referred to "my children" and "my house" as if Jack were no more than a tenant; for another, Gloria seemed to relish describing Jack's bullying behavior, as if proud of her ability to inspire it. I hadn't done a good legal interview, I realized; I had taken Gloria's statements at face value instead of pushing her closer to the limit, instead of determining how well her assertions would stand up under hostile questioning. We needed an affidavit we could argue not only in front of a judge but also defend against an opposing attorney.

When Gloria and Stephanie returned from their walk, all four of us talked in a conference room. Mary immediately began filling in the gaps I had left; she asked her questions directly but not harshly.

Did they have sexual relations after the incident?

Yes, that night.

Did she provoke him in any way?

Gloria grinned crookedly before responding. "I kicked him in the . . . you know . . ."

"The groin?"

"Yeah. And he got right back up — I couldn't believe it, I thought I was going to die right then."

Did she ever use or buy drugs?

No.

Mary rephrased a couple of questions from the official Application for Relief from Abuse.

Could she swear she was in imminent danger?

Gloria shrugged her shoulders, saying, "I guess, but do I have to swear it?"

Did she fear staying at home?

Gloria said she wasn't going to move into the women's shelter. And why should she? she added. It was her furniture, her house, her family's loans that made them possible.

Mary, I thought, would have been an excellent reporter. There was no judgment in her voice, only a sense that the truth must inevitably come out.

I left the room to revise the affidavit while Mary guided Gloria through the fee-waiver application — Jack, she said, had taken all the money out of their joint checking account. Mary and I then met again, alone.

Mary said she didn't believe Gloria's answer about drug

use and wondered what a judge would think if he heard Gloria had kicked Jack in the balls. What bothered her most, however, was Gloria's unwillingness to swear in open court that she was in imminent danger, for that was a key ingredient to a successful TRO application; it took fairly extreme circumstances for a court to grant an order on one person's unproved word. But we had no way of knowing, really, why Gloria couldn't answer the question. Was she reticent because she couldn't predict what Jack would do, or because she had exaggerated her fear, or because she simply didn't know the answer?

"As an officer of the court," Mary said, "I don't think I could argue for this real strongly." I didn't like to hear it, but I had to agree; though the affidavit was literally true, it gave an incomplete picture and stretched the definition of "imminent danger." Mary said she was willing to try to get the TRO despite her reservations, however; it wasn't our role, after all, to establish truth. She said, with a smile, "Let's let the judge decide."

By noon we had the complete package together — the affidavit, the application for relief, the fee-waiver form, its accompanying financial statement, a law-student-intern consent form, and an *ex parte* ("for one party") order for the judge to sign should he grant the TRO. It was hard to believe we had done all that in three hours. Mary, Gloria, Stephanie, and I marched off to Superior Court, Judicial District of New Haven, and within fifteen minutes Mary and I were sitting in a judge's chambers. Like Gloria — who remained with Stephanie in the courtroom, empty except for the clerk — I had not expected the wheels of justice to move so quickly.

After looking at the file for a moment, the judge said the *ex parte* form hadn't been filled out properly — I had put Gloria's address in the wrong box, and thus appeared to ask that Jack be kept away from his workplace rather than his home. I was more than a little embarrassed, and began to fear I would fall apart if the judge asked me to justify the TRO application then and there. The revised affidavit was more moderate than the first, but the doubts Mary had sown in my mind continued to fester. I was damned as an officer of the court if I went too far, it seemed, but damned as an advocate if I didn't go far enough.

Mary, fortunately, knew the judge well enough to be completely open with him. She really didn't know, she said, whether this case warranted a TRO or not. For a moment I wondered whether Mary's deference was straight-shooting or tactical maneuvering; by coming close to taking Jack's side she could virtually assume that the judge, being a lawyer, would take the opposite view and thus argue Gloria's position for her. I soon decided Mary considered law too important to treat like a game. It might not seem very lawyerly to present beliefs unadorned, to let a straightforward affidavit speak for itself, but I think the judge appreciated Mary's candor.

He eventually declared the case "pretty clear-cut." After a beat in which I feared the worst, he added, "This most recent incident is enough." He signed the TRO, and just like that, we had won.

"We learned something today," Mary said, after I closed the judge's door behind me. "That 'imminent' can mean different things to different people." We also learned how tense I had been, for I had to dash back into the judge's chambers to grab my briefcase.

Gloria seemed pleased at our news. Mary then went back to her office while I made photocopies of the TRO for Gloria and the county sheriff, who would serve Jack with the necessary papers. I told Gloria to keep the order with her at all times, as I had been instructed. If Jack tried to get into the house, I said, she should call the police; I also told her that once Jack was served, he could be arrested at the house for criminal trespass — a violation that brought up to a year in prison.

I told Gloria to call me for any reason and that I'd be in touch with her within a few days. Mary had invited me to join her and some of her partners for lunch when I was through at court, but I didn't get the chance; it took me a while to figure out which forms I was supposed to give the sheriff. If all went well, that was the last thing I had to do until the fourteen-day hearing, when I might have to argue against Jack's attorney for a continuance of the TRO. I tried to put that frightening prospect out of mind.

But things didn't go well, procedurally, and the hearing never took place. The sheriff's department called to say that Jack's workplace was beyond its jurisdiction, which meant I had to refile the TRO papers with a local address for Jack. Before I did so on the next working day, however, Gloria called Mary to say she wasn't sure the TRO was such a good idea. I don't know whether the delay in service contributed to Gloria's change of mind (or heart), but Mary, after ascertaining that Gloria wasn't being coerced into dropping her legal action, had to go along. Through some sixth legal sense, Mary had anticipated this outcome all along; she had felt Gloria wasn't yet ready to make the break with Jack.

But Gloria became ready, apparently, soon after. A few weeks later another student in the TRO program called me to ask whether I still had a copy of Gloria's file; Gloria had again called the women's hotline because Jack had "gone crazy." Gloria told the student she was now definite about wanting a TRO and filing for divorce.

I hoped she would get what she truly wanted this time,

but I had my doubts. Law, at bottom, could do very little for Gloria; its solutions, and dissolutions, couldn't help her solve her basic problem — the difficulty in deciding whether the changes she craved were worth the sacrifices they entailed. This was a cost/benefit analysis she had to make on her own, however much she wished that law would make it for her.

The TRO Project wasn't the only student-run program I became involved with during the spring semester. The Green Haven Prison Project was not a legal clinic, however; we didn't gather evidence for a class-action lawsuit over prison conditions, as students did in one program, or help individual inmates with legal problems, as they did in another. The nonclinical nature of the Green Haven Project was in fact part of its appeal, for I wasn't sure I could handle any legal responsibility beyond that required for a TRO. And in any case, I thought I had a duty to see what happened to a convicted defendant; for all I knew, the affidavit I had written might help put Gloria's husband behind bars some day.

The Green Haven Project consisted of seminars on legal issues, often conducted with the aid of a Yale Law faculty member, held in a maximum-security prison in lower New York State. They were intended to educate students about prison life as much as to educate inmates about law, but I came away from my handful of hours in Green Haven Correctional Facility — its official name — convinced that prison life was beyond my comprehension. I had expected to transcend my initial sense of voyeurism but transcendence never came; as soon as I saw bars and guns and uniforms and guard boxes, I found myself shutting down, unable to evoke even the desire to understand. The inmates' lives and experiences were so remote from my own that an unscalable wall remained between us even as we sat side by side, knees touching.

I first went to Green Haven in early spring. Seven of us — two first-years, two second-years, a third-year, the Yale Law librarian, and me — left New Haven in the late afternoon. We stopped two hours later, for a dinner of hastily eaten sandwiches at a gas station a few miles past the Connecticut border. It was somehow disturbing that the scenery became prettier the nearer we approached the prison; the ugly white ribbon of interstate concrete was behind us and only a couple miles of tree-lined country road lay ahead. I couldn't help remarking that "Green Haven Prison in Stormville, New York" sounded all wrong. Shouldn't it be "Stormville Prison in Green Haven," or "Storm Haven Prison in Greenville"?

It was a visceral shock, a few minutes later, to see the prison's smooth gray bastions rising from the gently sloping green fields. The student who ran the Green Haven Project, Paul, said the facility held more than two thousand inmates — it was, he said, just like a small city . . . an alien city, to be sure, looking both completely impenetrable and completely out of place. In the parking lot Paul gave us a quick run-down on prison rules and etiquette. Don't take anything, even messages, from the inmates; don't give legal advice; don't ask an inmate what he was convicted of, though it was usually okay to ask how much time he had left to serve.

Paul led us through the visitors' entrance, which opened into a large, fluorescent-lit room with scores of lockers on the right and a security station on the left. To get there we had to walk a gauntlet of waist-high walls that doubled back on itself before ending at a metal detector. Two guards, both with thick mustaches, watched us from behind a counter next to the detector as we made our way through the entrance maze. There were only two classes of people here: the observer and the observed.

A guard checked our group against the prison schedule. After asking for photo IDs, the other guard had us empty our pockets, one by one, onto the counter. He suggested I leave my Swiss army knife in a locker, and I did — along with my wallet, watch, and keys, as if I were more likely to be robbed in prison than in New Haven or New York. I set off the metal detector nonetheless, and the guard told me to remove my belt and shoes. "Steel shanks," he said, as I walked through the machine in my stockinged feet.

A third, burly guard escorted us to a steel-bar gate. We waited there until he received a signal that the hall before us, which ended in a similar gate twenty feet later, was secure. The first gate slid slowly aside to the sound of a whirring motor and metal scraping metal, and closed with a sharp slap behind us. It felt just like the movies, though not for long.

After passing through the next gate, we suddenly found ourselves outdoors again, but in what seemed to be a formal Georgian courtyard. This side of the prison wall was faced in warm red brick, and at its base were well-tended flower beds. It was bizarre to encounter a relatively bucolic scene inside a prison, and I assumed it existed primarily to impress visiting dignitaries. I didn't have time to think about it, however; another building loomed ahead — a cell block, I realized. The brief reunion with the evening sky only heightened my developing sense of dread.

We signed in at a security center, where each of us received a clip-on visitor badge. They were checked a few yards later by a guard standing outside a glass booth in which another guard sat watching a video monitor. Directly before us was another gate, and behind it a doorless hall that seemed to stretch on forever.

For the next five minutes we hiked down wide hallways and halted at steel gates. Occasionally we spotted other guards walking down perpendicular hallways, once in a while inmates — trusties, no doubt — carrying folders or mopping floors, but otherwise the prison was eerily quiet and empty. We made so many turns that by the time we got to an open doorway with a guard desk next to it, I doubted any of us could retrace his steps without getting lost.

We were ushered into a room off a short corridor behind the desk. The room was white, windowless, and harshly lit; empty plastic chairs were arranged roughly around the perimeter. The inmates arrived soon after, and before long numbered thirty or so. I took some comfort in the thought that while I was now surrounded by killers, rapists, arsonists, and other violent men, they were said to be the cream of the Green Haven crop — indeed, of the entire state prison system. Because of its proximity to New York City and thus most inmates' families, the authorities were said to transfer prisoners to Green Haven as a reward for good behavior — and transfer them out as punishment for bad. We had been assured, too, that inmates came to the seminar from genuine interest in legal issues; they didn't want anything from us except our time and intellectual stimulation.

I instinctively started to sit with the other students, but didn't want to betray my anxiety by seeming afraid to mingle. I considered settling down next to a well-groomed, silver-haired man wearing expensive, bright-white running shoes, but quickly dismissed the idea as equally subject to misinterpretation. My implicit assumption — that this white man was imprisoned for a white-collar crime while most of the blacks were imprisoned for violent crimes — was probably racist in and of itself, but it also turned out to be close to the truth.

I eventually sat between a large, skeptical-looking man and a younger, goateed inmate wearing his sweatshirt hood over his head. Both were dressed in the drab olive greens and browns that seemed to pass for a prison uniform. I thought about introducing myself, but decided against it; why risk breaking some unspoken prison code?

After the last inmate closed the door behind him — a prison college class had kept him overtime, he explained — Paul assured the gathering that the prison administration had no say over the content of these seminars. Anyone could say anything; no one was listening in, no one need fear reprisal. He then introduced the law school librarian, the evening's speaker.

The librarian gave a quintessentially librarianlike description of law resources and research methods. My mind strayed, and I wondered what the two female law students were feeling. Most of the inmates seemed to ignore them, quite aware of the tension any special notice would create, but two or three stared silently at the women, as if they were sculptures in a museum.

The inmates didn't seem much interested in the librarian's talk but became more involved during the question period. While few cared about the law's abstractions, many knew in detail the precedents and laws that bore on their own convictions and sentences; they peppered the librarian about ways of finding specific bits of legal information. I was most surprised by the fact that many of the inmates were very articulate, and before long was convinced that at least a couple knew as much law as some third-year students.

One inmate was a scraggly bearded, gnomelike man in his sixties. He turned out to be the prison's law librarian, and he offered to give us a tour of his domain. The library was cramped and disorganized but obviously well used; when the

Supreme Court handed down an important criminal law decision, the librarian said, the inmates sometimes lined up to read it. The image seemed funny at first — convicted lawbreakers belatedly anxious to learn law — but it brought up a serious issue for the prison librarian. The library needed more copies of legal materials, he said; if anyone should have easy access to such things, he seemed to be saying, it should be those whom they affect most.

Conversing with inmates seemed easier in the more familiar environment of the law library. I overheard one inmate trying to convince a student that he had been wrongly convicted through a misinterpretation of security law — he had been a lawyer himself before disbarment, the inmate explained. Another inmate whispered to me that the white man in the fancy running shoes was a CIA operative who had sold secrets — or guns or drugs, I don't remember which — to other countries; some inmates suspected he still worked for the government. When I mentioned to the law librarian that I was a journalist as well as a law student, he began telling me how many times he had been beaten up in prison for trying to exercise his First Amendment rights. One particularly well-spoken inmate, a writer who was having a play read in Manhattan a few weeks later, said that the Justice Department was attempting to sabotage his upcoming parole hearing for political reasons.

After a few more conversations I saw there was a common thread to much of the prisoners' talk — the idea that law was a grand conspiracy to subjugate those without access to power. To some extent I agreed, but was surprised to learn that even the most intelligent inmates believed that oppression was the primary intent of criminal law, not a side effect. And that brought to mind a bigger issue. If inmates came to this belief in prison, wasn't the institution fostering at least as much crime as it prevented? After doing his time — after paying his "debt to society," a metaphor that defines crime, significantly, as an economic transaction — an inmate with that attitude would feel no compunction about continuing to break laws. Rehabilitation in a "correctional facility" is a charade if inmates believe the legal system to be inherently unjust . . . and how could I say they were wrong?

The conspiracy theorists came to the fore on my second and last visit to Green Haven. They were spurred on by the topic Paul had chosen for the evening's discussion, which struck just about everyone in the room as daring, borderline foolish. The inmates laughed and looked at one another in disbelief when Paul opened the seminar by saying, "Tonight I'd like to suggest we talk about prison riots."

In some ways I was ready for just such a discussion. A few minutes earlier, at the visitors' entrance, I had been told I couldn't bring in an article on prison literature I had recently run across in a small-circulation magazine and intended to give to the inmate/playwright. I should have called ahead and gotten permission, the guard told me; besides, he added, I could always mail the article — an option I had already rejected because letters to inmates, I had heard from Paul and others, are often intercepted by prison staff. I could understand the security problems, but why embargo information? Literature? Knowledge? Inmate ignorance might ensure pliability in the short run, but over time it seemed a sure way to breed defiance.

The discussion of Paul's topic seemed to support the point.

A prison, said one inmate, is nothing but a business. Prisons were built not to house a growing criminal population but to create jobs in rural areas — for whites, I gathered. The police didn't fight crime so much as create it; their job was to round up and railroad blacks to fill up the new facilities. This analysis, offered without evidence, was followed by a general murmur of agreement.

A second inmate elaborated on the same theme by saying that the "enlightened" penology of recent years — since the Attica riots of 1971, essentially — was a calculated business decision. Prison riots had become few and far between because inmates were "pacified"; more recreation and television time, fewer lock-downs, marginally better food, easier access to families — all such improvements, he said, were brainwashing disguised as humanitarianism. Yale Law's prison project was itself being criticized, I saw, as being designed to coopt inmates — to make them "soft," prevent them from recognizing that correctional facilities are "full of political prisoners." This argument, too, was well received.

I couldn't tell whether these ideas commonly circulated among inmates. But it was clear that any inmate who had been in Attica during the riots — one or two were present that night — was regarded with enormous respect. It was horrifying to think a riot that killed more than forty people was now looked upon as the good old days, when guards were tough and inmates didn't eat quiche, but that seemed to be the case.

In retrospect, however, I began to understand that I had witnessed a textbook example of community-making. Forced to dress alike and live alike, told what to do and when to do it, the inmates reasserted their identities by creating an antithetical culture of their own. Unable to join society, they try to beat it, and at its own game — by making and enforcing their own form of law. The major effect of life in prison seemed to be to convince inmates that law is nothing but a euphemism for power. Curiously, law students learn a similar lesson during their legal education, and for many of the same reasons — though they, of course, usually end up on the accepted side of the law.

I left Green Haven for good in a somber mood. I fell behind the rest of the group while putting on my coat, and when we got to the cell-block exit, a heavy-faced guard put up his hand to stop my passage. I froze, thinking, "Oh shit, they know something." The rest of the group, talking softly among themselves, moved on.

The guard lifted my coat.

"You should wear it on the outside," he said, gesturing to my visitor's badge.

"Oh sure," I said, bathed in relief, and scrambled to catch up with the others.

Thirteen

Skill against Wisdom

[T]he chief source of our blundering ineptness in dealing with moral and political problems is that we do not know how to think about them except by quantitative methods. . . . In this sense we need to be, not more scientific, but less scientific, not more quantitative but other than quantitative. We must create and use methods of belief which are suitable to the study of men as self-governing persons. . . . [W]e invent and run machines of ever new and amazing power and intricacy. And we are tempted by that achievement to see if we can manipulate men with the same skill and ingenuity. But the manipulation of men is the destruction of self-government. Our skill, therefore, threatens our wisdom. In this respect the United States with its "know-how" is, today, the most dangerous nation in the world.

ALEXANDER MEIKLEJOHN
Free Speech and Its Relation to Self-Government
1948

Curiously, the most memorable episode from my trips to Green Haven had nothing to do with prisons or criminal law. The prison experience was vivid, to be sure, but not so different from what I expected. The incident that long haunted me was an ethical problem, and it underscored the inherent tension between law and journalism.

One of the students I met through the Green Haven program had spent the previous summer at a law firm frequently employed by a utility company. I asked Frank (as I'll call him) what he did there, how he liked the work, and so on, and he mentioned that one of the firm's ongoing projects was the attempt to open a nuclear power facility. I replied that representing a company involved in nuclear power must be personally troubling at times, given the fact that many people oppose it, and before long we were talking about ethical dilemmas.

It was an interesting conversation, and before long I was telling Frank my experience at law school had made me see that while both lawyers and journalists serve the same two masters — the public interest and their employers — they resolve conflicts between those masters in very different ways. When the journalist finds himself caught between serving his readers and serving his newspaper — when a company, say, threatens to withdraw its advertising because of an article he wrote — the journalist still feels obliged to argue the public's cause, if only to his editor; his first loyalty, he feels, is to the public. When the lawyer finds himself similarly caught, however — when he uncovers evidence, for example, establishing his client's guilt — the lawyer remains silent; his first loyalty is to his employer. The lawyer is trained, in short, to submerge common beliefs about justice beneath the legal system's rules of justice, even though those rules may ensure justice is *not* done.

How, I asked Frank rhetorically, can lawyers bear to work within such a system? Especially since they can't avoid knowing it is based on at least three fallacious assumptions: that every relevant point of view is represented in a case, that the advocates for those views are equally skilled, and that a judge will weigh their arguments impartially. Numerous legal rules and codes of ethics supposedly ameliorate those problems, but they only seemed to justify the status quo by implying that solutions can always be found within the prefabricated, lawyer-made legal system. Instead of illuminating professional choices in the light of ordinary moral conduct, instead of showing lawyers how to grow in response to hard questions, law's internal rules did just the reverse — allowed lawyers to dodge moral issues by narrowing them to fit the answers already available. Lawyers resolved conflicts by placing them in a hermetically sealed, self-referential loop that ignores precisely what it should encompass — the views of the millions of nonlawyers whose lives their decisions affect.

Frank was no doubt relieved when I wound down this speech. But he seemed to agree, on some level, for he told me about a legal conflict that confirmed my worst fears.

The previous summer, Frank said, a lawyer in his firm discovered during a routine legal check that the title to a parcel of land in the nuclear power plant site was "defective." It almost didn't matter whether the defective title was a minor glitch or a major calamity, for it was the lawyer's job to assume the worst — that the utility did not, and possibly could not, fully own the site. The lawyer brought the problem to other members of the firm and to the client, and before long the moral center of the problem had evaporated. The basic question was no longer "How shall we disclose this information to the public it affects?" but "Are attorneys obliged by law to reveal this fact?" and "How can we pretend this fact doesn't exist?" The issue was atomized, sanitized, and manipulated through legal analysis, in short, until its core was rendered irrelevant and therefore harmless. The utility ultimately decided to do nothing, advised by its lawyers that the state's statute of limitations would run in a few years . . . thus allowing it to gain clear title to the parcel through adverse possession (in nonlegal terms, by squatting).

Frank's disclosure, if true, was a bombshell, and I had no reason to disbelieve it. After reminding him I was a journalist, I asked for facts and dates and sequences of events, but did so with mixed feelings; there seemed no way to check out the story without implicating Frank as the source. If I published the allegations, his legal career was likely to be over before it began, for Frank had not only broken the attorney-client privilege but revealed information that directly harmed his client's interests — perhaps the worst sin a lawyer can commit.

I couldn't tell whether Frank told me the story to register his disagreement (at least in part) with the legal calculus his firm had made. But that seemed plausible; why else would Frank risk extreme fallout when silence on his part was not only acceptable but professionally required? At the same time, however, I suspected Frank had concluded he could clear his conscience only by lobbing this hot potato to somebody else . . . and I happened not only to be handy, but a journalist.

I had a number of options. I could (1) do nothing, like the utility; (2) try to confirm the story and hang Frank out to dry; (3) leak it to another journalist, possibly protecting Frank but gambling that the utility lawyers would not successfully stonewall the story; (4) check out the allegations only when, if confirmed, they might affect the facility's future; or (5) sit on the story until I published my book, hope that my understanding of Frank's description of the issues was essentially accurate, and address the larger issue — the legal profession's willingness to use its specialized beliefs and codes to influence public questions without the public's knowledge or consent.

I chose the last route, for it guaranteed that the story wouldn't deteriorate into a discussion among lawyers about evidentiary relevance and acceptable lawyer behavior. That was, after all, exactly my point — that the professional expertise lawyers bring to an issue automatically changes the issue and so any decision ultimately made. By taking the defective title dilemma at face value, too, I could pose a pleasing hypothetical of my own. If a nuclear power plant becomes operative because the legal profession's code of ethics prevents the revelation of a fact that would have otherwise ensured its demise, and a subsequent disaster at the plant kills thousands of people, can survivors sue the legal profession as a "racketeering enterprise" under the Racketeer Influenced and Corrupt Organizations Act, better known as RICO? It seemed reasonable to me — as reasonable, at least, as many of the cases I had read in law school.

Frank's disclosure did more than throw me into an ethical vacuum. It also forced me to rethink further my assumption that lawyers and journalists are quite different sorts of people. They have serious philosophical disagreements, to be sure, but they diverge in methods more than goals; both the lawyer and the journalist swear allegiance to truth and justice, but each believes only his profession is properly equipped for their definition and delivery. One trait the two professions unquestionably share is arrogance, and each feels threatened by the assurance with which the other seems to view the world.

The rivalry between lawyers and journalists was relatively subdued at Yale Law, for neither the M.S.L.s nor the professors were regularly on the front lines of their respective professions. But a rivalry did exist, and it wasn't hidden; indeed, it was sometimes prodded into open conflict, as if confrontation would help us understand one another better. Often, however, the effect was just the reverse, for when push came to shove the lawyers and journalists became defensive and refused to search for common ground, let alone common language; no one dared suspend professional beliefs, even for a moment, to entertain seriously another skilled perspective. The result was usually the substitution of lecturing discourse — at which those trained in law excelled — for any attempt at mutual comprehension.

I first glimpsed the depth of the lawyer/journalist communication gap at the fall conference on press issues. During a panel discussion of the public's "right to know," the Supreme Court reporter for the *Baltimore Sun*, Lyle Denniston, lashed into the legal profession for its secretiveness and arrogance. Arthur Liman (counsel to Congress, a few months later, during its investigation of the Iran-contra scandal) countered by saying lawyers frequently refuse to talk to reporters for the same reason journalists grant anonymity to sources: in order to preserve their ability to elicit difficult, hidden, often damaging information. Liman implied that journalists are hypocritical to berate lawyers for refusing to talk about their cases. If journalists commonly protect sources by withholding certain information from the public, why don't they respect lawyers' doing the same?

I might have believed Liman's argument had I not already unraveled its self-serving starting point. It's a false dichotomy to compare the lawyer's client with the reporter's source because the lawyer is not only paid by his client, but paid to mold facts one-sidedly on the client's behalf. I could see, however, how the parallel made sense to the legal mind. If you believe law to be more important than facts, it's easy to argue that lawyers serve the public interest even when representing clients who damage it; of paramount significance, from that point of view, is the legal *system*. Lawyers, in other words, presume justice and the justice system to be one and the same, and that intellectual leap permits them to rationalize virtually any professional action. They neatly jump the gap between theory and practice by telling themselves it doesn't exist.

The following months at Yale Law did nothing to diminish my sense that legal education encourages this spurious conflation. And journalists, of course, hindered that process, for they resisted the idea that justice should be defined and controlled exclusively by the legal profession. That was why, I thought, the M.S.L.s were no more than tolerated by most of the Yale Law faculty; while we often considered ourselves to be toilers in the same field as the lawyers, they regarded us as trespassers. For a time the M.S.L.s had biweekly lunches with professors to try to overcome our mutual distrust, but before long the professors' apparent disdain for journalism made the meals seem trivial. It seemed unproductive to converse with people who believed journalists had much to learn from lawyers but lawyers had nothing to learn from journalists.

It came as a surprise, consequently, when the M.S.L. dean asked in the spring whether the journalists would be interested in conducting a couple of workshops for faculty and students exploring how a reporter might cover a news story. We were skeptical but agreed nonetheless, grateful for the chance to demonstrate that journalism is a serious, rigorous endeavor.

For the workshop Alina invented a problematic news situation. Fifteen minutes before press-time, a reporter for an afternoon daily hears over the police radio that a fire has broken out in an abandoned warehouse next to a toxic waste dump and a block from a hospital. He calls the fire chief, who says that a fireman has been injured, arson has not been ruled out, containment is expected shortly, and — not for attribution — that the company which owns the dump site has failed to implement long-standing fire safety precautions. The reporter makes four more phone calls: to the dump owner, who doesn't answer; to an environmental group, which says the dump has not been cleaned up because the neighborhood is minority and poor; to a city councilman, who says he can't yet comment; and to an industry analyst, who says the dump company's safety record is generally good.

What is the story, Alina asked, and how should it be reported? Workshop members — seven or eight law students, two professors, and the M.S.L. dean — had ten minutes to write one up.

It seemed straightforward to me. The most important news was the fireman's injury, the question of arson, and the possibility that the fire could spread to the hospital and toxic waste dump. But when we talked about the various stories the class had come up with, one student, whom I'll call Tim, argued vehemently that it was wrong to make any reference to the dump.

"As far as the reporter knows," Tim said, hunching over the table around which we had gathered, "the dump didn't burn and wasn't likely to burn. I wouldn't call something 'news' if it hasn't happened yet. And in any case, all the bad things he's heard about the dump — and they don't amount to much — are hearsay. He shouldn't be publishing unfounded allegations."

Tim's tone was aggressive and condescending. The

M.S.L.s were taken aback; we hadn't expected such an instantly negative reaction . . . nor did we realize that we were
being set up.

Mackenzie, a television reporter, looked at Tim with exasperation. "The story isn't just the fire," she began. "It's the
dump, too. It was an accident waiting to happen. Maybe not
this time, but the next fire could —"

"But you don't *know* that!" Tim replied with increasing
heat. "The reporter doesn't have any evidence! The fire chief,
the environmentalist, what they said is speculation, it's rumor. Why does the dump company become the target when
it has nothing to do with the fire? He's going beyond the
facts as he knows them. You're saying that's good journalism?"

I was getting a little hot under the collar myself. Tim
seemed to think that facts didn't exist until they could be
scientifically proved, and that people like himself were the
obvious arbiters of proof. I thought that sort of positivism
had been thoroughly discredited decades ago; only the to-
bacco companies seemed to use it now, invariably claiming,
upon the release of the zillionth study linking lung cancer to
cigarette use, that no *real* scientist, no *objective* observer,
could agree with such findings.

Alina was also getting angry. "Look," she said, "the
dump has become news whether the owner likes it or not —
the fire chief and the environmental people made it news.
Just because a story hasn't been covered until something
brings it into the open doesn't mean it isn't news; the problem was there all along. Its time just came."

Tim was having none of it. He looked appalled, as if
personally shocked by what he had heard about journalistic
techniques. "You're saying the fire is a 'news hook'? Is that
right? That's just what the environmentalists were looking

for, and you gave it to them without even talking to the dump owner. How can you call it a balanced story without getting the company's side of things?"

"You're on deadline," Alina said, giving up. "You do everything you *can* do."

I realized two things in quick succession — that Tim was arguing that the reporter's standards should be the same as the lawyer's, and that he was playing devil's advocate. It didn't bother Tim that he had obliged listeners to take seriously an argument he didn't take seriously himself — in fact, that was the whole point. Tim could argue his position well precisely because he didn't care about its content; with content to one side, he could concentrate his energies on rhetorical technique.

What mattered to him wasn't the accuracy of his words but their effectiveness, even if their only effect was to antagonize and alienate. Indeed, perhaps he intended that result; angered, the M.S.L.s could do little more than splutter and fume and say the first half-baked thing that came to mind. Tim wanted to win a debate, not explain the truths in his position, and he didn't mind winning by intimidating those who disagreed with him.

I was dismayed to hear a significant issue treated so casually. I didn't speak my mind, however, afraid of loosing an *ad hominem* attack that would seem only to confirm Tim's disdain for nonlegal thinking. And in any case, we had already lost the exchange; by rising to Tim's bait, and thus acting defensive, we had let the workshop become a confrontation.

Barely controlling my voice, I replied that no reporter believes he can nail down the complete truth at any given instant. Sometimes he casts his net too widely, sometimes too narrowly, but the amazing thing is that he usually casts it fairly well. Most news stories are quite accurate and relatively complete, and most substantial inaccuracies and omission are eventually corrected. Sometimes the only way to flush out truth, I said, is to provide an incomplete picture that others can finish or revise.

The workshop ended soon after. That was fortunate, for it had degenerated into a turf battle. We were back to square one — the lawyers regarding the journalists' worldview as emotional and senseless, and the journalists regarding the lawyers' as reductive and beside the point. Why should I waste my time building bridges toward lawyers, I thought as I walked back to my apartment, if the only bridges lawyers would cross are one-way, of their own design, and radiating from the legal center?

During spring break the M.S.L.s had another chance to investigate the conflicts between law and journalism, on the program's annual field trip to Washington, D.C. The centerpiece was an interview with a Supreme Court justice (whose name I cannot divulge for reasons that will soon become clear), but we also talked about legal coverage with other judges and journalists. Going in, I assumed the experience would highlight the differences between the legal and journalistic frames of mind, but in the end those differences were overshadowed by the solipsistic worldview peculiar, it seems, to Washington.

Like many American teenagers, I had once spent a few summer days touring the nation's capital with my parents. I was duly impressed by the monumentality and profundity of the place, in spite of the fact (or perhaps because of it) that we visited in the midst of the Watergate hearings of 1973. It was clear by then that the Nixon administration was filled with lawbreakers, many of them lawyers, but the legal sys-

tem remained unimpeached; indeed, the entire nation could
see it throbbing away openly, directly, and with an air of
inevitability. The American legal system might be headed
toward a crisis, Watergate seemed to say, but the crisis could
be resolved within the existing structure.

I received no such message on this trip. The silence was
partly due to the fact that I was no longer an empty vessel,
but also a side effect, I think, of legal education. Law school
seemed to have taken away my ability to listen without
guile, to respond without caveats. The District's monumen-
talism, its love of institutions and institutional history, now
rang false, for the city's obsession with power, control, rules,
symbols, seemed destructive rather than heroic. Washington, I understood for the first time, invited the citizen to
marvel at law, not participate in it. Perhaps Chief Justice
John Marshall really was right, in his time, to call the United
States "a government of laws, and not of men" — but how
could he have foreseen that those laws would become so
closely identified with a class of men trained to think in the
same narrow, inbred, isolating way?

Washington was not, however, only bleak. What could
have been the city's most depressing monument, the memorial to Vietnam veterans, was its most stirring. Clad in
mourning black, sunk below ground like a tomb, it proclaimed that laws can be wrong, that ideas can kill, that a
government can ask too much. And the monument gave
names, almost every name; it listed mutely the price paid by
thousands to enforce others' beliefs. The Supreme Court,
which consistently refused to rule on the constitutionality of
the war in Vietnam, sat as far from the Vietnam memorial
as it's possible to get in central Washington, and the distance
seemed an apt metaphor for the gulf between law and life.
Reduce a conviction to words in an argument and you may

find yourself forced to fight on alien ground by alien rules.

The gulf did narrow a bit, though, soon after I walked into the Supreme Court for the very first time. The M.S.L.s had arranged to meet in the cafeteria, but I had come early to get some breakfast. As I read the newspaper, I noticed a group of high school students and, in their midst, a familiar face — that of Associate Justice Harry Blackmun. I was surprised to see, first, that he was such a small man, elfin with his big head and large eyes, and second, that he seemed to be listening and thinking as much as talking. If every justice made a point of talking with, and perhaps learning from, those whose lives he or she would affect for decades to come, law would surely cleave to common human experience. Wouldn't it?

When the other journalists and the M.S.L. dean arrived, we walked down a marble hall to the appropriate elevator, where a guard inspected our belongings. We got off on the next floor, found the right set of offices, and introduced ourselves to the secretary of the justice who had agreed to see us. Before long a door opened and the justice appeared in a dark suit. He invited us into his chambers, a large, high-ceilinged, wooden-paneled room that reeked of tradition — except for the computer that glowed on a table next to his desk. The text on the screen, I noted with some disappointment, was too far away to read.

The justice shook hands with each of us and motioned to some leather chairs. "Well, what do you want to know?" he asked, taking a seat himself. The words implied he had better things to do with his time, but the tone was friendly, as if he hoped someone would pose an unexpected, unprecedented query. We didn't. The questions — about cameras in the courtroom, the way draft opinions circulated, the quality of press coverage, the recent insider trading scandals — were predictable. And the answers were as well, though the justice replied openly and without hesitation. The comment I recall most vividly, in fact, came not from the justice but from the dean, when she remarked that the interview was, of course, off the record.

The dean spoke as if reminding the M.S.L.s of an agreed-upon precondition, but I, for one, knew nothing about it. I was tempted to tell the dean she had no right to dictate the rules of a game without first obtaining all the players' consent, but I wasn't about to ruin the interview for all concerned — nor suffer the probable humiliation of being told by a Supreme Court justice, even in jest, that ignorance of the rules is no excuse.

The justice made a couple of interesting comments in the course of the interview, however, and I repeat them because they illuminate the judicial mind. In answer to a question about the complexity of Supreme Court decisions, he said, "If it takes twenty-three pages, I write twenty-three pages; it if takes nineteen, I write nineteen." In answer to a question about whether he felt increased responsibility upon being elevated to the highest court in the land, he gave a terse "No."

The first reply was admirable. I was glad to hear a judge say he felt obliged to answer legal questions concisely, without fudging, in exactly as many words as the question deserved. Though it sounded like the response of a strict constructionist, I took the statement as commitment to the idea that judges must communicate in ways nonlawyers can understand.

The second reply, on the other hand, seemed to value concision for its own sake. Was the justice saying he felt no added responsibility because on lower courts he had always forced himself to rule as if his decisions were final? Or did his monosyllabic response mean something else entirely — that he didn't feel any additional pressure when sitting on the Supreme Court because he considered himself a tool of law, a mechanical translator? In that case, I thought, we were in trouble, for this justice had become all mind; he had remade himself to fit his image of what a judge should be. He might see himself as Law's slave, shaped to its intellectual expectations, but in fact he was its master, using law to shape other's lives.

I had a very different sense of the judge we talked to less than an hour later, at the court of appeals for the D.C. circuit (generally regarded as the second-most-important court in the nation). We got a warm reception here; as soon as we entered her chambers, Chief Justice Patricia Wald, a Yale Law graduate, said she had something for us. After rummaging in a bookcase she came up with a few copies of perhaps the most significant First Amendment case of the year, *Tavoulareas v. The Washington Post*, which her court had handed down (in favor of the newspaper) a few days earlier. Wald then invited us to sit down at her conference table and began signing copies of the decision for us.

She seemed to understand that journalists were natural allies, not natural enemies. I even thought Wald welcomed our intrusion because it lessened her sense of isolation — a universal feeling among judges, and unhealthy not only for them personally but for their decisions. As she would say of appellate judges later that year during an address at Yale Law, "On a day-to-day basis, humanity counts for just as much [as brilliance]." Isolation, Wald implied, might ensure judicial purity, but that purity could be dangerous in and of itself.

In some ways I wish our D.C. interviews had ended right there. The portrait of Justice we had received, to that point, was neat and clean: opposing legal philosophies illustrated by opposing judicial natures. But the interviews did continue, and one — with ABC television's Ted Koppel — put the balance out of kilter. He demonstrated that balance is an artificial state of mind.

The interview was memorable less for what Koppel said than what he did. He cross-examined the M.S.L.s, put words in our mouths, interrupted us, and argued with virtually anything and everything we said; he treated us, in short, as if we were guests on *Nightline*. We weren't surprised to learn that Koppel had taken some law school classes, but for once I couldn't attribute combativeness to legal training. It was *Nightline* itself, I suspect, that caused Koppel to badger; it was his way of creating the sparks required for "good TV." Like Tim at the lawyer/journalist workshop, Koppel seemed less interested in ideas than in demonstrating his ability to control a debate.

I realized again how difficult it is to get outside the conventions of one's profession. Koppel was hamstrung by the television interview form; judges, by the requirements of the judicial opinion and demeanor; lawyers, by procedural forms and codes; and I, soon, by editors' and readers' expectations about what a book should be. ("A successful book cannot venture to be more than ten percent new" — so said an editor to Marshall McLuhan after reading the manuscript of *Understanding Media*.) I had previously been able to avoid thinking seriously about the compromises produced by journalism's forms, but the interview with Koppel ushered them into the foreground. How could I say the conventions of law failed to do justice to reality if the conventions through which I articulated that idea — a book — were susceptible to the same criticism?

The issue stayed with me for the rest of the semester, and

indeed, throughout the writing of this work. In retrospect it could hardly have been otherwise, for the problem can't be solved; no thought goes uncompromised by the limitations of language and the writer's inability to escape subjectivity. And yet the distortions caused by form cried out for discussion, for both law and journalism thrive on the pretense that they are transparent, neutral interpreters of reality. And that, surely, is a major reason the general public mistrusts law and journalism more than other professions — because lawyers and journalists assume airs of authority they have not earned, because the images they provide are often too neat, too convenient, too arrogant.

And yet. . . . The Wizard of Oz was a con artist, no doubt. But stripped of his machinery, defrocked, made human once more, he needs no borrowed authority to live up to his promises. The capacity to realize — to make real, literally — has been within him, and within Dorothy, all along. It's possible; reality can be captured, truth does have the power to transform, inward vision may be the most powerful. Slender reeds from which to hang a book, but they were the only ones available. Aside, perhaps, from that offered by Beckett, a reed of unavoidable existentialism: I can't go on, I'll go on.

Spring break in Washington had quite a different effect than fall break in California, less than five months earlier. Both weeks illustrated the power of law, but in the spring that power was no longer appealing. If anything, I was beginning to feel a convert against law, at least as currently practiced.

The turning point came, I think, after I met with a media columnist for the *Washington Post*. I didn't know him very well, and telephoned just to say hello, but he suggested we meet for breakfast the following day. We did, and after an hour of talk about journalism, publishing, and law I said I had to make a couple calls. He suggested I accompany him to the *Post*'s offices, where I could phone in a warm room with a little privacy. I agreed; I could use every conceivable edge, for I was about to call one of the best-known literary agents in New York. I had recently sent her a proposal for a book on the genesis of the legal mind, and if she didn't like the idea, or my writing, I would consider dropping the project altogether.

The agent proved enthusiastic. I was somewhat surprised by her reaction but realized I shouldn't have been; in ordinary conversation it was largely lawyers who looked for an argument, a point of difference, a hidden contradiction. I had met the *Post* reporter only once previously, had never talked to this agent before, yet they were not only willing to talk to me, they were interested in what I had to say. They kept their truth channels open, and without effort, as all good media people do. On the train back to New York, and Lisa, I was glad to feel like a journalist again.

Law school, with the exception of Images, seemed much less interesting when classes resumed a few days later. Boredom set in — not the boredom of reading cases and learning law by rote, but boredom with legal analysis itself. It had lost its fascination for me; it now seemed but one way of thinking among many, and not a very attractive way at that. It was odd to find myself intellectually distanced from law school when it was the intellectual distance fostered by law school that made it seem so damaging, but that was perhaps the only recourse available. And with just seven weeks of classes remaining, and just one exam to study for, I could afford to stand back from the legal endgame. Moreover, now that I was fairly sure I was going to write a book about law school, I was almost compelled to regain some lost perspective.

Few events at law school, from this point onward, were memorable. There was "Law Revue," the annual production in which students wreak revenge on faculty members, often cruelly; Kahn Law was satirized as a game show in which contestants are forewarned that "anything you say can and will be used against you." There was the emergency "town meeting" in which Guido called the entire law school together to excoriate those responsible for the graffiti threatening campus gays with bodily harm; the dean described the recent incidents as some of the sickest, most repulsive actions he had ever encountered. There was the graduate student lunch with Professor Burke Marshall, assistant attorney general for civil rights in the Kennedy administration and former general counsel of IBM, who said two years of law school, and perhaps just one, was sufficient.

And there was graduation, on Memorial Day. I hadn't bothered to rent a cap and gown, thinking it silly to honor so formally an education dedicated to deflating similarly unthinking traditions, and so was shocked to find I was one of only two gownless students among the 180 or so receiving degrees. I was embarrassed to be dressed only in a suit — even if it was a handsome glen plaid made for my father in Berkeley in the 1940s, the very suit I had worn to my college graduation nine years earlier. I feared some parents would interpret my appearance as disrespect, but at most I wanted to express the sort of independence that law school, contrary to its reputation, ultimately discourages.

The commencement address was given, to everyone's surprise and delight, by Supreme Court Associate Justice William Brennan. He arrived at the podium, grinning and sprightly, to a standing ovation, and launched into a mild attack on lawyers' love of money. He concluded a few minutes later by saying that law school graduates must never forget that "the primary responsibility for maintaining the American dream is being passed on to you. Safeguard and cherish it."

The third-years listened raptly. Justice Brennan was telling them to live up to the ideals of law, not its reality, but I wondered whether the message had gotten through. Most of these students would be corporate lawyers within a year or two; would they remember then what the ordinary American's dream was like, or had law school, and law practice, permanently distorted their understanding of such simple things? Power, money, and prestige would be theirs for the next fifty years, but the price they paid might turn out to be a Faustian diminishment of the soul. The gowns worn by these new-made lawyers looked like regal judicial robes, but to me, at that time, in that place, they appeared an expensive kind of straitjacket.